LAUR

A Survey of Modernist Poetry

and

A Pamphlet Against Anthologies

LAURA (R DING) JACKSON (1901–1991) is a   l yet
misread rite   f the twentieth centu y SF   r her
Collected Poems pea   d in 1938 and a   work
which left its   n Auden, Ashbe y   llabo-
rations and her   ssays, stories and poems   ative
and critical de   urrounding twentieth-centu   nerican
literature. A g   t deal of her work is still being pu

ROBERT GRAVES (1895–1985) was a major lyric poet and – as the monumental three-volume *Complete Poems* (1995–9) demonstrates – an enormously prolific one. He was also an unusually versatile writer of prose: his works include historical novels, reworkings of mythology, the celebrated autobiography *Goodbye to All That* and *The White Goddess* (subtitled 'A Grammar of Poetic Myth'), as well as a wide range of literary criticism.

CHARLES MUNDYE is Lecturer in English at the University of Hull.

PATRICK MCGUINNESS is Lecturer in French and a Fellow of St Anne's College, Oxford. He is the editor of T.E. Hulme's *Selected Writings* for Carcanet.

Also by Laura Riding and Robert Graves from Carcanet

Essays from Epilogue

LAURA RIDING AND ROBERT GRAVES

A Survey of Modernist Poetry

and

A Pamphlet Against Anthologies

edited with notes and introduction by
CHARLES MUNDYE and PATRICK McGUINNESS

CARCANET

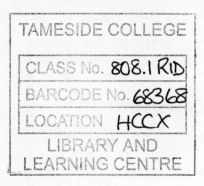
This edition first published in Great Britain in 2002 by
Carcanet Press Limited
4th Floor, Conavon Court
12–16 Blackfriars Street
Manchester M3 5BQ

A Survey of Modernist Poetry first published by Heinemann, 1927
A Pamphlet Against Anthologies first published by Garden City, 1928

A CIP catalogue record for this book
is available from the British Library

ISBN 1 85754 568 0

The publisher acknowledges financial
assistance from the Arts Council of England

Funded by
THE
ARTS
COUNCIL
OF ENGLAND

Typeset in Monotype Ehrhardt by XL Publishing Services, Tiverton
Printed and bound in England by SRP Ltd, Exeter

Contents

Introduction

Mistrust me not, then, if I have begun
Unwontedly and if I seem to shun
Unstrange and much-told ground:
For in peculiar earth alone can I
Construe the word and let the meaning lie
That rarely may be found.

> Laura Riding, from 'As Well as Any Other'

He continues quick and dull in his clear images;
I continue slow and sharp in my broken images.

He in a new confusion of his understanding:
I in a new understanding of my confusion.

> Robert Graves, from 'In Broken Images'

A Survey of Modernist Poetry and *A Pamphlet Against Anthologies* confront the difficult literature of early twentieth-century poetic modernism. They are not just works of literary criticism, however insightful their to-the-minute reflections on such writers as T.S. Eliot, W.B. Yeats, e.e. cummings, Gertrude Stein, Marianne Moore or Hart Crane may be, and however well they might serve to document the production and reception of experimental writing in the early twentieth century. In the 1920s both Riding and Graves were committed wholeheartedly to the cause of poetry, and these books eschew the analytical focus of 'objective' criticism. Partial, subjective and polemical, these are deeply serious works: not criticism or literary history in the conventional sense, but rather written with the passion and force of poetic manifestos.

Both books provide reflections by practising poets on the technical language of poetry, as well as on the means of poetry's production, marketing, packaging, and reception. They lead in many directions, engaging with (among other preoccupations) the emerging debates about Modernism and experimental poetry, Shakespeare criticism, literary democracy and elitism. Many of the questions they take up remain pertinent, while several of their categories – the 'plain reader', the 'difficult poem', 'live' and 'dead' movements – have stayed central to contemporary critical discourses on poetry and its audience.

Laura Riding and Robert Graves first met in early January 1926. Riding had developed a significant reputation in the United States, particularly for the poetry she published in *The Fugitive* magazine, to which Graves had also contributed poems. The relationship and working partnership they subsequently developed was one of the most productive literary collaborations in twentieth-century poetry. In 1926 Graves published *Impenetrability; or, The Proper Habit of English*, and *Another Future of Poetry*, both of which are dedicated to Riding (he had, as early as 1925, reprinted her poem 'The Quids' in full in his *Contemporary Techniques of Poetry: A Political Analogy*). In 1926 Riding also published her first collection of poems, *The Close Chaplet*, whose title is drawn, as the book's epigraph shows, from Graves's poem 'The Nape of the Neck'. Throughout the period of their association – which lasted more than fifteen years – they were to engage in many collaborative projects, most notably the co-founding of the Seizin Press (1927–1939, which published, amongst other writers, Gertrude Stein); the creation of the *Epilogue* periodical (1935–1938);[1] and, of course, the mutual authorship (described for both books as a 'word-by-word' collaboration[2]) of *A Survey of Modernist Poetry* and *A Pamphlet Against Anthologies*. These works emerge from a particularly intensive period of their professional and personal relationship; one during which the paths of their different longer-term preoccupations intersected.

Riding and Graves are among the first to employ 'modernist' as a literary descriptive and classificatory term, although readers will find that their use of it is not always consistent; confluent with current usages. *A Survey* engages with and partly endorses the modernist 'project', yet the neutral-seeming title masks an often personal agenda, as, like many poet-critics before them, they seek to create the standards by which they themselves

---

1   For a selection from *Epilogue*, see Laura Riding and Robert Graves, *Essays from 'Epilogue' 1935–1937*, edited with an introduction by Mark Jacobs (Carcanet, 2001).

2   The phrase is from the opening note to *A Survey of Modernist Poetry* and is repeated in the 'Foreword' to *A Pamphlet Against Anthologies*, in response to reviews of *A Survey* which had misrepresented or ignored their prefatory note on collaborative authorship. In the note to *A Survey*, the authors make clear that the last chapter is a collaborative revision of 'an essay separately written and printed by one of them'. The reference is to Laura Riding's essay 'The New Barbarism, And Gertrude Stein', which appeared in *transition*, 3 (June 1927), pp.153–168. The substance of the piece appears in Riding's *Contemporaries and Snobs* (1928) under the title 'T.E. Hulme, The New Barbarism, & Gertrude Stein'.

are to be judged. Indeed, in the chapter entitled 'The Making of the Poem', a previously unpublished Riding poem – 'The Rugged Black of Anger' – is presented anonymously to furnish a demonstration-example of the authors' recommended reading method for 'what might be called a modernist poem'. Their attitude is complex: both supportive and yet critical of modernist poetry, sympathetic to its aspirations but guarded about its methods, the *Survey* is more reactive than descriptive, and more polemical than explanatory:

> It [the modernist period in poetry] has been followed by a pause in which no poetry of any certainty is appearing at all, an embarrassed pause after an arduous and erudite stock-taking. The next stage is not clear. But it is not impossible that there will be a resumption of less eccentric, less strained, more critically unconscious poetry, purified however by this experience of historical effort.
>
> ('Conclusion', *A Survey of Modernist Poetry*)

Modernist writing, they suggest, was a necessary evil – but they claim that by 1927 it had served its purpose. Their sympathy with experiment is consequently tempered by their belief in the need for a less contorted and fractured poetic language. Among the most ambivalently treated of their poetic examples is cummings, whose 'Sunset' poem is, in Chapter One, rewritten by Riding and Graves as a poem influenced by the French Symbolist writer Remy de Gourmont, and written in a stale Georgian idiom. This attempt to 'restore the extinct poem' behind cummings's original is perhaps the most extreme example of their critical method, and it yields the following conclusion:

> the poetry of e.e. cummings is clearly more important as a sign of local irritation in the poetic body than as the model for a new tradition. [...] cummings in this poem was really rewriting the other poem which we gave into a good poem. But for the rarer poet there is no 'other poem'; there is only the poem which he writes. cummings' technique, indeed, if further and more systematically developed, would become so complicated that poetry would be no more than mechanical craftsmanship [...] Poets, however, do not pursue innovations for their own sake. They are on the whole conservative in their methods so long as these ensure the proper security and delivery of the poem.
>
> ('Modernist Poetry and the Plain Reader's Rights', *A Survey*)

Their contention is that Modernist writing is often a re-writing, masking its influences, kicking over its own traces, and laying claim to novelty which, on close examination, is merely cosmetic. Whilst such a statement clearly offends against the judgements of a current Modernist orthodoxy, it is indicative of the authors' determination to define for themselves a space for their own work. In the process, they draw on a formidable range of reference, though with a principally Anglo-American focus (Paul Valéry is the only non-English-language writer to receive more than a glancing mention). There are engagements with other writers from the 'Fugitive' circle, in particular John Crowe Ransom and Allen Tate (two key practitioners of what was to become the New Criticism); present also are such Georgian writers as John Drinkwater, and in addition to the now-canonical list of Modernists – Joyce, Stein, Pound, Eliot, Williams, Moore – there are some important considerations of more marginal, and indeed now merely curious, authors such as the Sitwells, Nancy Cunard, and Humbert Wolfe. Riding and Graves discuss, and mostly reject the validity of, poetic schools and movements: French Symbolism is criticized, while Georgianism and Imagism are both in one way or another perceived as 'dead' movements, movements which produce a poetry written to some preconceived notion of stylistic 'specification', and therefore lacking in integrity.

 Their criticisms are, however, not confined to the writers of poetry. The chapter entitled 'Modernist Poetry and the Plain Reader's Rights' suggests a sympathy with the frustrations of an audience confronted with the particular sorts of difficulty found in modernist texts ('Such poetry seems to say: "Keep out. This is a private performance"'). However, if the 'plain reader' is enlisted by Riding and Graves against difficult poetry, the same 'plain reader' is found, later in the *Survey*, to be wanting in the matter of active and discriminating reading:

> The chief condition the reader makes about the poetry he reads is that it shall not be difficult. For if it is difficult it means that he must think in unaccustomed ways, and thinking to the plain reader, beyond the range necessary for the practical purposes of living, is unsettling and dangerous; he is afraid of his own mind.
>
>   ('The Unpopularity of Modernist Poetry
>   with the Plain Reader', *A Survey*)

Mindful of the poet's freedoms as well as of the reader's rights, their analysis of what sort of audience modern poetry can deserve or expect reaches a more sophisticated position than is to be found in many contemporary debates about elitism and accessibility.

Perhaps the best-known (though often misconstrued) section of *A Survey* is the extended analysis of Shakespeare's Sonnet 129. The context, or platform, of this discussion is an underlining of the importance to a poem of its accurate typographical representation. However, this central point is used as a basis for exploring further issues of modernist formal experimentation – and particularly the innovations of cummings. At the same time Riding and Graves take issue with the carelessness of a publishing

industry, and especially an anthologist culture, that sanitises and dena-
tures poetic texts through decontextualization and regularization. Their
arguments have both stimulated and infuriated Shakespeare editors.[3] It is
also on contemporary record (notably from Empson himself and from I.A.
Richards, his supervisor) that their analysis of Sonnet 129 provided
William Empson with a starting-point for *Seven Types of Ambiguity*
(1930). However, it would be equally true to say that what Riding and
Graves explore as an analytical technique becomes, with Empson, a
complex and expansive critical system, and that there is no genuine
kinship of attitude between their respective critical practices. For
instance, Riding and Graves consider the sonnet as a kind of puzzle,
suggesting a search for closure to the poem once its most difficult meaning
(incorporating contiguous meanings) has been appreciated:

> All these alternate meanings acting on each other, and even other
> possible interpretations of words and phrases, make as it were a
> furiously dynamic crossword puzzle which can be read in many
> directions at once, none of the senses being incompatible with any
> others. This intensified inbreeding of words continues through the
> rest of the poem.
>
>   ('William Shakespeare and e.e. cummings:
>   A Study in Original Punctuation and Spelling', *A Survey*)

The enclosing of meaning implied in these metaphors (the crossword
puzzle and the 'inbreeding') is distinct from the Empsonian method,
which seeks to dissolve such precisions and allow ever more disparate
possibilities – a point forcefully made by Riding herself in a 1975 article
'On Ambiguity'.[4] To align the thrust of the Riding-Graves collaboration

---

3   Of the recent scholarly editions of the Sonnets Stephen Booth takes extended
issue with Riding and Graves; see *Shakespeare's Sonnets*, edited with analytic
commentary by Stephen Booth (New Haven: Yale University Press, 1977).
Booth's argument centres on the observation that for every ambiguity faithfully
preserved by the punctuation of the original many others remain, whether hidden
by that punctuation or unflaggable by any punctuation in its own power. Hence
the desire to preserve ambiguity offers no argument against any particular
proposed modernization of punctuation.
4   'And so the intricate little linguistic revelation made by the analysis of the
sonnet in the book in question (and elsewhere, there), a rather homely public trial
of a critical method [...] involving a principle of requisite checking for honest
linguistic substantiality in the using of words to *mean*, was stripped of its linguistic
good sense and presented as a gospel of ambiguity. Thus there sprouted what came
to be called the New Criticism', Laura (Riding) Jackson, *Modern Languages
Quarterly*, 36 (March, 1975), p.105. For a recent account of the relationship
between the Riding/Graves analysis of Shakespeare and Empson, see Jonathan
Bate, *The Genius of Shakespeare* (London: Picador, 1997), pp.302–311.

too closely with Empson's work (or indeed with what were to become the preoccupations of the New Criticism) would be to misconstrue the very particular, and writerly, preoccupations of Riding and Graves as they worked on *A Survey of Modernist Poetry*.

Riding and Graves argue for the absolute uniqueness of the poetic craft; what they take issue with is the desire of many writers to seek their paradigms for poetry among the other arts. Imagism is a 'dead' movement because, claim Riding and Graves, it seeks its paradigms in the pictorial arts; Symbolism by the same logic is condemned for aspiring to the condition of music. Riding and Graves are unwilling to allow that such paradigmatic restlessness can constitute openness to new forms, and that it reflects Modernist poetry's desire to seek new modes of expression. Beneath the often aggressive posturings of the modernist writers, Riding and Graves detect a profound lack of confidence in the autonomy of the poetic craft. This is exemplified in the work of T.E. Hulme, whose urge to organize the arts according to a single analogical system is, they claim, both flawed and naive:

> The fundamental fallacy in such an attempted co-ordination appears with the difficulty which poetry has to face in entering a new artificially barbaric era. In painting and sculpture neither colour nor stone had been intrinsically affected by the romantic works in which they had been used. To escape the Renaissance, painting and sculpture merely had to revert to barbaric modes – negroid, Oceanic, Aztec, Egyptian, Chinese, archaic Greek – creating modern forms as if in primitive times; forms primitive, obedient to conventions which they accepted, therefore final, absolute, 'abstract'. But poetry could not seemingly submit itself to an *as if*, because its expressive medium, language, had been intrinsically affected not only by the works in which it had been used but also by all the non-poetic uses of which language is capable. This difference between poetry and more regular arts points to a variance in poetry and suggests the probable falsity of all philosophical generalizations on art. The falsity is the falsity of analogy; yet analogy is the strongest philosophical instrument of co-ordination. Since poetry as an art is not sufficiently regular, not sufficiently professional, it is to become so by being made more sculptural or pictorial, by having grafted on it the values and methods of more professional arts.

> ('Conclusion', *A Survey*)

There exist few pithier diagnoses of the anxiety of Modernist literary endeavour than this passage. They do not do justice to Hulme's thought, but justice is not the aim of this polemical book: Riding and Graves assert poetry's separate and indivisible entity against those poets who try to harness poetry to paradigms drawn from other arts. For Riding and Graves, poetry cannot be measured, described or evaluated in terms borrowed (however temporarily and however figuratively) from any medium, process or field other than its own. As they claim in the course of their discussion of Imagism:

> The ideal modernist poem is its own clearest, fullest, and most accurate meaning. Therefore the modernist poet does not have to talk about the use of images 'to render particulars exactly', since the poem does not give a rendering of a poetical picture or idea existing outside the poem, but presents the literal substance of poetry, a newly-created thought-activity: the poem has the character of a creature by itself. Imagism, on the other hand, and all other similar dead movements, took for granted the principle that poetry was a translation of certain kinds of subjects into the language that would bring the reader emotionally closest to them. It was assumed that a natural separation existed between the reader and the subject, to be bridged by the manner in which it was presented.
>
> ('Modernist Poetry and Dead Movements', *A Survey*)

This lies at the centre of their respective philosophies of poetry, philosophies which, for the duration of the writing of *A Survey*, coincide and find expression. Riding and Graves challenge the break up of the organic but irreducible craft of poetry into various mere subdepartments of technique:

> For the virtue of the poem is not in its being set down on paper, as a picture's is in the way it is set down on canvas. Genius in the poet is a sympathy between different parts of his own mind, in the painter between his paint-brush and his canvas. Method in poetry is therefore not anything that can be talked about in terms of physical form. The poem is not the paper, not the type, not the spoken syllables. It is as invisible and as inaudible as thought; and the only method that the real poet is interested in using is one that will present the poem without making it either visible or audible, without turning it into a substitute for a picture or for music.
>
> ('Modernist Poetry and the Plain Reader's Rights', *A Survey*)

It is ironic that a book so insistent on the irreducibility of good poetry, maintaining that poems are their own best explanation, should have become best-known for a critical method based around explication and close reading. The same philosophy which impels Riding and Graves to think of the irreducibility of form also drives their discussion of poetry collections and anthologies in *A Pamphlet Against Anthologies*. Anthologies take poems from their contexts, remove them from their sustainable environments. Poems displaced from their original context are in danger of being misunderstood, or not understood at all, and anthologies (especially the more 'cynical' trade anthologies) uproot poems and transplant them into artificial environments created around false confluences of theme, form, or period. 'Poetry has no intrinsic categories', they state in *A Pamphlet*, in which the vagaries of publishing, as seen from the ironic and often sardonic perspective of the professional writer, are acerbically documented. Riding and Graves, for all the integrity of their intellectual positions, show themselves keenly aware of the practicalities of the business of literature and of the relations between poet, reader and publisher in the modern literary marketplace.

Note on the Texts used
A Survey of Modernist Poetry, by Laura Riding and Robert Graves. London, William Heinemann Ltd., 1927. 295pp.
A Pamphlet Against Anthologies, by Laura Riding and Robert Graves. London, Cape, 1928. 192pp.

Typographical errors in the original texts have been silently corrected. Riding and Graves' footnotes are marked with asterisks. Our own endnotes are numbered.

Acknowledgements
The editors are grateful to Alan J. Clark, compiler of the Laura (Riding) Jackson bibliography, for his help and suggestions throughout the project, and Mark Jacobs and William Graves for their interest and advice. Thanks go also to Clare Brind and Rowland Cotterill.

                                        Charles Mundye and Patrick McGuinness

LAURA RIDING and ROBERT GRAVES

A SURVEY OF
MODERNIST POETRY

NOTE

This book represents a word-by-word collaboration; except for the last chapter, which is a revision by both authors for the purposes of this volume of an essay separately written and printed by one of them.

Contents

CHAPTER I

Modernist Poetry and the
Plain Reader's Rights

IT must be assumed for the moment that poetry not characteristically 'modernist' presents no difficulty to the plain reader; for the complaint against modernist poetry turns on its differences from traditional poetry. These differences would seem to justify themselves if their effect was to bring poetry any nearer the plain reader; even traditional poetry, it is sometimes charged, has a tendency to withdraw itself from the plain reader. But the sophistications of advanced modern poetry seem only to make the breach wider. In the poetry of e.e. cummings, for example, who may be considered conveniently to illustrate the divorce of advanced contemporary poetry from the common-sense standards of ordinary intelligence, is to be found apparently not only a disregard of this intelligence, but an insult to it. Such poetry seems to say: 'Keep out. This is a private performance.'

What we have to do, then, is to discover whether or not the poet means to keep the public out. If, after a careful examination of poems that seem to be only part of the game of high-brow baiting low-brow, they still resist all reasonable efforts, then we must conclude that such work is, after all, merely a joke at the plain reader's expense and let him return to his newspapers and to his Shakespeare (who we are for the moment assuming is understood without difficulty). But if, on the other hand, we are able to get out of these poems the experiences we are accustomed to expect of poetry, or at least see that the poet originally wrote them as poetry and not as literary tricks, then the plain reader must make certain important alterations in his critical attitude. In the first place, he must admit that what is called our common intelligence is the mind in its least active state: that poetry obviously demands a more vigorous imaginative effort than the plain reader has been willing to apply to it; and that, if anthologies compiled to refresh tired minds have indulged his lazy reading habits, the poet can be excused for using exceptional means to make him do justice to his poems, even for inventing a new kind of poem in this end.[1] Next he must wonder whether such innovations have not a real place in the normal course of poetry-writing. Finally, if these things are so, he must question the depth of his understanding of the poetry which, like Shakespeare's, is taken for granted and ask whether a poet like e.e. cummings must not be accepted, if not for his own sake, at least for his effect on the future reading of poetry of any age or style.

To begin with, we shall choose one of e.e. cummings' earlier and simpler poems, one which will nevertheless excite much the same hostility as his later work. It is unusually suitable for analysis, because it is on just the kind of subject that the plain reader looks for in poetry. It appears, moreover, in Mr Louis Untermeyer's popular *Anthology of Modern American Poetry* side by side with the work of poets more willing than e.e. cummings to defer to the intelligence-level of the plain reader.[2] It is all the more important to study, because Mr Untermeyer seems personally hostile to cummings' work and yet to have been forced by the pressure of more advanced critical opinion to include it in a book where modernism in poetry means, in Mr Untermeyer's own definition, simplicity ('the use of the language of everyday speech' and the discarding of that poetical padding which the plain reader and the plain critic enjoy more than Mr Untermeyer would admit). But Mr Untermeyer is speaking of a modernism no longer modern, that of such dead movements as Georgianism and Imagism which were supposedly undertaken in the interests of the plain reader.[3] We are dealing here with a modernism with apparently no feelings of obligation to the plain reader, undertaken, presumably, in the interests of poetry.

SUNSET[4]

stinging
gold swarms
upon the spires
silver

      chants the litanies the
great bells are ringing with rose
the lewd fat bells
         and a tall

wind
is dragging
the
sea

with

dream

-S

With so promising a title, what barriers does the poem raise between itself and the plain reader? In what respects does it seem to sin against the common intelligence? To begin with, the lines do not begin with capitals. The spacing does not suggest any regular verse-form, though it seems to be systematic. No punctuation marks are used. There is no obvious grammar either of the prose or of the poetic kind. But even overlooking these technical oddities, it still seems impossible to read the poem as a logical sequence. A great many words essential to the coherence of the ideas suggested have been deliberately omitted; and the entire effect is so sketchy that the poem might be made to mean almost anything or nothing. If the author once had a precise meaning it was lost in the writing of the poem. Let us, however, assume for the sake of this argument that it is possible to discover the original poem at the back of the poet's mind; or at least to gather enough material from the poem as it stands from which to make a poem that would satisfy all formal requirements, the poem that cummings perhaps meant to hint at with these fragments. Just as the naturalist Cuvier could reconstruct an extinct animal in full anatomical detail from a single tooth, let us restore this extinct poem from what cummings has permitted to survive.

First we must decide if there are not positive features in the poem which make it possible to judge it in these respects as a formal poem and which should occur in any rewriting of the poem with much the same emphasis. The title might undergo some amplification because of a veiled literary reference in lines five and six to Rémy de Gourmont's *Litanies De La Rose*:[5] it might reasonably include some acknowledgement of the poet's debt to French influences, and read 'Sunset Piece: After Reading Rémy de Gourmont'; although the original title *Sunset* would be no less literary. The heavy alliteration in *s* in the first seven lines, confirmed in the last by the solitary capitalized *S*, cannot be discarded. The context demands it – certain inevitable associations are connected with the words as they stand. The first word, *stinging*, taken alone suggests merely a sharp feeling; its purpose is only to prepare for the poem and supply an emotional source from which the other *s* ideas may derive. In the second line *swarms* develops the alliteration, at the same time colouring *stinging* with the association of golden bees and softening it with the suppressed idea of buzzing. We are now ready for the more tender *s* word, *spires*, in the third line. *Silver*, the single word of the fourth line, brings us back to the contrast between cold and warm in the first and second lines (*stinging* suggests cold in contrast with the various suggestions of warmth in the *gold swarms*) because *silver* reminds one of cold water as *gold* does of warm light. Two suppressed *s* words play behind the scenes in this first part of the poem, both disguised in *silver* and *gold*, namely, *sea* and *sun*. *Sea* itself does not actually occur until the twelfth line, when the *s* alliteration has flagged: separated from alliterative associations, it becomes the definite image *sea* and the centre around which the poem is to be built up. But once it has appeared there is little more to be said; the poem trails off, closing with the large *S* echo of the last line. The hyphen before this *S* detaches it from *dream* and sets it apart as the alliterative summary of the poem; in a realistic sense *-S* might stand for the alternation of quiet and hiss in wave movement. As a formal closing it leaves us with a feeling like the one we started with, but less acute, because the *z* sound has prevailed over the *s* sound with which the poem was begun. The sunset is over, the final impression is darkness and sleep, though the *-S* vaguely returns to the two large *S*'s of the title.

Another feature which would recur in the rewriting is the slowing down of the rhythm in the last half of the poem, indicated by the shortening of the line and by the double spacing. In regular verse this would naturally mean line lengthening, the closing of a ten-syllabled line series with a twelve-syllabled couplet, for example. Though no end-rhymes occur in the poem as it stands, the rhyme element is undoubtedly strong. The only obvious rhyme sympathy is between *stinging* and *ringing*, but many suppressed rhymes are present: not only *swinging* accompanying the idea of bells but other new rhyme suggestions such as *bees* and *seas*, *bells* and *swells*, *spires* and *fires*. In the rewritten poem a definite metrical scheme would have to be employed, but the choice would be governed by the character of the original poem. The rhythm would be gentle and simple, with few marked emphases. Monosyllables would prevail, with a noticeable recurrence of *ing* words; and *bells* would have to be repeated. Here, then, is a poem embodying the important elements of e.e. cummings' poem, but with each line starting with a capital, with normal spacing and punctuation, and with a regular verse-form. It contains no images not directly suggested by him, but links up grammatically what appeared to be an arrangement based on caprice.

SUNSET PIECE

After reading Rémy de Gourmont

> White foam and vesper wind embrace.
> The salt air stings my dazzled face
> And sunset flecks the silvery seas
> With glints of gold like swarms of bees
> And lifts tall dreaming spires of light
> To the imaginary sight,
> So that I hear loud mellow bells
> Swinging as each great wave swells,
> Wafting God's perfumes on the breeze,
> And chanting of sweet litanies
> Where jovial monks are on their knees,
> Bell-paunched and lifting glutton eyes
> To windows rosy as these skies.

And this slow wind – how can my dreams forget –
Dragging the waters like a fishing-net.

This version shows that cummings was bound to write the poem as he did in order to prevent it from becoming what we have made it. To write a new poem on an old subject like sunset and avoid all the obvious poetical formulas the poet must write in a new way if he is to evoke any fresh response in his readers at all. Not only does the rewritten poem demand much less attention than the first poem; but it is difficult to feel respect for a poem that is full of reminiscences not only of Rémy de Gourmont, but of Wordsworth ('To the imaginary sight'), Milton (in the metrical variations taken from L'Allegro), Messrs Belloc and Chesterton ('Where jovial monks …' etc.) and Tagore in English translation ('Dragging the waters like a fishing net').[6] Stale phrases such as 'vesper wind' and 'silver seas' have come to mean so little that they scarcely do their work in the poem. And yet we shall see that such phrases cannot be avoided if we are to revise the poem for the plain man. 'White foam' is understood from the sea setting, the movement of the poem, the cold hissing implied in the sequence of *s*'s. 'Vesper wind' is suggested by *sunset, spires, monks, bells, tall wind*. 'Salt air', as well as resulting from the embrace of 'white foam' and 'vesper wind', is built up from *stinging, sea,* and *wind*. The transformations are fairly obvious in the next three lines. 'Imaginary sight' is necessary to remind the plain reader that the poem is not to be taken literally, a hint that e.e. cummings disdained to give. It should be noticed that 'imaginary' is the longest and slowest word in the poem but adds nothing to the picture; in fact, makes it less real. The seventh and eighth lines express the connection between bells and waves that cummings leaves the reader to deduce, or not. The ninth line is the expansion of the rose idea demanded by the context: *Monks, spires, litanies* are all bound up with the Catholic symbolism of the rose; and in rewriting the poem it is impossible not to develop the literary associations of the rose as well (wafting, perfumes). The rose-windows of cathedrals are also obviously suggested. Unfortunately *lewd*, too strong a word for a formal sunset piece, has to be broken up into *jovial* and *glutton*, recalling the Christmas-annual type of monk. The analogy between *great bells* and *fat monks* has to be made definite, thus introducing gratuitous words like *mellow, bell-paunched, on their knees*, etc. Instead of taking advantage of the natural associations in certain highly pictorial words, we have had to go over much unnecessary ground and ended by being merely dull and banal. In lengthening the metre in the last two lines to match the slowing down in the original piece it will be noticed how many superfluous words and images have had to be introduced here too. First of all, *slow* itself, as weakening to the concentration of the poem as the line 'To the imaginary sight'. Then, '– how can my dreams forget –', to account grammatically for the vivid present tense in which the whole poem is written, and to put *dream* in its more logical position, since in the original poem it is doing double duty for a specific image (*fishing-net*, following from *dragging*) and the vagueness with which the image is felt.

The conclusion to be drawn from this exercise might be that poems must in the future be written in the cummings way if poetry is not to fall to pieces altogether. But the poetry of e.e. cummings is clearly more important as a sign of local irritation in the poetic body than as the model for a new tradition. The important thing to recognize, in a time of popular though superficial education,[7] is the necessity of emphasizing to the reading public the differences between good and bad poems, just such differences as we have been pointing out here. Poems in such a time, indeed, may forget that they have any function other than to teach the proper approach to poetry: there is an exaggerated though excusable tendency to suspend the writing of all poetry not intentionally critical. (There are, of course, always exceptions: poets whose writing is so self-contained that it is not affected by stalenesses in traditional poetry or obliged to attack them or escape from them.) cummings in this poem was really rewriting the other poem which we gave into a good poem. But for the rarer poet there is no 'other poem'; there is only the poem which he writes. cummings' technique, indeed, if further and more systematically developed, would become so complicated that poetry would be no more than mechanical craftsmanship, the verse patterns growing so elaborate that the principal interest in them would be mathematical. In their present experimental stage, and only in their experimental stage, these patterns are undoubtedly suggestive. Poets, however, do not pursue innovations for their own sake. They are on the whole conservative in their methods so long as these ensure the proper security and delivery of the poem.

For the virtue of the poem is not in its being set down on paper, as a picture's is in the way it is set down on canvas. Genius in the poet is a sympathy between different parts of his own mind, in the painter between his paint-brush and his canvas. Method in poetry is therefore not anything that can be talked about in terms of physical form. The poem is not the paper, not the type, not the spoken syllables. It is as invisible and as inaudible as thought; and the only method that the real poet is interested in using is one that will present the poem without making it either visible or audible, without turning it into a substitute for a picture or for music. But when conservatism of method, through its abuse by slack-minded poets, has come to mean the supplanting of the poem by an exercise in poet-craft, then there is a reasonable place for innovation, if the new method defeats the old method and brings up the important question: how should poetry be written? Once this question is asked, the new method has accomplished its end. Further than this it should not be allowed to go, for poems cannot be written from a formula. The principal value of a new method is that it can act as a strong deterrent against writing in a worn-out style. It is not suggested here that poets should imitate cummings, but that poems like cummings' and the attention they demand should make it harder for the standardized article to pass itself off as poetry. If we return to the two versions of the 'Sunset' piece, it will be seen just how this benefit is conferred. We may not accept the cummings version, but once we have understood it we cannot return with satisfaction to the standardized one.

Turning back for a more direct comparison of these two versions, we perceive how much of the force of the original has been lost in the second. We have used capitals throughout as in formal verse, but have thus eliminated the large final *S*, which was one of the most important properties of the original, and given a look of unnecessary importance to words like *And*, *To*, and *So*. By substituting normal spacing and verse-form we have had to disregard the significance of the double spacing and indentation, and of the variation in the length of the lines. Formal indentation can either be a guide to rhyming pairs or a sign that the first part of a line is missing, but it cannot denote musical rests of varying value as with cummings. We have also expanded the suggested ideas by grammatic means and supplemented them with the words that seemed to have been omitted. But in so doing we have sacrificed the compactness of the previous poem and introduced a definiteness which is false to its carefully devised dreaminess. So by correcting the poem in those poetic features in which it seemed deficient we have not added anything to it but on the contrary detracted from it.

What, now, has happened to the formal features of the cummings poem when reproduced in the rewritten poem? The expansion of the poem by the addition of the suppressed words has necessarily multiplied the number of *s*'s in the poem, because these suppressed words show a high proportion of *s*'s. This alliteration, sustained over several couplets, does not match the alliteration of the shorter poem, especially since we have been obliged to use many *s*'s that have no alliterative significance ('To windows rosy as the skies'). Neither has the gradual slowing down of the rhythm in the last half of the poem been effectively reproduced. In the actual poem the slowing down extends over the sestet of this fragmentary sonnet (the fragmentary line, -*S*, being an alliterative hang-over). But as in the formal treatment cummings' simple octave develops a prolixity which destroys the proper balance between it and its sestet, we have had to abandon the sonnet form and pack into two lines words which should have had the time-value of six. The best we have been able to do is to keep fourteen lines (or rather seven rhyming couplets, one of which has an extra line). The rhymes, too, in the new poem have mutilated the sense: they express the remoteness of the scene by a series of echoes instead of by silences: for cummings' lines can definitely be regarded as sonnet-lines filled out with musical rests. So by putting the poem into a form in which a definite metrical scheme could be recognized we have entirely altered the character of the poem. We have not even been able to save the scraps of quite regular iambic rhythm with which we started.

Certain admissions must, therefore, be made. We have not only rejected the formal poem in favour of the cummings poem: we have seen that the cummings poem itself was an intensely formal poem. Indeed, its very technicalities caused it to be mistaken for a mere assemblage of words, a literary trick. But as it is apparently capable of yielding the kind of experiences customarily expected from poetry, in fact the most ordinary of such experiences, our conclusion must be that the plain reader's approach to poetry is adequate only for poems as weak as the critical effort that he is ready to apply to them; and that cummings, to disregard the satiric hilarity in which many of his poems are written, really means to write serious poetry and to have his poetry taken seriously, that is, read with the critical sympathy it deserves. The importance of any new technical methods that he makes use of to bring this about lies not in their ultimate permanence or impermanence, but in their establishment of what the poet's rights are in his poem: how free he is to proceed without regard to the inferior critical efforts to which the poem will probably be submitted. What, then, of the plain reader's rights? They are, presumably, like the poet's, whatever his intelligence is able to make them.

It must be admitted that excessive interest in the mere technique of the poem can become morbid both in the poet and the reader, like the composing and solving of crossword puzzles. Once the sense of a poem with a technical soul, so to speak, is unriddled and its patterns plainly seen, it is not fit for re-reading; as with the Sphinx in the fable, allowing its riddle to be guessed is equivalent to suicide. A poem of this kind is nevertheless able to stave off death by continually revealing, under examination, an unexpected reserve of new riddles; and as long as it is able to supply these it can continue to live as a poem. Yet at some stage or other the end must come. If it is asked: 'Is this really a poem?' the answer must be: 'Yes, as long as one can go on discovering new surprises in it.' But clearly the surprises cannot last for ever; nor can we, as in the indestructible poem whose soul is not technical, go back to the beginning and start all over again as with a new poem. The obvious weakness in the surprise-poem is that it encourages the reader to discover many things not consciously intended by the poem. But, while there is no way of being absolutely sure that the steps taken in unravelling the poem are the same as those involved in inventing the poem, the strength of such a poem is proved by the room it allows for surprises thus improvised by the reader, by the extent to which it is tactically disposed to resist critical attacks. As long as a poem is so disposed, it justifies itself. One thing we can be sure of, that this particular poem of e.e. cummings was not examined in this way by Mr Untermeyer. Otherwise he would not have included it as an example of poetry that 'does not provoke the reader to anything more than irritation' in an anthology whose principal aim is to soothe, not irritate. He would have left it out, because it could no longer serve as a foil to the more formal poem, seeing that it was a formal poem.

How much more life is left in the poem at this point? Have we come to an end; or are there still further reasons why it should continue to be called a poem, since it is only a poem as long as there is a possibility of its yielding still more meaning? Did we not, without assuming any formal verse-pattern, give a satisfactory explanation of the poem? Did we not also find it possible to give an entirely new view of it on the basis of its being a suppressed sonnet? Did we not accept the poem as a non-grammatic construction and make sense of it nevertheless? Could we not show it to be potentially or even actually grammatic and make sense of it because it was grammatic? By reading *swarms* and *chants*, which we have probably been regarding as nominative plural nouns, as third person singular verbs, and by reading *silver* and *gold* not as adjectives but as nouns? The poem would then stand grammatically as follows:

> Stinging gold swarms upon the spires.
> Silver [*i.e.* a voice or tone of silver] chants the litanies
> The great bells are ringing with rose –
> The lewd fat bells –
> And a tall wind is dragging the sea with dreams.

Nor could we allow ourselves to be stopped by the length of the poem, since by thus limiting the number of possible discoveries to its length we should be implying that the virtue of a poem was in its length. Even if we had exhausted all the possibilities in a poem of thirty-one words – the grammar, the metre and other technical aspects, the context and the association of images – we should still have the fact that the poem had thirty-one words, and perhaps find in it another formalism. Can it be a coincidence that this is also the standard length of the tanka, the dominant verse-form in Japanese poetry – thirty-one syllables, each of word value? The Japanese influence is further intimated by cummings' tendency to suggest and symbolize rather than to express in full. In Japanese, according to the conventional arrangement of the thirty-one word-units in lines of five, seven, five, seven, seven, this poem would be set down like this:

> stinging gold swarms upon the
> spires silver chants the litanies the great
> bells are ringing with rose
> the lewd fat bells and a tall
> wind is dragging the sea with dreams.

But stronger than the Japanese influence in modern English and American poetry is the French, which in turn has borrowed so much from the Japanese. Mallarmé, the father of French symbolism, turned the art of suggestion in poetry into a science. He found the tradition of his national poetry so exhausted by sterile laws of prosody that he had to practise poetry as a science to avoid malpractising it as an art. Rimbaud, with all Mallarmé's science behind him and endowed with a natural poetic mind as well, was able to practise poetry as an art again. Similarly cummings and other experimentalists – cummings is to be regarded rather as an inspired amateur than a scientist – may be preparing the way for an English or American Rimbaud. As Paul Valéry, the French critic and poet, says of Mallarmé and Rimbaud, discussing their employment of the vehicles of sense in poetry: 'What is only a system in Mallarmé becomes a domain in Rimbaud'. So modernist poets are developing resources by mechanical means to which a future poet will have easy access when he turns the newly opened-up territory into a personal poetic domain.

Although an elaborate system of poetry-writing can go into the making of a natural poet like Rimbaud, it may on the other hand end in mere preciousness, which in turn may harden into a convention as tyrannic as the one it was originally invented to criticize. There is more danger of this, however, in French poetry than in English. Paul Valéry has even been made a member of the French Academy, in recognition, presumably, of his formal influence on contemporary poetry. Like cummings, although as classical in form as cummings is romantic, he relies almost entirely on the effectiveness of images – on their power to evoke sensations and on their strangeness. To describe how night hid from Narcissus his own beloved image in the fountain, he says that night slid between him and his image like 'a knife sheåring a fruit in two'.[8] What he means is that Narcissus and the image form a whole as symmetrical as the two halves of an apple before they are divided. cummings' images are as strange and vivid as this ('gold swarms' or 'ringing with rose', for example); but we do not suggest making an academician of cummings or calling his most recent and more methodical phase 'Pope-ian' as Valéry's last phase is known by his admirers as 'Racinian', after the master craftsman of the most formal period in French poetry.

Modernist English poetry also imitates the French in the use of combinations of sounds to give a musical picture. This is, of course, no new thing in English poetry. Gray, one of the most traditional of all English poets, wishing to give the picture of slow and painful descent down a steep mountain, writes:

> As down the steep of Snowdon's shaggy side
> He wound with toilsome march his long array.[9]

But this usage has never been applied except in occasional decoration, and even as such has been discouraged rather than encouraged by criticism. It may escape adverse criticism only where the combinations of sounds add musicalness without taking away from the meaning; but never where they over-represent the meaning. For example, Milton's *Lycidas* and Tennyson's *Blow, Bugle, Blow* have been praised, because the predominance of l's, *m*'s, *n*'s, and *r*'s in the former and the variation of vowel sounds in the latter please the ear by acting as a musical accompaniment to the idea and cannot be regarded as in any sense containing the idea itself. The only general principle implied in such practice is that poetry should be, where possible, as pleasing to the ear as to the mind. The danger in it is that it can have the effect of allowing the thought of the poem to be controlled by its ability to please musically, as in Victorian poetry.

But musicalness in modern French verse means something else, the treating of word-sounds as musical notes in which the meaning itself is to be found. This makes poetry curiously like acrostics and takes it even further from its natural course than Victorianism in its worst coloratura effects. The bond between the Victorian poet and his reader was at least an agreement between them of a common, though not an original, sentiment. The meaning of a poem was understood between them beforehand from the very title, and the persuasion of the word-music was intended to keep the poem vibrating in the memory long after it had been read. The bond, however, between the French modernist poet and his reader is one of technical ingenuity, in the poet in setting the meaning down in combinations of sounds, in the reader in interpreting words as combinations of sounds rather than as words. Actually there is very little poetic thought in Victorian poetry because of the compromise it makes between ideas and their pleasurable expression. But the compromise in this other poetry, though less apparent, is still more destructive of poetic thought. It is between ideas and typography, and as such means the domination of ideas by mechanics. By giving the letters of words a separate personality we have a new psychology of letters entirely distinct from the psychology of images. A striking illustration of the attempt to reconcile these two psychologies is a poem of Rimbaud's on the colours of the vowels.[10] It is plain that the colours associated with vowels will vary widely with the person and may be determined by so irrelevant a cause as the colour of the alphabet blocks which one used as a child. A better case might perhaps be made for the meaning-associations of consonants, particularly of combinations of consonants such as *st*, as in *stinging*, *strike*, *stench*, to denote sharp assault, and the final *nch*, as in *clinch*, *munch*, *wrench*, to denote strain. But such imitation by the letters of a word of its meaning is only occasional: it cannot be made a general rule. There are many more instances of letters out of harmony with word-meanings than in harmony with them. The word *kiss*. *Is* this *iss* any gentler than the *iss* of *hiss?* Or is the *k* in *kiss* gentler than the *k* of *kick?* Logically such a theory should mean that a French poem written in this way would produce the same effect on a person who did not understand French as on one who did.

When it is remembered how such theories fill the literary air, it will be realized what great restraint e.e. cummings imposed on himself in the matter of alliteration and other tricks with letters. He would not, we feel, let such theories run away with him to the extent of forcing his choice of words to depend more on the sense of their sounds than on the sense of their images. His choice of *swarms*, for instance, is primarily determined by the three meanings combined in the word (the crowding sense, the bee-buzzing sense, and another hitherto not noted – the climbing sense associated with *spires* and the eye looking up to the light); not by the occurrence of *s* and *z* or by the presence of *warm* in *swarm*, though these are accidents of which he takes every advantage. And this is the way such things should happen in poetry, by coincidence. The poet appreciates and confirms rather than elaborately stage-manages. A certain amount of superstitious faith in language is necessary if the poet is going to perform the sort of miracles expected of and natural to poetry.

CHAPTER II

The Problem of Form and Subject-Matter in Modernist Poetry

MODERN French poetic theory lays a great deal of emphasis on the phonetic sense of words; and has done so increasingly since the symbolists. For a long time, indeed, the French have been dissatisfied with the success of poetry as compared with other arts, and have attempted to remedy its supposed deficiencies by bringing it closer to music. To do this they have had to insist on a musical meaning accompanying the word-meaning, on introducing a system of letter-notation similar to musical notation. Three lines from Paul Valéry will illustrate this picture-making in poetry by the help of sounds:

> Il se fit Celui qui dissipe
> En conséquences son Principe,
> En étoiles, son Unité.[1]

Now, since we are able to recognise *dissipe*, *conséquences*, *Principe*, and *Unité* by their English parallels, we must rewrite these lines in some practical phonetic notation which will completely divorce them from any associated meaning, if we would test their direct phonetic value:

> Eel s' fee s' lwee kee deesseep p'
> Ahng kohnsaykahng s' sohng Prangseep p',
> Ahng aytwal l', sonn Ewneetay.

This is the best rough phonetic approximation that we can make without the use of a formal phonetic system. We are immediately impressed by the recurrence of the strong *s* and the narrow *ee* sound, as we are supposed to be. This might denote a number of things: a man whetting a scythe, a child writing on a slate, or a serpent trying to talk. On the other hand, such sounds might have nothing to do with the subject; as in the couplet:

> As fleecy sheep we leap
> Across this grassy sweep;

the *s* and *ee* sounds are contrary to the sense. Suppose, however, we did actually choose the idea of a serpent's talking, as we were meant to. What, then, is our clue to what the serpent is talking about? Or are the lines merely meant to represent a serpent talking, without any collateral meaning? No. They represent, as a matter of fact, a serpent talking about God. But how are we to deduce God from the sound of the poem or know indeed when the alliteration is to indicate the subject or the elocutionist? We must admit that for the special purpose of representing a serpent sneering at God such sound-combinations may be very wittily employed. But as a general thing a poetic practice like this becomes as tiresome and puerile as, say, the incessant puns and jokes of Goldsmith, Hood, or Calverley. Wit in poetry should be devoted to the irony in ideas rather than in phonetics. Phonetics, if they get the upper hand in a poem, turn it into an exercise in elocution.

But let us try another Valérian specimen, one in which there is no speaking in character:

> Vous me le murmurez, ramures! ... O rumeur déchirante.[2]

Because *murmurez* and *rumeur* are suggestive of their meanings in English, we might be able to get something of the intended sense (the murmur of wind among leaves) and even make a good guess at the meaning of the other words; if only because we have Tennyson's

> immemorial elms
> And murmur of innumerable bees,[3]

as a class-room quotation to help us to it. Could we not, however, easily improvise a line of the same musical character but with a totally different meaning?

> More ordure never will renew our midden's pure manure.

This line will show how misleading to the sense letters can be, and makes us suspect that the aim of such poetry as Valéry's is to cast a musical enchantment unallied with the meaning of a poem. The meaning becomes merely a historical setting for the music, which the reader need or need not be aware of. We are made to feel that the poet would not object to his reader's adopting the same attitude to his poems as his own *Mme Teste* to lofty and abstract questions:[4] instead of being bored by them, she was musically entertained by them. Valéry, perhaps realizing the strain put upon his reader by the preciousness of his images, holds his attention by the masterly skill of these musical distractions.

It is here important to understand the close connection between Paul Valéry and e.e. cummings, and the question of impressionism. The chief claim of impressionism is that the realistic truth about anything may be conveyed better by the impressions it gives the observer, however disjointed or irrelevant these may seem, than by systematic reasoning or study. Impressionist poetry describes an object by creating in the reader the indefinite feelings he would have on seeing it, not by giving definite facts about it. This is a method in poetry first formally recommended by Poe,[5] borrowed from him to justify and explain the things that began to happen to French poetry with Baudelaire, and re-imported into America when French poetry had carried Poe's theory far beyond his intentions, which had to do more with the sentiment than with the technical theory of poetry. Poe defined poetry as a combination of music and an idea, resulting in indefinite feelings. But this is, after all, only a re-statement of the most historically familiar definition of the aim of poetry: to create a pleasant effect on the reader; while formal impressionism aims at a technical correctness – it wishes the reader to have the same frame of mind as the poet had when he wrote, to help the reader to rewrite the poem for himself with the poet's mind. These so-called 'indefinite feelings' of impressionism, therefore, must be expressed in painstakingly precise images, since the whole effect of the poem depends on an accurate identity of the reader's feelings with the poet's.

If, then, the poet practises impressionism according to its literal meaning, it is unfair to call him an impressionist in the loose, popular sense of the word. He rejects reason and logic as poetic aids, not because they lead to definite feelings, but because the feelings they lead to are not definite, not subtle enough for his purpose. 'Indefinite' should be understood in its opposite sense, namely, not to be defined by the more ordinary methods of speech; so *definite*, in fact, that ordinary methods of measurement are not accurate enough. Images in poetry that seem strained and obscure are often like distances so small or so large that the foot-rule is of no use in measuring them, so that one has to work in abstract mathematics, though the distances are real. Suppose a poet wishes to describe a sunset. He can say in substance: 'It was beautiful. The sea was flecked with gold as the sun sank into it. Above my head floated rosy clouds. At my feet hissed the silvery foam. Bells were ringing somewhere. There was a salt taste in the air and the evening wind blew slowly in from the sea as night drew on.' Or he can say: 'It was beautiful. At first I felt invigorated. My eyes ached with the dazzle of the sun and the saltiness of the air. As I looked up to the rosy glory above me, a great religious feeling overcame me; I seemed in the presence of God. There was a ringing in my ears. I felt warm and cold at once. But after a time the wind made me feel sleepy, so I turned in.' Now it would be possible to call either of these poems impressionist in the colloquial sense, for they would record objectively or subjectively the poet's impressions with a view to reproducing them in the reader. In reality, however, they would convey only a vague and somewhat insincere atmosphere, as would a formalized version of cummings' early poem 'Sunset'. For an actual experience of this sunset one would have to go to some such poem as cummings'. In it would be found a complicated recipe for a sunset experience, as if for a pudding, not merely a description of what the pudding looked like or how it tasted. For such a method turns the reader into a poet.

This 'Sunset' poem of Mr cummings, then, is not, strictly speaking, Mr cummings' poem, but the poem of anybody who will be at pains to write it. What at first sight strikes the plain reader as external peculiarities that hindered him from approaching the meaning of the poem – its oddness of form – now appear to be the poet's means of avoiding that conventional form which generally does stand between the reader and the poem. Indeed, if we look upon form as something distinct from the subject-matter of a poem, in this sense true impressionist poems are usually without form; or rather they are capable of having a new form with every reader. The poet blends the subject of the poem with the feelings that the subject arouses into one expression. This unity makes the poem a living whole; it is impressionistic, but not because the subject and the feelings it arouses become indefinite in the combination. They make a blend, not a blur.

Looking on impressionism as one of the earliest manifestations of the general modernist tendency to overcome the distinction between subject-matter and form, we realize that Valéry draws the same old-fashioned line between *music* and idea that Poe did; that he subscribes, in fact, to the historically most familiar conception of poetry. He is a classicist in the musical associations he gives his poems, all intricately designed to create the indefinite feelings that he desires to arouse in the reader. Although in his choice of the images through which he conveys poetic ideas he is a modernist, the images apparently intended, that is, to arouse *definite* feelings, these feelings are really more like the physical sensation a thing gives than the idea of itself it gives. To these definite feelings provoked by the images, or, we might say, the thought, of a poem of Valéry's, the indefinite feelings provoked by the *sounds* of the words form a musical background. In fact, paradoxically, it is in this musical background that the ideas are suggested rather than in the logical thought of the images. Valéry deliberately suppresses Reason in poetry; but he allows the musical background to make the logical connections between the images. And this is what we mean by calling him a classicist in form and a modernist in the thought-content of his poems. He handles the modernist problem of achieving a unity between form and subject-matter by letting form suggest the subject of the poem and thought-content do all that form is ordinarily supposed to do. The only reason for calling this method impressionistic is that it does not and could not succeed in arriving at an ingenious balance between the two sets of feelings, definite and indefinite, which are supposed to combine to give the poetry meaning; all it results in is the vague blur that impressionism has come to stand for in its most derogatory sense.

Valéry is only one familiar contemporary example of these modern French theories of poetry which have had such an abnormal and unwholesome influence on the younger poets of America and England. In cummings' defence it should be said that, though his poetry by its immediate effect of oddness does invite labels, it is possible to understand it without reference to labels. Particularly as regards the label *impressionism* – it is not necessary to associate him with it in order to explain the poem 'Sunset'; although as an impressionist he makes a very good case for impressionism. But any fairly good poet can be used to justify any practicable theory of poetry, however inadequate a theory it may be by which to write poetry. Shakespeare, indeed, can be used to justify impressionism or any other poetic theory simply because he is such a good poet. It would be as reasonable to explain Shakespeare, who was independent of poetic theory, in terms of impressionism as by any of the poetic theories prevailing at his time. It would be wrong to overlook the influence on Shakespeare of contemporary theories, but it would be false to say that he wrote as he did from a conscious use of these theories. If Shakespeare had been critical in the way a good poet is generally supposed to be, then we should expect to find in Shakespeare merely evidences of well-chosen poetic theories. As a matter of fact, his work was such a clearing-house of good and bad elements in contemporary poetry and drama that they cannot have been introduced by any conscious critical choice.

It would be as absurd to say that cummings sat down to write a poem with all the rules of impressionism before him as to say that Shakespeare sat down to write a play with all the theories of the so-called 'university wits' before him. These men – Lodge, Peele, Greene, Nashe, Lyly, and Marlowe – had to set themselves the deliberate task of compromising between the old popular type of play, which was very violent, disorderly and exciting, and the new blank-verse play on the classical model, which was very orderly and very dull. They had for the time being to treat the drama as a scientific problem. But when we get past Marlowe's early work and past Kyd's *Spanish Tragedy* we find the drama no longer treated as a problem; it is already a successful convention; the London theatres are paying concerns, and Shakespeare, fortified by his long apprenticeship in these theatres, has nothing to worry about. These dramatic experimenters provided him with a legacy; but he was the natural heir to it by the right of his genius. What were conscious theories in the dramatists of the previous generation became in him native habits. We may say generally that there are no technical inventions in Shakespeare's plays or sonnets. The nearest thing to invention in Shakespeare is his original use of other people's inventions. The convention of the Court Fool, introduced by the wits to make a link between the old farcical play and the new classical tragedy, was no longer with Shakespeare mere comic relief, but a living, even a serious, part of the tragedy itself. Likewise with the sonnet: though pre-Elizabethan experiments with the sonnet, which little by little removed it from the Italian model, were made by Wyatt and Surrey, the

Elizabethan sonnet is nevertheless called after Shakespeare, in spite of the fact that Shakespeare made no new experiments with it, that by the time it reached him it had been successfully used by all the Elizabethan small fry. Yet the sonnet theory can be proved in Shakespeare's sonnets as all pre-Shakespearian dramatic theories can be proved in his plays.

An undue prominence is given to poetic theories either when people who are not real poets are encouraged by the low state of poetry to try to write it themselves: such poets must obviously depend on theories in proportion as they are wanting in genius. Or when critics without any poetic sense attempt to explain changes in poetry to themselves and to the reading public. No genuine poet or artist ever called himself after a theory or invented a name for a theory. And it was surely a critic who first pointed out the distinction between subject-matter and form, and from this began to philosophize on form; as it is surely criticism which has always stood between poetry and the plain reader, made possible the writing of so much false poetry and, by granting too much respect to theories, lost the power of distinguishing between what is false and what is true.

The struggle on the part of poets to make subject-matter and form coincide in spite of criticism is an old one, as old, perhaps, as the first critic. It should not be confused with attempts to make form suit subject-matter (as the Pindaric Ode was cast to contain any stately flattery); or to suit subject-matter to a popular form (as the sonnet has become a general utility form designed to do for a variety of subjects). The whole trend of modern poetry is toward treating poetry like a very sensitive substance which succeeds better when allowed to crystallize by itself than when put into prepared moulds: this is why modern criticism, deprived of its discussions of questions of form, tries to replace them by obscure metaphysical reflections. Modern poetry, that is, is groping for some principle of self-determination to be applied to the making of the poem – not lack of government, but government from within. Free verse was one of the largest movements toward this end. But it has too often meant not self-government but complete laissez-faire on the part of the poet, a licence to metrical anarchy instead of a harmonious enjoyment of liberty. Strangely enough, when we come upon an example of free verse that shows clearness and restraint and proportion, we do not think of it as free verse, though we do not think of it, on the other hand, as poetry of a traditional form. And this is as it should be. An example is the opening of a poem by Hart Crane, 'Passage':

> Where the cedar leaf divides the sky
> I heard the sea.
> In sapphire arenas of the hills
> I was promised an improved infancy.[6]

The rhyme between *sea* and *infancy* is not strong enough to mislead one into construing this as a regular stanza. The impression of regularity comes from a careful alternation of images, from a regularity of design more fundamental than mere verse regularity. The authorized version of the Bible, in passages where the original text was in poetic form, is the most familiar example of this:

> The beauty of Israel is slain upon thy high places:
> How are the mighty fallen!
> Tell it not in Gath,
> Publish it not in the streets of Askelon;
> Lest the daughters of the Philistines rejoice,
> Lest the daughters of the uncircumcised triumph.[7]

The effect of regularity is here again achieved by the recurrence of ideas in varying alternations to show the movement of the poem. As in Mr Crane's poem a parallelism exists between the first and third lines and the second and fourth, the third and fourth carrying the imaginative experience of the first and second to a more specialized meaning, from which the direction of the remainder of the poem may be taken; so in the Biblical lines quoted a parallelism also exists between the *beauty of Israel* and *the mighty*, and between *slain upon thy high places* and *fallen* of the first and second lines. The scorn with which the last four lines here must be pronounced is obviously dictated by the ironic contrast between the *high places* of Israel and the *streets* of Gath and Askelon (the streets of these cities being generally trenches below ground-level) and between the *beauty of Israel* and the *daughters of the Philistines*. In Mr Crane's poem the sympathetic connection between the first four lines and the rest of the poem depends not so much on the general technical symmetry of the poem as on the use of the images directly stated in these lines in a more indirect and complicated sense in the following lines. Poetry so treated is nothing more than a single theme subjected to as many variations as its first or simplest statement will allow, even to the point where it ironically contradicts itself. There is in it no room for, and no reason for, a separate element of form. Obvious mechanical form imposed on a poem, unless the poem is deficient in the balance of its ideas, is like architectural dressing that spoils the natural proportions of a building and has not even structural usefulness.

How, now, does the question of form affect the long poem? Let us take Tennyson's *In Memoriam*, which embroiders the theme of his friend's death in a sequence of episodes, and T.S. Eliot's poem, *The Waste Land*, which enlarges the introductory theme of the death and decay implicit in Spring to embrace the death and decay implicit in all forms of hopeful human energy.[8] In the first, the same rhymed stanza is maintained through all the varying moods of the poem; in the second the progress of the poem is marked by the most sensitive change – not only from episode to episode but from passage to passage. It is just at these delicate transitions from one atmosphere to another, where the separate parts are joined into a single continuous poem, that the poetic quality is to be looked for. No such transitions are to be found in Tennyson's poem, or for that matter in a poem like the *Aeneid*: length in such poems means bulk. The poem is as long as the poet's endurance and the reader's patience permit.

Just how long this will be depends on the period in which it is written: we generally find long poems when poetic themes are limited to a few approved subjects, such as war, religion, lamentation or love. The length of the poem is then only a sign of the dignity of the subject. It has not until recent times been considered as something beside dignified bulk. A long poem was not thought to need the same unity as a short poem: the unchanging metre was enough to keep the loosely connected parts of the poem together. This is the case with *In Memoriam*, where the different sections are digressive rather than progressive. But *The Waste Land* has to be read as a short poem: that is, as a unified whole. The reader can no more skip a passage in it than a line in a short poem and expect to understand the poem. For it is not a long poem in the usual sense of being a number of short poems in a uniform metre, joined by mere verse padding.

> When lovely woman stoops to folly and
> Paces about her room again, alone,
> She smoothes her hair with automatic hand,
> And puts a record on the gramophone.

This formal rhymed stanza, reminiscent of Goldsmith, is by Mr Eliot ironically applied to a sordid modern love-scene. We are to go from here back to a romantic picture of Queen Elizabeth and Leicester in amorous progress down the same Thames over whose waters the noise of this gramophone is now carried. How is the transition between these two passages made? The ten-syllabled iambic line of the stanza quoted turns into blank verse beginning with a romantic quotation from *The Tempest*, getting more and more ragged as the music is interrupted by the Thames-side noises, and finally trailing off with syncopated phrases suggested by a mandoline.

> 'This music crept by me upon the waters'
> And along the Strand, up Queen Victoria Street.
> O City city, I can sometimes hear
> Beside a public bar in Lower Thames Street,
> The pleasant whining of a mandoline
> And a clatter and a chatter from within
> Where fishmen lounge at noon: where the walls
> Of Magnus Martyr hold
> Inexplicable splendour of Ionian white and gold.

The step is now made from the riverside to the river by allowing the rhythm to break up into short verse units proper to a river song.

> The river sweats
> Oil and tar
> The barges drift
> With the turning tide
> Red sails
> Wide
> To leeward, swing on the heavy spar.
> The barges wash
> Drifting logs
> Down Greenwich reach
> Past the Isle of Dogs.
>> Weialala leia
>> Wallala leialala

The lyrical quality of this passage is, according to the poet's explanatory note, to be associated with the song of the Rhinedaughters in *Götterdämmerung*. And this operatic atmosphere imposed on a modern river-scene makes the fitting transition to the picture of Elizabeth and Leicester not in a barge foul with oil and tar but in a gilded state-barge:

> Elizabeth and Leicester
> Beating oars
> The stern was formed
> A gilded shell
> Red and gold
> The brisk swell
> Rippled both shores
> Southwest wind
> Carried down stream
> The peal of bells
> White towers
>> Weialala leia
>> Wallala leialala

In contrast with this apparently irregular transition, let us consider three successive sections of *In Memoriam*: 119, 120, 121. The first is a return in reverie to the early days in Cambridge when Tennyson and his dead friend were undergraduates. Arthur Hallam seems to stand before him as in life:

> And bless thee, for thy lips are bland,
>> And bright the friendship of thine eye;
>> And in my thoughts with scarce a sigh
> I take the pressure of thine hand.

This stanza closes the first section. The next section continues in exactly the same metre. But not only are the sections separated by a double space and further cut off from each other by a new numbering; when we begin to read section 120 we seem to be in an entirely different poem.

> I trust I have not wasted breath:
>   I think we are not wholly brain,
>   Magnetic mockeries; not in vain
> Like Paul with beasts, I fought with death;

We find him here right in the midst of an elementary philosophical discussion of Darwinism and the materialistic conception of the universe. Apparently we are supposed to read in this the triumph of mind over matter as particularly shown by the poet's persistence in regarding his friend as still alive. This may also be a reminiscence of undergraduate discussions on the same subject. But we only make these connections in default of a true connection between the texts of the separate sections. This is not a case of making the lazy reader think and work along with the poet, but of the lazy poet taking advantage of his reader's faith and industry. The next section begins:

> Sad Hesper o'er the buried sun
>   And ready, thou, to die with him,
>   Thou watchest all things ever dim
> And dimmer and a glory done:

Here again no strict connection can be construed. That the section opens in this strain is probably due to a reaction against the prosy scientific language he used in the previous section. Casting about for a more elegiac tone, the poet is naturally brought back to Milton's *Lycidas*, from which he borrows the image of the setting sun, emblem of his dead friend. It is all very well to be able to account for Tennyson in this way. It does not, however, justify his binding together of random leaves from his poetic notebook into a long poem. The division into sections has certainly done away with the padding that would have been necessary had the poem been treated as a continuous piece without breaks. But it does not conceal the fact that these sections have no logical connection with one another. Deprive the poem of its sectional division; deprive it of its metrical regularity; and it will appear the loose and ill-assorted bundle of lost ideas it really is. Such feeble and false material would certainly not be tolerated in a poem which, like *The Waste Land*, had to invent its metrical changes as it went along. It is especially in the long poem that the distinction between form and subject-matter has the most vicious effect. In a short poem, even if form and subject-matter are not made identical, it is possible to keep them proper to each other: as in Milton's 'L'Allegro'. Compare this with its companion piece *Il Penseroso*, which is a praise of pensive melancholy as the former is a light-hearted denial of melancholy; and the metre will be found to be identical, though it is used with a different effect in both.

> But come thou Goddes fair and free,
> In Heav'n ycleap'd Euphrosyne,
> And by men, heart-easing Mirth,
> Whom lovely Venus, at a birth
> With two sister Graces more
> To Ivy-crownèd Bacchus bore;

is exactly the same metre as:

> But hail thou Goddes, sage and holy,
> Hail divinest Melancholy,
> Whose saintly visage is too bright
> To hit the sense of human sight;
> And therefore to our weaker view,
> Ore laid with black staid Wisdom's hew.

But in the first all is hurried, little punctuation is used; in the second all is slowed down, there is comparatively more punctuation, we get heavy internal rhymes, such as *Ore laid* with *black staid*, and the rhythm is further delayed by *s's* used in close juxtaposition, as *Goddes, sage, Whose saintly visage*, etc. Neither the tripping movement nor the slow-pacing movement, however, could have been effectively kept up if the poems had been any longer. Certainly if they had been printed together as the two halves of a single poem, the contrastive use of the metre would have not been so striking, a greater uniformity would have been necessary.

It must be concluded from this that even more strictness is to be demanded of the long poem than of the short poem. A long poem must give good reason for its length, it must account strictly for every line. Often the greater part of a long poem would be more properly put in a prose footnote. The apology of a long poem should be: 'I am really a long *short* poem.' Poe was the first modern critic to explode the dignity of the long poem of major poetry. In his *The Poetic Principle* he writes: 'That degree of excitement which would entitle a poem to be so called at all, cannot be sustained throughout a composition of any great length. After the lapse of half an hour, at the very utmost, it flags – fails – a revulsion ensues – and then the poem is, in effect, and in fact, no longer such.' Although he saw that the long poem was of necessity weak in structure, that length in itself was destructive of poetic form; by form he meant that regular form imposed on subject-matter which we have here been questioning in both the short and long poem. Modernist poetry seems to be composed chiefly of short poems – *The Waste Land*, one of the longest modernist poems, is only 433 lines long. But this is not because of a belief in the short poem *per se* as against the long poem. It is rather a result of a feeling that form and subject-matter are structurally identical; which affects the short and the long poem alike. Well-controlled irregularity instead of uncontrollable regularity makes *short* and *long* obsolete critical standards. The very purpose of this 'irregularity' is to let the poem find its own natural size in spite of the demands put upon poetry by critics, booksellers and the general reading public.

CHAPTER III

William Shakespeare and e.e. cummings: A Study in Original Punctuation and Spelling

THE objections that are raised against the 'freakishness' of modernist poetry are usually supported by quotations from poems by e.e. cummings and others which are not only difficult in construction and reference but are printed queerly on the page. The reader naturally looks for certain landmarks in the poem before he can begin to enjoy it: as the visitor to Paris naturally sets his mental map of the city by the Eiffel Tower and, if the Eiffel Tower were to collapse, would have a difficult time finding his way about for a few days. Modernist poets have removed the well-known landmarks and the reader is likewise bothered. The reasons given for this removal are that landmarks tend to make paths, that paths grow to roads, that roads soon mean walls and railings, and that the pedestrian or motorist, who must keep to the roads, never sees any new scenery.

> because
> you go away i give roses who
> will advise even yourself, lady
> in the most certainly (of what we
> everywhere do not touch) deep
> things;
>   remembering ever so ... etc.[1]

This is the beginning of one of Mr cummings' poems. The first obvious oddity is the degrading of the personal pronoun 'I' into 'i'. This has a very simple history. The 'upper case' was in mediaeval times used for all nouns and proper names and the adjectives formed from them; for the Deity; for Royalty (in 'We' and 'Our'); for certain quasi-divine abstractions such as Mystery, Power, Poetry; and sometimes for 'She' and 'Thou' and so on, where love gives the pronoun a quasi-divine character. Mr cummings protests against the upper case being also allotted to 'I': he affects a casualness, a humility, a denial of the idea of personal immortality responsible for 'I'. Moreover 'i' is more detached: it dissociates the author from the speaker of the poem. This use of 'i' is in keeping with his use of the word 'who', instead of 'which', to qualify the roses; the roses become so personal as to deserve the personal rather than the neutral relative. His next idiosyncrasy is his refusal of a capital letter to each new line of the poem. Now, if this convention were not so ancient, it would seem as odd and unnecessary as, for instance, quotation-marks seem in eighteenth-century books enclosing each line of a long speech instead of occurring only at the beginning and end of a passage. The modernist rejection of the initial capital can be justified on the grounds that it gives the first word of each line, which may be a mere 'and' or 'or', an unnatural emphasis. If for special reasons the poet wishes to capitalize the first word, the fact that it is anyhow capitalized like all the other initial 'And's' and 'Or's' makes any such niceness impossible. Later in the poem cummings uses the capital letter at the beginning of a new sentence to call attention to the full-stop which might otherwise be missed: but the 'because' at the beginning of the poem need not be capitalized because it obviously is the beginning. Similarly, he has suppressed the conventional comma after 'lady' because the end of the line makes a natural pause without punctuation. Commas he uses to mark pauses, not merely as the geographical boundaries of a clause. He has even in another poem inserted one between the 'n' and 'g' of the word 'falling' to suggest the slowness of the falling. Colons and semicolons and full stops he uses to mark pauses of varying length. To give a longer pause still he will leave a blank line. In the quotation just given, the new line at 'remembering' is to mark a change of tone, though the pause is not longer than a semicolon's worth. Parentheses he uses for *sotto voce* pronunciation; or, if they occur in the middle of the word, as in 'the taxi-man p(ee)ps his whistle', they denote a certain quality of the letters enclosed – here the actual sharp whistling sound between the opening and closing (the two p's) of the taxi-man's lips.[2] When this system is carried to a point of great accuracy we find lines like the following:

with–ered unspea–king: tWeNtY, f i n g e r s, large[3]

which, quoted detached from their context, seem to support any charge of irrational freakishness, but in their context are completely intelligible. Moreover, Mr cummings is protecting himself against future liberties which printers and editors may take with his work, by using a personal typographical system which it will be impossible to revise without destroying the poem.

It may be that he has learned a lesson from the fate that has overtaken Shakespeare's sonnets: in which not only have changes in spelling and pronunciation been used to justify the liberties that have been taken in 'modernizing' the texts; but certain very occasional and obvious printer's errors in the only edition printed in Shakespeare's lifetime have been made the excuse for hundreds of quite unjustifiable emendations. Mr cummings and Shakespeare have in common a deadly accuracy, and that accuracy makes poems difficult rather than easy. It is this accuracy that frightens Mr cummings' public, it was Shakespeare's accuracy that provoked his editors to meddle with his texts as being too incomprehensible as they were written. Actually we shall find that Shakespeare is more difficult than Mr cummings in thought, though his poems have a more familiar look on the page: Mr cummings expresses with an accuracy peculiar to him what is common to everyone, Shakespeare expresses in the conventional form of the time, with greater accuracy, what is peculiar to himself. Let us print two versions of a sonnet by Shakespeare, first the version found in the *Oxford Book of English Verse* and other popular anthologies which have apparently chosen this sonnet from all the others as being particularly easy to understand, and next the version printed in the 1609 edition of the *Sonnets*, and apparently, though pirated, printed from Shakespeare's original manuscript. The alterations, it will be noticed in a comparison of the first with the second, are, with a few exceptions which we will point out later, chiefly in the punctuation and spelling. By showing what great difference in the sense the juggling of punctuation marks has made in Shakespeare's original sonnet, we shall perhaps be able to sympathize somewhat with what seems typographical perversity in a poet like Mr cummings. The modernizing of the spelling is not quite so serious a matter, though we shall see that to change a word like *blouddy* to *bloody* makes a difference not only in the atmosphere of the word but in its sound as well.

I

Th' expense of Spirit in a waste of shame
Is lust in action; and till action, lust
Is perjured, murderous, bloody, full of blame,
Savage, extreme, rude, cruel, not to trust;
Enjoy'd no sooner but despised straight;
Past reason hunted; and, no sooner had,
Past reason hated, as a swallow'd bait
On purpose laid to make the taker mad:
Mad in pursuit and in possession so;
Had, having, and in quest to have, extreme;
A bliss in proof, and proved, a very woe;
Before, a joy proposed; behind, a dream.
    All this the world well knows; yet none knows well
    To shun the heaven that leads men to this hell

II

(No. 129)

Th' expence of Spirit in a waste of shame
Is lust in action, and till action, lust

Is periurd, murdrous, blouddy full of blame,
Sauage, extreame, rude, cruell, not to trust,
Injoyd no sooner but dispised straight,
Past reason hunted, and no sooner had
Past reason hated as a swollowed bayt,
On purpose layd to make the taker mad.
Made In pursut and in possession so,
Had, hauing, and in quest, to have extreame,
A blisse in proofe and proud and very wo,
Before a joy proposd behind a dreame,
    All this the world well knowes yet none knowes well,
    To shun the heauen that leads men to this hell.[4]

    Let our method first be, before trying to match our own intelligence with Shakespeare's intelligence, to compare these two versions, the original one and the modern one, in order to feel as intimate with the language in which the poem was written as if all these years did not stand between ourselves and Shakespeare. First, then, as to the spelling. As a matter of course the *u* in *proud* and *heauen* changes to *v*; the Elizabethans had no typographical *v*. There are other words in which the change of spelling does not seem to matter. *Expence, cruell, bayt, layd, pursut, blisse, proofe, wo* – any of these words taken by themselves are not necessarily affected by modernization; but undoubtedly much of the original atmosphere of the poem is lost by changing them in the gross. Sheer facility in reading a poem is no gain when we are trying to discover what the poem was like for the poet. And when one considers all that has happened to the language since Shakespeare's time one can understand why Mr cummings should set his poems down so that when read they are read as 'in the original'. But other changes to make this sonnet comprehensible to modern readers have involved more than changes in spelling. *Periurd* to *perjured* would have meant, to Shakespeare, the addition of another syllable, as *murdrous to murderous*. *Injoyd*, with the same number of syllables as *periurd*, is however made *Enjoy'd*; while *swollowed*, which must have been meant as a three-syllabled word (Shakespeare used *ed* as a separate syllable very strictly and did frequently allow himself an extra syllable in his iambic foot) is printed *swollow'd*. When we come to *dispised*, we find in the modern version an accent over the last syllable. By apostrophes and accents and changes of spelling the rhythm and the consistency in spelling of the original is sacrificed; and without making it an easier poem, only a less accurate one. The sound of the poem suffers through respelling as well as through false alterations in the rhythm. *Blouddy* was pronounced more like *blue-dy* than *bluddy*; the *ea* of *extreame* and *dreame* were sounded like the *ea* in great; *Injoyd* was pronounced as it was written; *periurd* was probably pronounced *peryurd*. But the changes in punctuation do the most damage:

not only to the personal atmosphere of the poem but to the meaning itself. In the second line a semicolon after the first *action* instead of a comma gives a longer rest than Shakespeare gave; but it also cuts off the idea at *action* instead of keeping *in action* and *till action* together as well as the two *lust*'s. A comma after *blouddy* separates it from *full* with which it really forms a single word meaning 'full as with blood'. Next come several semicolons for commas; these introduce pauses which break up the continuous flow of ideas treading on one another's heels. (If Shakespeare had wanted such pauses he would have used semicolons as he does elsewhere.) Particularly serious is the interpolation of a comma after *no sooner had*; for this confines the phrase to a special meaning, *i.e.* 'lust no sooner had is hated past reason', whereas it also means 'lust no sooner had *past reason* is hated past reason'. The comma might as well have been put between *reason* and *hated*; it would have limited the meaning but no more than has been done. On the other hand a comma is omitted where Shakespeare actually did put one, after *bayt*. With the comma, *On purpose layd* – though it refers to *bayt* – also takes us back to the original idea of *lust*; without the comma it merely carries out the figure of *bayt*. In the original there is a full stop at *mad*, closing the octave; in the revised version a colon is used, making the next line run right on and causing the unpardonable change from *Made* to *Mad*. The capital *I* of *In* shows how carefully the printer copied the manuscript. Shakespeare undoubtedly first wrote the line without *Made*, but probably deciding that such an irregular line was too bold, added *Made* without changing the capital *I* to a small one. *Made* logically follows from *make* of the preceding line: 'to make the taker mad, Made (mad)'; but it also returns to the general idea of lust. This change from *Made* to *Mad* limits the final *so* of this line to *Mad* and provokes another change from comma to semicolon, *i.e.* 'Mad in pursut and in possession so (mad)', whereas the idea of *Mad* is only vaguely echoed in this line from the preceding line. The meaning of the line might reasonably be restricted to: 'Made In pursut and in possession as follows': since it is the first line of the sestet, it is more likely to refer forward than back. As a matter of fact, it does both.

The comma between *in quest* and *to have extreame* has been moved forward to separate *have* from *extreame*. The line originally stood for a number of interwoven meanings:

1. The taker of the bait, the man in pursuit and in possession of lust, is made mad, is made like this: he experiences both extremes at once. (What these extremes are the lines following show.)

2. The *Had, having, and in quest*, might have been written in parentheses if Shakespeare had used parentheses. They say, by way of interjection, that lust comprises all the stages of lust: the after-lust period (*Had*), the actual experience of lust (*having*), and the anticipation of lust (*in quest*); and that the extremes of lust are felt in all these stages (*to have extreame*,

i.e. to have extremes, to have in extreme degrees).

3. Further, one stage in lust is like the others, as extreme as the others. All the distinctions made in the poem between *lust in action* and lust *till action*, between lust *In pursut* and lust in *possession* are made to show that in the end there are no real distinctions. *Had, having, and in quest* is the summing up of this fact.

4. The *Had, having,* separately sum up *possession:* that is, the *action* of lust includes the *expence of Spirit, the waste of shame.* The *in quest,* naturally refers to *In pursut.*

5. It must be kept in mind throughout that words qualifying the lust-business refer interchangeably to the taker (the man who lusts), the bait (the object of lust) and lust in the abstract. So: *Had* may mean the swallowing of the bait by the taker, or the catching of the taker by the bait, or 'lust had', or 'had by lust'; *having* and *in quest* are capable of similar interpretations.

These are the numerous possibilities in the line if the original punctuation is kept. But in the revised punctuation it has only one narrow sense, and this not precisely Shakespeare's intention. By the semicolon placed after *so* of the preceding line, it is cut off from close co-operation both with the line before and the other preceding lines. By the shifting of the comma not only is a pause removed where Shakespeare put one and the rhythm thus changed, but the line itself loses its point and really does not pull its weight in the poem. In this punctuation the *whole* line ought to be put into parentheses, as being a mere repetition. The *to have* linked with *in quest* is superfluous; *extreme* set off by itself like this is merely a descriptive adjective already used. Moreover, when the line is thus isolated between two semicolons (after *so,* after *extreme*) *Had, having,* etc., instead of effecting a harmony between the various senses given to *lust* (taker, bait, lust in the abstract), disjoint them and become ungrammatical. *Mad in pursuit, and in possession so*; only refers to *the taker mad. A bliss in proof, and proved, a very woe*; can only refer to lust in the abstract. Thus this intervening line is just a pompous confusion. The next line (*A blisse in proofe and provd and very wo,*) should explain *to have extreame*; it is not merely another parenthetical line as in the revised version. To fulfil the paradox implied in *extreame* it should mean that lust is a bliss during the proof and after the proof, and also *very wo* (real woe) during and after the proof. The altered line only means that lust is a bliss during the proof but a woe after the proof, denying what Shakespeare has been at pains to show all along, that lust is all things at all times. Once the editors tried to repunctuate the line they had to tamper with words themselves in the text. A comma after *proof* demanded a comma after *proved. A* comma after *proved* made it necessary to change *and very wo* to apply to *provd* only. Another semicolon at the end of this line again detaches a line and further breaks the continuity of the poem. Specifically, by cutting off the following line from itself, it in turn does to the following line what the preceding line did to it: makes it only another antithesis or rhetorical balance ('a joy in prospect, as against a dream in retrospect', to repeat the sense of a bliss during proof as against a woe after proof) instead of permitting it to carry on the intricate and careful argument that runs without a stop through the whole sestet. The important thing about this line is that it takes all the meanings in the poem one stage further. Lust in the extreme goes beyond both bliss and woe; it goes beyond reality. It is no longer lust *Had, having, and in quest*, it is lust face to face with *love*. Even when consummated, lust still stands before an unconsummated joy, a proposed joy, and proposed not as a joy possible of consummation but one only to be desired through the dream by which lust leads itself on, the dream behind which this proposed joy, this love, seems to lie. This is the final meaning of the line. It is inlaid with other meanings, but these should follow naturally from the complete meaning, it should not be built up from them. For example the line may also be read: 'Before a joy (lust) can be proposed, there must be a dream behind, a joy lost by waking' ('So that I wake and cry to dream again'); or: 'Before a joy can be proposed, it must first be renounced as a joy, it must be put behind as a dream; you know in the pursuit that possession is impossible'; or: 'Before the man in lust is a prospect of joy, yet he knows by experience that this is only a dream'; or: 'Beforehand he says that he definitely proposed lust to be a joy, afterwards he says that it came as a dream'; or: 'Before (in face of) a joy proposed only as a consequence of a dream, with a dream pushing him from behind'. All these and even more readings of the line are possible and legitimate, and each reading could in turn be made specially to explain why the taker is made mad or how lust is *to have extreme* or why it is both *a bliss* and *very wo*. The punctuated line in the revised version, cut off from what has gone before and from what follows, can only mean: 'In prospect, lust is a joy; in retrospect, a dream.' Though a possible contributory meaning, as the *only* meaning it makes the theme of the poem that lust is impossible of satisfaction, whereas the theme is, as carried on by the next line, that lust as lust *is* satisfiable but that satisfied lust is in conflict with itself. The next line, if unpunctuated except for the comma Shakespeare put at the end, is a general statement of this conflict: the man in lust is torn between lust as he well-knows it with the world and lust in his personal experience, which crazes him to hope for more than lust from lust. The force of the second *well* is to deny the first *well*: no one really knows anything of lust except in personal experience, and only through personal experience can lust be known *well* rather than 'well-known'. But separate the second *well* from the first, as in the revised version, and the direct opposition between *world* and *none*, *well knowes* and *knowes well* is destroyed, as well as the whole point of the word-play between *well knowes* and *knowes well*; for by the removal of the comma after the second *well*, this is made merely an adverb to modify *To shun* in the following line – *well* here means merely *successfully* with *To shun*, not *well enough* with *knowes*. This repunctuation also robs *All this* of its real significance, as it refers not only to all that has gone before but to the last line as well: 'All this the world well knows yet all this none knows well' (*i.e.* the character of lust), and 'All this the world well knows yet none knows well' the moral to be drawn from the character of lust (*i.e. to shun the heaven that leads men to this hell*). The character and the moral of lust the whole world well knows, but no one knows the character and the moral really well unless he disregards the moral warning and engages in lust, no one knows lust well enough to shun it because, though he knows it is both heavenly and hellish, lust can never be recognized until it has proved itself lust by turning heaven into hell.

The effect of this revised punctuation has been to restrict meanings to special interpretations of special words. Shakespeare's punctuation allows the variety of meanings he actually intends; if we must choose any one meaning, then we owe it to Shakespeare to choose at least one he intended and one embracing as many meanings as possible, that is, the most difficult meaning. It is always the most difficult meaning that is the most final. (There are degrees of finality because no prose interpretation of poetry can have complete finality, can be difficult enough.) Shakespeare's emendators, in trying to make him clear for the plain man, only weakened and diluted his poetry. Their attempts to make Shakespeare easy resulted only in depriving him of clarity. There is but one way to make Shakespeare clear: to print him as he wrote or as near as one can get to this. Making poetry easy for the reader should mean showing clearly that it is difficult.

Mr cummings makes himself safe from emendation by setting down his poems, which are really easy as poetry, so that their most difficult sense strikes the reader first. By giving typography an active part to play he makes his poems fixed and accurate in a way that Shakespeare's are not. In doing this he loses the fluidity Shakespeare got by not cramping his poems with heavy punctuation and by placing more trust in the plain reader – by leaving more to his imagination than he seems to have deserved. The trouble with Mr cummings' poems is that they are too clear, once the plain reader puts himself to work on them. Braced as they are, they do not present the eternal difficulties that make poems immortal, they merely show one difficulty, how difficult it is for Mr cummings or for any poet to stabilize a poem once and for all. Punctuation marks in Mr cummings' poetry are the bolts and axels that make the poem a methodic and fool-proof piece of machinery requiring common-sense for its operation rather than imagination. The outcry against his typography shows that it is as difficult to engage the common-sense of the reader as his imagination. A reviewer of Mr cummings' latest book, *is 5*, writes:

I know artists are always saying that a good painting looks as well upside down as any other way. And it may be true. The question now arises: does the same principle apply to a poem? But it is not necessary to answer the question; if a poem is good, people will gladly stand on their heads to read it. It is conceivable, if not probable, that the favourite poetic form of the future will be a sonnet arranged as a crossword puzzle. If there were no other way of getting at Shakespeare's sonnets than by solving a crossword puzzle sequence, I am sure the puzzles would be solved and the sonnets enjoyed. But what about Mr cummings? Can his poems surmount such obstacles? Well, perhaps if they cannot survive as poems they can survive as puzzles.

This may be the immediate verdict on Mr cummings' typography; but one thing cummings can be sure of that Shakespeare could not have been sure of, is that three centuries hence his poems if they survive (and worse poets' have) will be the only ones of the early twentieth century reprinted in facsimile, not merely because he will be a literary curiosity but because he has edited his poems with punctuation beyond any possibility of re-editing. The Shakespeare to whose sonnets this reviewer makes a rhetorical appeal is the popular Shakespeare of the anthologies and not the facsimile Shakespeare. How many of those who read this had ever before read Sonnet 129 in the original? So few, surely, that it is safe to conclude that no one is willing to stand on his head to understand Shakespeare, that everyone wants a simplified Shakespeare as well as a simplified cummings. Indeed, very few people can have looked at Shakespeare's sonnets in the original since the eighteenth century, when the popular interest in Shakespeare's more high-spirited comedies sent a few dull commentators and book-makers to his poems. In 1766 George Steevens printed the *Sonnets* in the original and without annotations apparently because he thought they were not worth them. Twenty-seven years later he omitted the *Sonnets* from an edition of Shakespeare's works 'because the strongest Act of Parliament that could be framed would fail to compel readers into their service'. People were certainly not more ready to stand on their heads to understand Shakespeare in that time than in this and Malone, who undertook in 1780 to justify Shakespeare to an apathetic public by simplifying the difficult originals (crossword puzzles, if you like), was considered by Steevens to be 'disgracing his implements of criticism by the objects of their culture'. Steevens' view was the general one; (Chalmers reaffirmed it in 1810), and if Malone by his emendations, which have become the accepted Shakespearian text, had not overridden the general critical opinion of the *Sonnets* and presented them filleted to the plain man, the plain man of today would undoubtedly be unaware of the existence of the *Sonnets*. Unlike cummings' poems, Shakespeare's

Sonnets would not even have 'survived as puzzles'.

Thus far does a study of the typography of Shakespeare take one. The lesson of this for modernist poetry is an appreciation of the difficulties of a poet with a large audience to whom his meanings are mysteries and for the most part must remain mysteries. The modernist poet handles the problem by trying to get the most out of his audience; Shakespeare by trying to get the most out of his poem. Logically, the modernist poet should have more readers than Shakespeare with an elementary under-standing of his poems, and Shakespeare only a few readers, but these with an enlarged understanding of his poems. The reverse, however, is true because the reading public has been so undertrained on a simplified Shakespeare and on anthology verse generally, that modernist poetry seems as difficult as Shakespeare really ought to seem. Typography, we see, then, is really the subject of the fate of poetry with its audience. Since it is, even at its worst, the least disturbing method of communication, both for the ideas communicated and for the audience, it is still the surest guide to the understanding of a poem that we have – even when the typography of a poem has been through a whole history of misunderstanding.

Only a few points in Sonnet 129 have been left uncovered in our typo-graphical survey of the poem, and these occur principally in the first few lines; for these suffer less from emendations than the rest of the poem. The very delicate interrelation of the words of the first two lines should not be overlooked: the strong parallelism between *expense* and *waste* and *Spirit* and *shame* expressing in the very first line the terrible quick-change from lust as lust-enjoyed to lust as lust-despised; the double meaning of *waste* as 'expense' and as 'wilderness', the *waste* place in which the Spirit is *wasted*; the double meaning of *expense* as 'pouring out' and as the 'price paid'; the double meaning of *of shame* as 'shameful', *i.e.* 'deplorable' and as *ashamed*, *i.e.* 'self-deploring'; the double meaning of *shame* itself as 'modesty' and 'disgrace'; again the double meaning of *lust in action* as 'lust' unsuspected by man 'in his actions' because disguised as 'shame' (in either sense of the word) and condemned by him because he does not recognize it in himself, and as 'lust in progress' as opposed to 'lust contemplated'. All these alternate meanings acting on each other, and even other possible interpretations of words and phrases, make as it were a furiously dynamic crossword puzzle which can be read in many directions at once, none of the senses being incompatible with any others. This intensified inbreeding of words continues through the rest of the poem. *Periurd is* another obvious example, meaning both 'falsely spoken of' and 'false'. Again, *heaven* and *hell* have the ordinary prose meaning of 'pleasure' and 'pain', but also the particular meanings they had in Shakespeare's poetic vocabulary. 'Heaven' to Shakespeare is the longing for a temperamental stability which at the same time he recognizes as false. 'Hell' is Marlowe's hell, which

> hath no limits nor is circumscribed
> In one selfe place, for where we are is hell.

The reader complaining of the obscurity of modernist poets must be reminded of the intimate Shakespearian background he needs to be familiar with before he can understand Shakespeare. The failure of imagination and knowledge in Shakespeare's emendators has reduced Shakespeare to the indignity of being easy for everybody. Beddoes, an early nineteenth century imitator of Shakespeare, said:

> About Shakespeare. You might just as well attempt to remodel the seasons and the laws of life and death as to alter one 'jot or tittle' of his eternal thoughts. 'A Star', you call him. If he was a star all the other stage-scribblers can hardly be considered a constellation of brass buttons.

The modernist poets are not many of them Stars but they are most of them very highly polished brass buttons and are entitled to protect themselves from the sort of tarnishing from which Shakespeare, though a Star, has suffered.

Shakespeare's attitude toward the perversely stupid reorganizing of lines and regrouping of ideas is jocularly shown in the satire on repunctuation given in the prologue of *Pyramus and Thisbe* in his *A Midsummer Night's Dream*.

> *Bottom.* If we offend, it is with our good will.
>   That you should think, we come not to offend,
> But with good will. To show our simple skill,
>   That is the true beginning of our end.
> Consider, then, we come but in despite.
>   We do not come, as minding to content you,
> Our true intent is. All for your delight,
>   We are not here. That you should here repent you
> The actors are at hand; and by their show,
>   You should know all, that you are like to know.

> *Theseus.* – This fellow doth not stand upon points. His speech was like a tangled chain, nothing impaired but all disordered.

CHAPTER IV

The Unpopularity of Modernist Poetry with the Plain Reader

THE eighteenth-century reading public had poetry made clear for it, both by the way in which new poetry was written and previous poetry, early English and Classical, rewritten. But the eighteenth century had a very limited recipe for poetry; for metre the heroic couplet, which broke thought up into very short lengths; for language a stock poetical vocabulary of not more than a couple of thousand words. Anybody could write poetry then if he obeyed the rules, without necessarily being a poet. In the nineteenth century, because of a reading public enlarged by democracy, clearness meant not so much obeying rules as writing for the largest possible audience. The twentieth-century reaction in poetry against nineteenth-century standards is not against clearness and simplicity but against rules for poetry made by the reading public, instead of by the poets themselves as they were in the eighteenth century. This is why so many modern poets are forced to feel themselves in snobbish sympathy with the eighteenth century. The quarrel now is between the reading public and the modernist poet over the definition of clearness. Both agree that perfect clearness is the end of poetry, but the reading public insists that no poetry is clear except what it can understand at a glance; the modernist poet insists that the clearness of which the poetic mind is capable demands thought and language of a far greater sensitiveness and complexity than the enlarged reading public will permit it to use. To remain true to his conception of what poetry is, he has therefore to run the risk of seeming obscure or freakish, of having no reading public; even of writing what the reading public refuses to call poetry, in order to be a poet. The only fault to be found with a poet like e.e. cummings is that he has tried to do two things at once: to remain loyal to the requirements of the poetic mind for clearness, and to get the ordinary reading public to call the result 'poetry'. He has tried to do this by means of an elaborate system of typography, and the only gratitude he has had from the reading public is to be called freakish and obscure because of his typography.

The following is a poem describing day-break seen through a railway carriage window in Italy.

Among
    these
        red pieces of
day (against which and
quite silently hills
made of blueandgreen paper
scorchbend ingthem
– selves – U
pcurv E, into:
        anguish (clim
b)ing
s-p-i-r-a
l
and, disappear)
       Satanic and blasé

a black goat lookingly wanders

There is nothing left of the world but
into this noth
ing il treno per
Roma si-gnori?
jerk.
ilyr, ushes.[1]

The cleverness of this as mere description can be shown by putting the poem into ordinary prose with conventional typography; and afterwards showing how the unconventional typography improves the accuracy of the description:

Among these red pieces of day (against which – and quite silently – hills made of blue and green paper, scorch-bending themselves, upcurve into anguish, climbing spiral, and disappear), satanic and blasé, a black goat lookingly wanders. There is nothing left of the world; but into this nothing 'il treno per Roma signori?' jerkily rushes.

'Red pieces of day' suggests sunset fragments – the disintegration of the universe as the train moves toward night. The hills become as unreal as blue and green paper. The rocking of the train seems to give their rounded outlines, as they stream past, the sort of movement a long strip of paper makes when it curls up in the heat of fire, or that the pen makes when it writes u's and e's in copperplate handwriting. As the train comes close up to the hills their rounded outlines seem to spiral upward against the red pieces ('into anguish') because the eye strains itself looking up at them:

they can only just be seen by pressing the face against the window, and as the train gets nearer still, they are no more visible. The eye is forced to drop to the foreground and there exchanges glances with a diabolic-looking goat. The traveller is utterly confused by these perceptual experiences: when the line of hills that he has been watching is snatched away from his eyes it seems like the end of the world, like death, and the goat seems like the Devil greeting the dead. He pulls himself together. 'Where am I?' The movement of rocking and jerking continues. He remembers the last words he has heard spoken, the question 'The Rome train, gentlemen?' which is all that he can think of to account for the motion.

This is not the prose summary of the poem, that is to say, the common-sense substitute for a piece of poetical extravagance. A prose summary cannot *explain* a poem, else the poet, if he were honest, would give the reader only a prose summary, and no poem. The above is rather the expansion, the dilution, even the destruction of the poem which one reader may perform for another if the latter is unable to face the intensity and compactness of the poem. The indignity of literary criticism is largely due to the fact that it has had to perform this levelling service for generations of plain readers. It has never yet performed any services for poetry itself, which it tries to suit either to philosophy or to the reader. Poetry cannot be judged by its adaptability to a philosophical system, and criticism's services to the reader are doubtful. By encouraging him in his reading vanity and in his demand for poems to be written down to him it has reduced him to critical imbecility. Perhaps from the above expansion of the poem the spoiled reader may be able to infer the greater accuracy and truthfulness of the poetic version. The irregularity of the lines as printed in the poem is evidently intended to give two movements in one, the jerking and the rocking of the train. 'Blueandgreen' is printed as a single word to show that it is not parti-coloured paper but paper which is blue and green at once, the colours run together by the rocking motion. 'scorchbend ingthem' represents the up-and-down rhythm of the diagonal spiral movement. '– selves –' stresses the realistic character of this movement. The capitalized 'U' and 'E' enlarge the mounting copperplate curves. The parentheses enclosing the syllable 'climb' means perhaps a slight catch of the breath at that point. The comma after the 'E', the colon after 'into' are used as pauses of a certain length marking the rhythm of the spirals. The word 'spiral' is distended by hyphens to mark the final large spiral that sweeps the sky out of view at the letter 'l'. 'Satanic' is capitalized to make the goat personally diabolic. The full stop after 'jerk' probably marks a sudden jolt back to a consciousness of the inside of the train and the purposefulness of the journey.

There is no experience here with which the plain reader cannot sympathize, and only a little imaginative recollection has been needed to make this analysis; no key from the author except the poem itself. The poem combines two qualities of clearness: clearness of composition in the interests of the poem as a thing in itself, clearness of transmittance in the interests of the reader. It is obvious that the poet could have given the poem this double accuracy in no other way. Can it be that the poet has been wrong in paying too much attention to the rendering of the poem for the reader: that if he had allowed it to be more difficult, if he had concentrated exclusively on the poem as a thing in itself, it would have seemed less freakish?

The 'freakishness' and abnormality of feeling with which the modernist poet is often charged, it needs to be explained, are not due to the fact that this is not an age for poetry and that therefore to write poetry at all is a literary affectation. The trouble is rather that ordinary modern life is full of the stock-feelings and situations with which traditional poetry has continually fed popular sentiments; that the commonplaces of everyday speech are merely the relics of past poetry; so that the only way for a modern poet to have an original feeling or experience that may eventually become literature is to have it outside of literature. It is the general reading public, indeed, which gets its excitement from literature and literary feelings instead of from life. To appreciate this fully it must be realized that it is always the poets who are the real psychologists, that it is they who break down antiquated literary definitions of people's feelings and make them or try to make them self-conscious about formerly ignored or obscure mental processes; for which an entirely new vocabulary has to be invented. The appearance of freakishness generally means: poetry is not in a 'poetical' period, it is in a psychological period. It is not trying to say 'Things often felt but ne'er so well expressed' but to discover what it is we are really feeling.

One of the first modernist poets to feel the need of a clearness and accuracy in feelings and their expression so minute, so more than scientific, as to make of poetry a higher sort of psychology, was Gerard Manley Hopkins, a Catholic poet writing in the eighties. We call him a modernist in virtue of his extraordinary strictness in the use of words and the unconventional notation he used in setting them down so that they *had to be understood as he meant them to be, or understood not at all* (this is the crux of the whole question of the intelligibility of 'difficult' poetry). Hopkins cannot be accused of trying to antagonize the reading public. In 1883 he wrote about the typographical means he used in order to explain an unfamiliar metre and an unfamiliar grammar:

There must be some marks. Either I must invent a notation throughout, as in music, or else I must only mark where the reader is likely to mistake, and for the present this is what I shall do.[2]

In 1885 he wrote again:

This is my difficulty, what marks to use and when to use them: they are so much needed and yet so objectionable. About punctuation my

mind is clear: I can give a rule for everything I write myself, and even
for other people, though they might not agree with me perhaps.

These lines from a sonnet written in his peculiar metre will show to what
an extent he is a modernist.

> Soul, self; come, poor Jackself, I do advise
> You, jaded, let be; call off thoughts awhile
> Elsewhere; leave comfort root-room; let joy size
> At God knows when to God knows what; whose smile
> 's not wrung, see you; unforeseen times rather – as skies
> Betweenpie mountains – lights a lovely mile.

First of all *Jackself.* The plain reader will get no help from the dictionary
with this, he must use his wits and go over the other uses of *Jack* in
combination: jack-screw, jackass, jack-knife, Jack Tar, Jack Frost, Jack of
all trades, boot-jack, steeple-jack, lumber-jack, jack-towel, jack-plane,
roasting-jack. From these the central meaning of 'jack' becomes clear. It
represents a person or thing that is honest, patient, cheerful, hard-
working, undistinguished – but the fellow that makes things happen, that
does things that nobody else would or could do. (Tom in English usage is
the mischievous, rather destructive, impudent and often unpleasant
fellow – tomboy, tomcat, tomfoolery, tomtit, peeping Tom, etc.).
'Jackself', then, is this workaday self which he advises to knock off work
for awhile; to leave comfort or leisure, crowded out by work, some space
to grow in, as for flowers in a vegetable garden; to have his pleasure and
comfort whenever and however God wills it, not, as an ordinary Jackself
would, merely on Sundays (Hopkins uses 'God knows when' and 'God
knows what' as just the language a Jackself would use). God's smile cannot
be forced from him, that is, happiness cannot be postponed until one is
ready for it. Joy comes as suddenly and unexpectedly as when, walking
among mountains, you come to a point where the sky shines through a
cleft between two mountains and throws a shaft of light over a mile of
ground thus unexpectedly illumined for you. We must appreciate the
accuracy of the term *Betweenpie.* Besides being again just the sort of
homely kitchen language that the Jackself would use to describe how sky
seems pressed between two mountains (almost as a smile is pressed
between lips) it is also the neatest possible way of combining the patching
effect of light – as in the word 'pied' (The Pied Piper of Hamelin) or in
'magpie' – with the way this light is introduced between the mountains.

Of Hopkins, who carefully observed so many rules, his editor, Dr
Robert Bridges, who postponed publication of his poems for thirty years,
thus making Hopkins even more of a modernist poet, writes:

> Apart from faults of taste … affectations such as where the hills are
> 'as a stallion stalwart very-violet-sweet' or some perversion of

human feeling, as, for instance, the 'nostrils' relish of incense along the sanctuary side', or 'the Holy Ghost with warm breast and with ah! bright wings', which repel my sympathy more than do all the rude shocks of his purely artistic wantonness – apart from these there are faults of style which the reader must have courage to face. For these blemishes are of such quality and magnitude as to deny him even a hearing from those who love a continuous literary decorum.

Why cannot what Dr Bridges calls a fault of taste, an affectation, in the description of hills as 'a stallion stalwart very-violet-sweet' be, with the proper sympathy for Hopkins' enthusiasm, appreciated as a phrase reconciling the two seemingly opposed qualities of mountains, their male, animal-like roughness and strength and at the same time their ethereal quality under soft light for which the violet in the gentle eye of the horse makes exactly the proper association? What Dr Bridges and other upholders of 'literary decorum' object to most in a poet is not as a matter of fact either 'faults of taste' or 'faults of style' (in Hopkins supposedly consisting chiefly in the clipping of grammar to suit the heavily stressed metre) but a daring that makes the poet socially rather than artistically objectionable. As a reviewer in the *Times Literary Supplement* states the grievance against modernist poetry:

> It is as if its object were to express that element only in the poet's nature by virtue of which he feels himself an alien in the universe, or at least an alien from what he takes to be the universe acknowledged by the rest of mankind.

But the truth is that 'the rest of mankind' is for the most part totally unaware of the universe and constantly depends on the poet to give it a second-hand sense of the universe through language. Because this language has been accepted ready-made by 'the rest of mankind' without understanding the reasons for it, it becomes, by 'progress' stereotyped and loses its meaning; and the poet is called upon again to remind people what the universe really looks and feels like, that is, what language means. If he does this conscientiously he must use language in a fresh way or even, if the poetical language has grown too stale and there are few pioneers before him, invent new language. But, if he does, he will be certain to antagonize for a while those who keep asking poetry to do their more difficult thinking for them; for they have a proprietary affection for the old language, however meaningless it may have become, and do not realize that it must be brought up to date or, if need be, entirely recast if poetry is to do its job properly. How irate they become can be seen from a further statement by the same reviewer.

Language itself is an accepted code: and if the poet is really to be the

man who cannot accept what others do, he ought to begin squarely at
the beginning and have nothing to do with their conventional jargon.

But let the poet begin squarely at the beginning in order to discover
whether there is anything to accept and the cry will be immediately raised:
'Language is an accepted code.'

It is easy in any period to look back with satisfaction on the growth of
language and, for instance, to accuse the early nineteenth century of dull-
ness and conservatism for being so slow to recognize the services to the
refreshment of poetry rendered by Wordsworth, Coleridge, Shelley and
Keats. But it is natural for every period to regard itself as the final stage of
everything that has come before it, so that it can only imagine new poets,
of an originality equal to that of Wordsworth and others in their own day,
as writing now exactly as they wrote then. The same is true in music: the
charge of freakishness has been brought by critics in their time against
Debussy, Wagner and even Brahms. Literary critics who bring charges of
freakishness against modernist poets find it possible to tolerate
modernism in contemporary music; as conservative musical critics will
not be so hard on modernism in literature – the proprietary interest in
their medium is not threatened in either case.

In the midst of this conflict stands the plain reader, the timid victim of
orthodox criticism on the one hand, and unorthodox poetry on the other
(unorthodox criticism overlooks him entirely, which is perhaps the most
severe affront he has to bear). His attitude toward poetry has, therefore, to
be one of self-defence. He must be cautious in his choice of what he reads.
He must not make a fool of himself by reading anything in which he may
be called on to rely on his own critical opinion. He must not read anything
which will be a waste of time, anything not likely to last for a long time,
not destined to be a classic. Forced to be on his guard, he will be inclined
to emphasize the value of the 'practical' things which are not poetry, such
as time in the quantitative, financial sense; also to develop a shrewd sense
of the 'practical' value of poetry: he will avoid new poetry about which no
final judgement has been made, whatever its emotional appeal may be –
poetry that seems too different from the poetry that has lasted to be a good
investment, poetry likely to prove a dead movement. His poem must not
only be plain, it must correspond with what he accepts, by reputation, as
classics. And to a certain extent he is right in this, for there is a great deal
of waste material left behind by dead movements in poetry; but only to a
certain extent, for a great many really bad poems also survive as classics
because of the plain reader's literary conservatism: he will prefer an
unoriginal but undisturbing poem to an original but disturbing one.

The plain reader is, in fact, more conservative in poetry than in any
other thing but religion; and in poetry more than in religion. The reader
who may be said to occupy an enlightened middle position toward various

historical changes he must face in his life is generally many generations behind himself in poetry and religion. This is perhaps not out of incapacity, but because he realizes that the demands put upon him by religion and poetry are too pressing, too personal. It is a case of all or nothing. So it is nothing; because no common Christian could seriously turn the other cheek when smitten or sell all that he had and give it to the poor, and no common poetry reader could bring himself without great effort to meet the demands of thought put upon him by an authentic poem. An advocacy in modern Christianity of the turning of the other cheek and of the communalizing of private property would be regarded as an obnoxious modernism in the most devout Christian; as an increase in poetry of the demands put upon the plain reader antagonizes him against modernist poetry no matter how much he loves poetry in general. Poetry, then, like religion, has to be dissociated from practical life, except as a sentimentality: he will give a saint or a poet lip-service, but only lip-service: particularly he must reject a saint or a poet if he is still living, for it is only time that reveals to a worshipper or a reader which of the saints or poets are real and which are charlatans. The common Christian will prefer a popular preacher of the orthodox type to a 'fanatic' like General Booth: this preserves his self-respect. We purposely make this analogy between poetry and religion, which is a false one, because it is a traditional analogy and largely accountable for readers' shyness of poetry. Religion can be in actual conflict with social principles; to turn the smitten cheek is to abandon the virtue of self-pride, is to compromise 'honour'. Poetry, on the other hand, in its more exacting side, makes no demands of a social nature, no demands which exceed the private intimacy of the reader and the poem; particularly when, as now, the poet asks for no personal bays or public banquets. But the plain reader is even more afraid of the infringements that poetry may make on his private mental and spiritual ease than of the social infringements that modernism in religion would lead him to. And undoubtedly the way that anything can interfere most with an individual's privacy is by demanding criticism (complete attention, complete mental intimacy and confidence) for itself from him.

So it is that when Wordsworth and Coleridge were producing their best poetry the plain reader would have nothing to do with them but was reading dull writers such as Shenstone and Meikle, who are now mere names in literary history; when Keats and Shelley were writing their best he was reading Thomas Moore and Samuel Rogers; when he should have been reading the early Tennyson he was reading Mrs Hemans and Martin Tupper; when he should have been reading Whitman he was reading Robert Montgomery and the later Tennyson. And so on to the present day: when even the plain reader trying to keep up with the poetry of his time will be more likely to choose a poet such as the American Carl Sandburg or the English John Drinkwater, belonging to a dead movement which has reached its limit and will expire with the death of its authors, than one belonging to a live movement (such as e.e. cummings or John Crowe Ransom) which asks him to risk his critical judgement.

Let us compare a poem of Carl Sandburg's, who tried to create a democratic poetry in the spirit of the American Middle West by using free verse, slang and sentimental lower-class subjects, with a poem of John Crowe Ransom's, who, without making a sensational appeal to the locality in which he lives or to a particular social class, yet has a colloquial dignity and grace which it is possible to call Southern and a quality in his poetry that is definitely aristocratic.[3] Strangely enough, it is Sandburg whose work is in the natural course of events shelved among the dull relics of dead movements and Ransom, though his poems are a formal and careful evasion of violence, who represents poetic modernism to the plain reader – which is the same to him as sensationalism. Here is a poem of Carl Sandburg's, then, especially designed to match the intelligence-level of the plain reader and present him with no allusions that may mystify him.

MAMIE

Mamie beat her head against the bars of a little Indian town and dreamed of romance and big things off somewhere the way the railroad trains all ran.

She could see the smoke of the engines get lost down where the streaks of steel flashed in the sun and when the newspapers came in on the morning mail she knew there was a big Chicago far off, where all the trains ran.

She got tired of the barber shop boys and the post office chatter and the church gossip and the old pieces the band played on the Fourth of July and Decoration Day.

And sobbed at her fate and beat her head against the bars and was going to kill herself,

When the thought came to her that if she was going to die she might as well die struggling for a clutch of romance among the streets of Chicago.

She has a job now at six dollars a week in the basement of the Boston Store

And even now she beats her head against the bars in the same old way and wonders if there is a bigger place the railroads run to from Chicago where maybe there is
    romance
    and big things
    and real dreams
    that never go smash.[4]

Perhaps this poem will show why the plain reader prefers bad contemporary poetry to good contemporary poetry: the former can give him as much innocent enjoyment as a good short story or his newspaper or an up-to-date jazz orchestra, the latter, because it is good yet too novel for any of the ordinary tests for a Classic to apply to it, demands an effort of criticism which robs him of his power of enjoying it. Poetry, like fashions in clothes, has to be 'accepted' before the man in the street will patronize it. Next to the permanently 'accepted' literature, the plain reader places literature of dead movements of his own time, literature that does not have to be accepted. 'Modern' poetry means to him poetry that will pass; he has a good-humoured tolerance of it because he does not have to take it seriously. 'Modernist' poetry is his way of describing the contemporary poetry that perplexes him and that he is obliged to take seriously without knowing whether it is to be accepted or not. The cautiousness of the plain reader's opinion creates an intermediary stage between himself and this poetry: the literary critic. However, such public authority is usually slower-acting and slower-witted than private taste. For, thinking the plain reader more stupid than he really is, the literary critic is in his turn cautious in what he recommends to him, being anxious not to earn his disapproval. Therefore much modernist poetry has been confined to limited editions for connoisseurs whose private taste is not dependent on the literary critic; which further antagonizes the plain reader, since whatever is patronized by a *few* seems self-condemned as a high-brow performance for a snobbish cult. So the plain reader gets the impression that this poetry was never meant to be common literature and so is only too glad to leave it alone; and it never reaches him except in pieces torn out of their context by the literary critic, for ridicule, to justify his ignoring them. This vicious circle repeats itself when the modernist poet, left without any public but the highly trained literary connoisseur, does not hesitate to embody in his poems remote literary references which are unintelligible to a wider public and which directly antagonize it. The following is an example of the sort of poetry which, because it is too good, has to be temporarily brushed aside as a literary novelty.

CAPTAIN CARPENTER

Captain Carpenter rose up in his prime
Put on his pistols and went riding out
But had got wellnigh nowhere at that time
Till he fell in with ladies in a rout.

It was a pretty lady and all her train
That played with him so sweetly but before
An hour she'd taken a sword with all her main
And twined him of his nose forever more.

Captain Carpenter mounted up one day
And rode straightway unto a stranger rogue
That looked unchristian but be that as may
The Captain did not wait upon prologue.

But drew upon him out of his great heart
The other swung against him with a club
And cracked his two legs at the shinny part
And let him roll and stick like any tub.

Captain Carpenter rode many a time
From male and female took he sundry harms
He met the wife of Satan crying 'I'm
The she-wolf bids you shall bear no more arms.'

Their strokes and counters whistled in the wind
I wish he had delivered half his blows
But where she should have made off like a hind
The bitch bit off his arms at the elbows.

And Captain Carpenter parted with his ears
To a black devil that used him in this wise
O Jesus ere his threescore and ten years
Another had plucked out his sweet blue eyes.

Captain Carpenter got up on his roan
And sallied from the gate in hell's despite
I heard him asking in the grimmest tone
If any enemy yet there was to fight?

'To any adversary it is fame
If he risk to be wounded by my tongue
Or burnt in two beneath my red heart's flame
Such are the perils he is cast among.

'But if he can he has a pretty choice
From an anatomy with little to lose
Whether he cut my tongue and take my voice
Or whether it be my round red heart he choose.'

It was the neatest knave that ever was seen
Stepping in perfume from his lady's bower
Who at this word put in his merry mien
And fell on Captain Carpenter like a tower.

I would not knock old fellows in the dust
But there lay Captain Carpenter on his back
His weapons were the old heart in his bust
And a blade shook between rotten teeth alack.

The rogue in scarlet and grey soon knew his mind
He wished to get his trophy and depart
With gentle apology and touch refined
He pierced him and produced the Captain's heart.

God's mercy rest on Captain Carpenter now
I thought him Sirs an honest gentleman
Citizen husband soldier and scholar enow
Let jangling kites eat of him if they can.

But God's deep curses follow after those
That shore him of his goodly nose and ears
His legs and strong arms at the two elbows
and eyes that had not watered seventy years.

The curse of hell upon the sleek upstart
Who got the Captain finally on his back
And took the red red vitals of his heart
And made the kites to whet their beaks clack clack.[5]

    In the first place this is a ballad, and the plain reader will insist that a
ballad in the old style like 'Chevy Chace', or 'Sir Patrick Spens', or the
Robin Hood Ballads may be imitated by a modern hand, but imitated with
an affected simplicity like that of 'The Schooner Hesperus' or of 'The
Ancient Mariner'. 'Captain Carpenter' makes use of an old ballad metre
and of an archaic vocabulary; the poet even goes so far as to imitate the
typography of the first ballads set down in print, by omitting all incidental
punctuation. But this is not enough for the plain reader: the poet has
committed the unforgivable modernist sin of allowing the audience to
have more than one possible reaction to a single poem. Indeed to such a
poem as this a variety of reactions are possible; and it is the balance of
these various possible reactions that should form the reader's critical atti-
tude toward the poem. But the ordinary reader does not want to have a
critical attitude, only a simple pleasure or pain reaction. He does not want
to understand poetry so much as to have poetical feelings. He wants to
know definitely whether he is to laugh or cry over Captain Carpenter's
story and if he is not given a satisfactory clue he naturally doubts the
sincerity of the poet, he becomes suspicious of his seriousness and leaves
him alone. The plain reader makes two general categories for poetry; the
realistic (the true), which is supposed to put the raw poetry of life felt
dumbly by him into a literary form, a register of the nobler sentiments of
practical life; and the non-realistic or romantic (the untrue), which covers
his life of fantasia and desires, the world that he is morally obliged to treat
as unreal. Now this particular poem is based on an interplay between these
two worlds in which fact and fancy have equal value as truth. Captain
Carpenter is both the realistic hero or knight-errant, who is bit by bit

shorn of his strength until there is nothing left but his hollow boasts, and the fairy-tale hero who is actually reduced bit by bit to a tongue; and the double meaning has to be kept in mind throughout. The ordinary psychology, therefore, of the reader trained to look for a single reaction in himself is upset, and modernist poetry becomes the nightmare from which he tries to protect his sanity.

When examined, *Captain Carpenter* reads innocently enough. There are a few literary echoes of the old ballads, such as the use of *twined* for 'robbed' and *jangling* for 'making a discordant noise', but for the most part they are very familiar archaisms. There are also references to the old ballads, typically eighteenth century words like *rout* for 'dance', Victorian expressions like *with gentle apology and touch refined*, and unmistakably modern usages like *the shinny part, like any tub.* But this mixture of styles is only an amiable satire of styles (the same sort of satire more violently employed in prose by James Joyce in the second part of his *Ulysses* against successive period styles) which only adds to the charm of Captain Carpenter's character, thus seen as a legendary figure of many successive ages. But the chief feeling against the poem would be that Captain Carpenter is not an easily defined or felt subject, neither a particular historical figure nor yet a complete allegory. He confounds the emotions of the reader instead of simplifying them and provides no answer to the one question which the reader will ask himself: 'Who or what, particularly, is Captain Carpenter?' The chief condition the reader makes about the poetry he reads is that it shall not be difficult. For if it is difficult it means that he must think in unaccustomed ways, and thinking to the plain reader, beyond the range necessary for the practical purposes of living, is unsettling and dangerous; he is afraid of his own mind. The poet is expected to respect this fear in the plain reader if only because he himself is supposed to have a mind much more obsessed with imaginative terrors. The difference is that the poet is on intimate terms with these terrors or mental ghosts; but how intimate the plain reader is unwilling to recognize. A certain convention has existed until recently restraining the poet from troubling the public with the more unsettling forms of thought, which are vaguely known to be involved in the making of poetry but not supposed to be evident in the reading of poetry. Caliban, for example, is just such a mental ghost of Shakespeare's. But by giving him a physical personality in a drama ('to airy nothing, a local habitation and a name') he makes him a fairy-story character, more realistic, less real. The modernist poet at his best neither conceals his private mind nor sends Calibans or Hamlets out upon the stage while he remains behind the scenes. His mind, if we may so put it, puts in a personal appearance; and it is the shock of this contact that the plain reader cannot bear.

CHAPTER V

Modernist Poetry and Dead Movements

THE refusal of the reading public to spend time on contemporary poetry can to a great extent be excused when we recall the decrepitude to which poetry was reduced by the death of the great Victorians and the survival of too many of the small ones. By domesticating itself in order to be received into the homes of the ordinary reading public and by allowing its teeth to be drawn so that it would no longer frighten, poetry had grown so tame, so dull, that it ceased to compete with other forms of social entertainment, especially with the new religion of sport. Callow or learned echoes of accepted poetry have now become as unattractive to the plain reader as the poetry he would classify as dangerous; and he does not realize that the alarming 'new' poetry with which he is at present surrounded is at least acting as a deterrent against the production of old-fashioned trash. For modernist poetry, if it is nothing else, is an ironic criticism of false literary survivals.

The feebleness with which poetry survived the poets who had made it feeble caused a general depression in the market-interest of all poetry except for academic or devotional purposes. To choose between such lines of John Drinkwater's as:

> O fool, o only great
> In pride unhallowed, O most blind of heart.
> Confusion but more dark confusion bred,
> Grief nurtured grief, I cried aloud and said,
> 'Through trackless ways the soul of man is hurled,
> No sign upon the forehead of the skies,
> No beacon, and no chart
> Are given to him, and the inscrutable world
> But mocks his scars and fills his mouth with dust.'[1]

and of Marianne Moore's *(To a Steam Roller)* as:

> The illustration
> is nothing to you without the application.
>   You lack half wit. You crush all particles down
>   into close conformity, and then walk back and forth on them.

Sparkling chips of rock
are crushed down to the level of the parent block.
   Were not 'impersonal judgement in aesthetic
      matters a physical impossibility,' you

might fairly achieve
it. As for butterflies, I can hardly conceive
   of one's attending you, but to question
      the congruence of the complement is vain, if it exists.[2]

involves an effort of criticism in the reader which it is not worth his while
to make, when so many other alternative possibilities of enjoyment are
offered outside of poetry. The first piece obviously takes him nowhere.
The second (an insulting address to a man with a steam roller mind,
lacking that half of wit which is to leave the whole unsaid) presupposes in
the reader a critical attitude toward poetry; assumes that he is willing to
part with the decayed flesh of poetry, the deteriorated sentimental part,
and to confine himself to the hard, matter-of-fact skeleton of poetic logic.
The plain reader may be brought to admire such a poet's puritanical
restraint in resisting the temptation to write an emotional poem of abuse
in the style of Mr Drinkwater, in conveying her meaning as dryly and
unfeelingly as a schoolmistress would explain a mathematical problem.
But while he may desire a reformation in poetry, he is interested only in
results, not in the technical discipline to which poetry must perhaps be
submitted. And Miss Moore's poetry is wholly concerned with such disci-
pline. The reader will therefore not sympathize with the prose quotation
in the above poem which its author thought necessary as the documentary
justification of her tirade, or appreciate the logical application of *butter-
flies*; a butterfly being the mathematical complement to a steam roller,
and, as a metaphorical complement, suggesting the extreme, unrelieved
dullness of this steam roller mind that has no possible complement, even
in metaphor. Anything indeed which reveals the poet at work, which
reveals the mechanism of his wit, is obnoxious to the plain reader. The
poetic process, he declares, is a mystery; and any evidence, therefore, of
what he may consider the technical aspect of poetry marks a poem as
incomprehensible. Miss Moore, who turns her poetry into matter-of-fact
prose demonstrations in order to avoid mystery, thus expresses the plain
reader's antagonism to poetry that perplexes rather than entertains. He
might not understand her sympathy, but he would undoubtedly agree
with her sentiments.

POETRY

I too, dislike it:
there are things that are important beyond all this fiddle.
The bat, upside down; the elephant pushing,

a tireless wolf under a tree,
the base-ball fan, the statistician –
'business documents and schoolbooks' –
these phenomena are pleasing,
but when they have been fashioned
into that which is unknowable,
we are not entertained.
It may be said of all of us
that we do not admire what we cannot understand;
enigmas are not poetry.[3]

It would be foolish to ask the plain reader to accept poetry that he does not understand; but it can perhaps be suggested to him, with more success than to the literary critic, that it would be wise to refrain from critical comments such as 'that is incomprehensible' unless he is willing to make the effort of criticism. If he does this, much that at first glance antagonized him will appear not incomprehensible but only perhaps difficult or, if not difficult, only different from what he has been accustomed to consider poetical. He may even train himself to read certain contemporary poets with interest; or, if he persists in keeping the critical process separate from the reading process, have at least a historical sense of what is happening in poetry.

It may be objected that modern poetry does not leave the plain reader alone, that it is constantly making advances to him; if not conciliatory advances, at any rate challenges which his self-respect does not permit him to overlook. It is true that modern poetry is full of noticeable peculiarities toward which the reader is bound to have some reaction either of sympathy or self-defence. But an important distinction must be drawn between peculiarities resulting from a deliberate attempt to improve the status of poetry by jazzing up its programme and those resulting from a concentration on the poetic process itself. The first class of peculiarities are caused by a desire to improve the popularity of poetry with the public and constitute a sort of commercial advertising of poetry. The second, while equally provoked by the cloud under which poetry has fallen, are concentrated on improving its general vitality, even to the point of making it temporarily more unpopular than ever: but for reasons opposite to those which reduced it to the state of disfavour in which it found itself at the beginning of this century. The plain reader has an exaggerated antagonism toward poetry of this second sort because it is too serious to permit of a merely neutral attitude in him and because, instead of presenting him with the benefits of its improvements, the poet seems impudently intent on advertising poetry for its own sake rather than for the reader's. A false sympathy, therefore, is likely to spring up between the plain reader and poetry especially designed to recapture his interest. This poetry attains a disproportionate importance and is artificially prolonged beyond the length of life to which it is naturally entitled. So has the long sequence of dead movements which have confused the history of contemporary poetry been perpetuated.

A dead movement is one which never had or can have a real place in the history of poets and poems. It occurs because some passing or hitherto unrealized psychological mood in the public offers a new field for exploitation, as sudden fashion crazes come and go, leaving no trace but waste material. In poetry such dead movements do not even survive as literary curiosities. From the eighties onward the writing of real poetry has been postponed by an increasing succession of such dead movements: the use of playful French forms for drawing-room occasions, of which the triolet became the most popular, by Austin Dobson, Arthur Symons and Sir Edmund Gosse; the wickedness movement of the Nineties, also of French origin, the characteristic words of whose poetical vocabulary were *lutany*, *arabesque*, *vermilion*, *jade*, *languid*, *satyr*; then a long end-of-the-century lull; then a new train of dead movements, only more interesting because they belong to a more alarming phase of world history. None of these movements which we call 'dead' because they never had any real poetic excuse for being, made any lasting contribution to English poetry: they were all merely modernized advertisements of the same old product of which the reader had grown tired.

Imagism is one of the earliest and the most typical of these twentieth-century dead movements. It had the look of a movement of pure experimentalism and reformation in poetry. But the issuing of a public manifesto of Imagism, its massed organization as a literary party with a defined political programme, the war it carried on with reviewers, the annual appearance of an Imagist anthology – all this revealed it as a stunt of commercial advertisers of poetry to whom poetic results meant a popular demand for their work, not the discovery of new values in poetry with an indifference to the recognition they received. The Imagists had decided beforehand the kind of poetry that was wanted by the time: a poetry to match certain up-to-date movements in music and art. They wanted to express 'new moods', and in free verse (or cadence). They *believed* in free verse; and to believe in one way of writing poetry as against another is to have the attitude of a quack rather than of a scientist toward one's art, to be in a position of selling one's ideas rather than of constantly submitting them to new tests. That is, they wanted to be *new* rather than to be poets; which meant that they could only go so far as to say everything that had already been said before in a slightly different way. 'Imagism refers to the manner of presentation, not to the subject.' Authentic 'advanced' poetry of the present day differs from such programmes for poetry in this important respect: that it is concerned with a reorganization of the matter (not in the sense of subject-matter but of poetic thought as distinguished from other kinds of thought) rather than the manner of poetry. This is why the plain reader feels so balked by it: he must enter into that matter without expecting a cipher-code to the meaning. The ideal modernist poem is its own clearest, fullest and most accurate meaning. Therefore the modernist poet does not have to talk about the use of images 'to render particulars exactly', since the poem does not give a rendering of a poetical picture or idea existing outside the poem, but presents the literal substance of poetry, a newly created thought-activity: the poem has the character of a creature by itself. Imagism, on the other hand, and all other similar dead movements, took for granted the principle that poetry was a translation of certain kinds of subjects into the language that would bring the reader emotionally closest to them. It was assumed that a natural separation existed between the reader and the subject, to be bridged by the manner in which it was presented.

Georgianism was a dead movement contemporary with Imagism. Although not so highly organised as Imagism, it had a great vogue between the years 1912 and 1918 and was articulate chiefly upon questions of style. Its general recommendations seem to have been the discarding of archaistic diction such as 'thee' and 'thou' and 'floweret' and 'whene'er' and of poetical constructions such as 'winter drear' and 'host on armèd host' and of pomposities generally. Another thing understood between the Georgians was that their verse should avoid all formally religious, philosophic or improving themes, in reaction to Victorianism; and all sad, wicked café table themes in reaction to the nineties. It was to be English yet not aggressively imperialistic; pantheistic rather than atheistic; and as simple as a child's reading book. This was all to the good, perhaps, but such counsels resulted in a poetry that could rather be praised for what it was not than for what it was. Eventually Georgianism became principally concerned with Nature and love and leisure and old age and childhood and animals and sleep and other uncontroversial subjects. Unfortunately there was no outstanding figure either among the Imagists, the Vers Librists generally, or among the Georgians, capable of writing a new poetry within these revised forms. So in both cases all that happened was that the same old stock-feelings and situations were served up again, only with a different sauce. And poetry became shabbier than ever. The extent of this shabbiness was concealed by the boom which the War brought about in poetry, as part of the general mobilization of public industries. A great many poets were carried through to popular recognition on the wave of the War who would otherwise never have been heard of again. Alan Seegar is an American example of this temporary immortalization.[4] The place of Rupert Brooke in English tradition is likely to be more secure only because this tradition has more powerful methods of literary propaganda: Rupert Brooke,[5] writing at the present moment unconnected with the war idea would be as coldly disregarded as indeed he was before his death on active service, when practically all the poems for which he has since become famous had already appeared. War-poetry was Georgianism's second-wind, for the contrast between the grinding hardships of trench-service – which as a matter of fact none of the early-Georgians experienced and the Georgian stock-subjects enumerated above was a ready poetic theme. Imagism also profited by the war, though, as it was more an American than an English product, it was only mobilized for war-service when neo-Georgianism had already made a good start. The expansion of feminism in poetry as in other war-services introduced a number of other dead movements which had, roughly speaking, one of two common sentimental 'tones': daintiness or daring. The 'daintiness' movements employed an Elizabethan or Cavalier atmosphere and were a form of escape from the War; they were further characterized by 'cuteness' (in the American sense), archness, slyness and naughtiness; the impression they left was of an argument in which the poet always won by having the last word. The 'daring' movements used for the most part free, very free, verse; they were 'confessing' movements in which the poet, under the influence of war-excitement, indulged in one burst of confidence after another. Imagism may be said to have engaged only the upper half of the plain reading public. But Georgianism in England and the daintiness and daring movements in America made poetry pay for a long time; until the poets and the plain readers grew tired, at about the same time. It can be said unreservedly that of all that creative and reading enthusiasm *nothing* remains except, perhaps, a few shadowy names. Of the war poets whose works were temporarily advertised by their death in action only three can be regretted: Sorley, Rosenberg and Owen.

Of the Imagists H.D. (Hilda Doolittle) was the most publicly applauded; all we have left of her now is the blushing memory of a short-lived popularity in the more adventurous reviews, and a few false metaphors. What disappears first in the poetry of dead movements is the personal reality of the poet, which has been represented with false intensity to make a romantic personal appeal to the reader (an appeal which does not appear so extravagantly in modernist poetry); the poetry itself drags on a little longer, waste.

> O night,
> you take the petals
> of the roses in your hand
> but leave the stark core
> of the rose
> to perish on the branch.[6]

Compare this metaphor with an equally eccentric one of Emily Dickinson's, a poet belonging to no 'movement' and whose personal reality pervades her work, though she kept it strictly out of her work:

Victory comes late
And is held low to freezing lips
Too wrapt with frost
To take.[7]

The only excuse to be made for those who once found H.D. 'incomprehensible' is that her work was so thin, so poor, that its emptiness seemed 'perfection', its insipidity to be concealing a 'secret', its superficiality so 'glacial' that it created a false 'classical' atmosphere. She was never able, in her temporary immortality, to reach a real climax in any of her poems.

I can almost follow the note
where it touched this slender tree
and the next answered –
and the next.

Shall I let myself be caught
in my own light?
shall I let myself be broken
in my own heat?
or shall I cleft the rock as of old
and break my fire
with its surface?[8]

All that they told was a story of feeble personal indecision; and her immortality came to an end so soon that her bluff was never called.

All dead movements are focussed on the problem of style. To the Imagists style meant the 'use of the language of common speech', but in a very careful way, as a paint-box. Language in poetry should not be treated as if it were a paint-box, or the poem as if it were something to be hung on the wall, so to speak. The reader should enter the life of the poem and submit himself to its conditions in order to know it as it really is; instead of making it enter his life as a symbol having no private reality, only the reality it gets by reflection from his world. Style may be defined as that old-fashioned element of sympathy with the reader which makes it possible for the poem to be used as an illustration to the text of the reader's experience; and much modernist poetry may be said to be literally without style, at least in so far as it is possible for poetry to make a radical change in a tradition within the memory of that tradition. So the modernist poet does not have to issue a programme declaring his intentions toward the reader or to issue an announcement of tactics. He does not have to call himself an individualist (as the Imagist poet did) or a mystic (as the poet of the Anglo-Irish dead movement did) or a naturalist (as the poet of the Georgian dead movement did). He does not have to describe or docket himself for the reader, because the important part of poetry is now not the personality of the poet as embodied in a poem, which is its style, but the personality of the poem itself, that is, its quality of independence from both the reader and the poet, once the poet has separated it from his personality by making it complete – a new and self-explanatory creature.

Perhaps more than anything else characteristic modernist poetry is a declaration of the independence of the poem. This means first of all a change in the poet's attitude toward the poem: a new sense has arisen of the poem's rights comparable with the new sense in modern times of the independence of the child, and a new respect for the originality of the poem as for the originality of the child. One no longer tries to keep a child in its place by suppressing its personality or laughing down its strange questions, so that it turns into a rather dull and ineffective edition of the parent; and modernist poetry is likewise freeing the poem of stringent nursery rules and, instead of telling it exactly what to do, is encouraging it to do things, even queer things, by itself. The poet pledges himself to take them seriously on the principle that the poem, being a new and mysterious form of life in comparison with himself, has more to teach him than he it. It is a popular superstition that the poet is the child. It is not the poet, but the poem: the most that the poet can do is to be a wise, experimenting parent.

Experiment, however, may be interpreted in two ways. In the first sense it is a delicate and constantly alert state of expectancy directed towards the discovery of something of which some slight clue has been given; and system in it means only the constant shifting and adjustment of the experimenter as the unknown thing becomes more and more known: system is the readiness to change system. The important thing in the whole process is the initial clue, or, in old-fashioned language, the inspiration. The real scientist should have an equal power of genius with the poet, with the difference that the scientist is inspired to discover things which already are (his results are facts), while the poet is inspired to discover things which are made by his discovery of them (his results are not statements about things already known to exist, or knowledge, but truths, things which existed before only as potential truth). Experiment in the second sense is the use of a system for its own sake and brings about, whether in science or poetry, no results but those possible to the system. As it is only the scientific genius who is capable of using experiment in the first of these senses, and as the personnel of science must be necessarily far more numerous than that of poetry, experiment in the second sense is the general method of the labouring, as against the inventive, side of science, perhaps properly so.

Poets, then, who need the support of a system (labourers pretending to be inventors, since in poetry, unlike science, there is no place for labourers) are obliged to adopt not only the workshop method of science, but the whole philosophical point of view of science, which is directly

opposite to the point of view of poetry. For in science there is no person-
ality granted to the things discovered, which are looked upon as soulless
parts of a soulless aggregate, with no independent rights or life of their
own. Such poets, therefore, produce poems that are only well-ordered
statements about chosen subjects, not new, independent living organisms;
facts, not truths; pieces of literature, not distinct poetic personalities.
Poetry of this sort (and there has been little poetry of any other sort, as
there have been few real poets) is thus the science of poem-training
instead of the art of poem-appreciation. The real poet is a poet by reason
of his creative vision of the poem, as the real parent is a parent by reason
of his creative vision of the child: authorship is not a matter of the right
use of the will but of an enlightened withdrawal of the will to make room
for a new will.

It is this delicate and watchful withdrawal of the author's will at the
right moments which gives the poem or the child an independent form.
But as the creative will is of as rare appearance in poetry as in parenthood,
there are, in its absence, very few real poems and very few real children.
Or if a real poem or child occurs in spite of its absence, the poem or child
will have to stand in the relation of a creator to itself, which means a
dangerous enlargement of the creative will in either of them, an enlarge-
ment that we may call genius. But with genius there is as much chance of
self-destruction as of fulfilment of the creative will. And therefore the
poem which survives great odds, the poem of genius, is as rare as the child
who survives to become the poet of genius. Most real poems and real poets
have come to be in this way, it being as impossible to arrange that the poet
with a capacity for writing real poems should have any to write as that two
people with a capacity for being the right parents for a real child should
have one who could benefit by this capacity. All that can be done is to
encourage an attitude toward the poem and the child which shall provide
for the independence of either in proportion to its power of independence.
In poetry at least this would mean that people would not write poems
unless they were complete ones, that is, they would not force a poem by
violent training to behave independently when it had no independence. In
general it would mean that people would not have to be 'geniuses' (*i.e.*
turn sports in order to survive the odds against them) to use their creative
will freely, to behave with genius.

When we say, then, that the modernist poet has an experimental atti-
tude toward the poem, we do not mean to imply that he is experimenting
with the poem in order to prove some system he has developed. This is
properly only the attitude of such a dead movement as Imagism, merely a
sign that something is wrong with the education of the poem (literally, the
'drawing out' of it). The Montessori system of education, for example,
corresponds in the history of pedagogical reform with Imagism and other
such systems in the reformation of poetry. Both are schools with new

systems of training or form to replace old systems: they do not imply the existence of a new kind of relationship between the parent and the child, the poet and the poem, a feeling of mutual respect favourable to the independent development of each and therefore to a maximum of benefit of one to the other. Of course, if the poem is left to shift entirely for itself and its independence is really only a sign of the irresponsibility of the poet, then its personality, by its wildness, is likely to be as indecisive as the personality of the formalized poem is by its reliance on discipline.

The policy of leaving the poem to write itself makes it only a form of automatic writing which inevitably leads to the over-emphasis of the dream element in the writing of poetry. It is true that dreams seem to exercise the same kind of control over the mind as the poem does over the poet. But in dreams we have thought in an uncreative state running itself out to a solution out of sheer inertia, unrefreshed by any volitional criticism of it; a solution which is like a negative image of the solution which thought would arrive at in a creative, waking state, refreshed by volitional criticism. The dream solution is therefore as arbitrary a substitute for the solutions of waking thought as the dream-poem (or automatic poem) is for the poem that would naturally result from the deliberate adjustment of the creative will to the solution which seems to come nearer and nearer as the creative will grows more and more discreet. The problem of preventing poetry from sinking into rapid decline and disuse does not seem to point, then, to a sense of responsibility in the poet toward the reader as shown in the use of a carefully designed 'style'. It points rather to the responsibility which the poet owes to the poem because of its dependence on him until it is complete, a dependence which shall not, however, be reflected as a weakness in the poem after it has been completed; as childhood should survive in a person as the element of continuous newness in him, not as the permanent bad effect of discipline that made him less, rather than more, independent as he grew.

CHAPTER VI

The Making of the Poem

A DECLARATION of the independence of the poem naturally causes a change in the attitude of the poet towards himself. This does not mean that the poet ceases to be important; he merely acquires a new sense of privacy which his relation to the poem in the old regime made impossible. He shrinks from the strenuous publicity into which he might be dragged by the author-worship of traditional poetry or the abnormal sense of self-importance usually displayed in the official programmes of such dead movements as Imagism. e.e. cummings' foreword to his volume *is 5* is undoubtedly inspired by a distaste for the sentimental display by which the poet has in the past been expected to advertise himself; and perhaps explains his tendency, the modernist tendency in general, to let the poem take precedence over the poet:

> On the assumption that my technique is either complicated or orig-
> inal or both, the publishers have politely requested me to write an
> introduction to this book.
>
> At least my theory of technique, if I have one, is very far from
> original; nor is it complicated. I can express it in fifteen words, by
> quoting The Eternal Question And Immortal Answer of burlesk,
> viz. 'Would you hit a woman with a child? – No, I'd hit her with a
> brick.' Like the burlesque comedian, I am abnormally fond of that
> precision which creates movement.
>
> If a poet is anybody, he is somebody to whom things made matter
> very little – somebody who is obsessed by Making. Like all obses-
> sions, the Making obsession has disadvantages; for instance, my
> only interest in making money would be to make it. Fortunately,
> however, I should prefer to make almost anything else, including
> locomotives and roses. It is with roses and locomotives (not to
> mention acrobats Spring electricity Coney Island the 4th of July the
> eyes of mice and Niagara Falls) that my 'poems' are competing.
> They are also competing with each other, with elephants and with
> El Greco.
>
> Ineluctable preoccupation with The Verb gives a poet one price-

less advantage: whereas non-makers must content themselves with the merely undeniable fact that two times two is four, he rejoices in a purely irresistible truth (to be found, in abbreviated costume, upon the title page of the present volume).

cummings, then, writing according to what would seem to the reader to be a very carefully constructed poetic system, refrains from delivering a critical key to his poems except as a semi-prefatorial confidence. Indeed the more independent poems become, the less need or sense there is in accompanying them with a technical guide for their understanding. This would seem to imply that, the more difficult poems become, the less chance there would be of understanding them. But in fact it would only mean that the reader was becoming less and less separated from poetry by the technique that had formerly been concentrated on connecting him with it. Technique itself has then taken on a different character; it is no longer the way a poem is presented to the reader, but the way it corresponds in every respect with its own governing meaning. For in making a poem the poet may be said to be governed by this meaning, which may only be the necessity of the poem to be written: in this foreshadowing, inevitable meaning in the poem really exists even before it is written. This it is that cummings should mean by 'the obsession of making' and this it is that the reader will have to reckon with if poetry continues in its present tendency of forcing him inside the framework of the poem and making him repeat the steps by which it came to be. So that technique in the modernist definition does not refer to the method by which a poem is written but that evolutionary history of the poem which is the poem itself. The Eternal Question And Immortal Answer of burlesque in literary terms are: 'Do you write poems with a prearranged technique? – No, I write them with a pen.' Meaning: the question of technique in the writing of a poem is irrelevant to the writing of it. If one talks about poems as being mechanically put together by the poet, then the pen is the thing that does it. Like the brick, it is the only practical answer possible to a theoretical question conditioned by an irrelevant practical qualification.

This brings us to the crucial complication in the adjustments to be made between poetry itself and the reader of poetry, who is unable to have a free and straightforward personal intimacy with a poem but is continually haunted by the idea of the presence of the poet in the poem. Between the reader and the poem therefore there is this embarrassment caused by the reader's awareness of the poet. He is not at his ease with the poem: it is never entirely his own – he reads the poem with the uncomfortable feeling that the poet's eyes are on him and that he will be expected to say something when he is finished. The reader cannot get over the idea that the poet had designs on him in writing the poem, to which he must respond. With traditional poetry the reader is less embarrassed because, although he is aware of the poet in a formal way, he is not made particularly self-conscious by him. He knows what to expect, since traditional poetry is formed with an eye to its serviceability as reading matter. We may compare traditional poetry in this sense with the conservative, well-appointed restaurant where the customer is placed in a soft light, the waiters address him in a respectful monotone and he is left to himself to eat. Modern poetry of the dead-movement sort, of which Imagism is a complete example, bears a resemblance to the 'artistic' tea-room where the customer finds himself besieged by orange curtains, Japanese prints, painted furniture, art-china instead of the plain white service of the ordinary restaurant, and conversational waitresses in smocks who give the personal touch with a cultured accent. As a result, the plain eater goes back to his corner restaurant and the tearoom becomes a dead movement. *Modernist* as distinct from *modern* poetry is, at its most uncompromising, neither the corner restaurant nor the tea-room. It seems inaccessible to the plain reader: the approach to it is like the front of a private residence and he is afraid that he is expected to lunch personally with the poet. So in this case again he goes back to the corner restaurant where he can at least reduce the personality of the waiters to a minimum. Actually, if the plain reader could conquer his initial self-consciousness before it he would find an interior in which it should be possible to be on completely unembarrassed and impersonal terms with poetry: he would find himself alone with it. But this is only theoretically possible. For the plain reader does not really want to be left all alone with poetry. The mental ghosts, which only poets are supposed to have natural commerce with, assail him. The real discomfort to the reader in modernist poetry is the absence of the poet as his protector from the imaginative terrors lurking in it.

What the reader, then, calls the clearness of a poem often means merely its freedom from those terrors which he, in his defence against them, attacks as obscurities. Clearness for him is really the suppression of everything in the poem over and above the average standard of comprehension – of everything likely to disturb normal ease. A poem, therefore, that really is potentially superior to the average standard of comprehension and which nevertheless conforms to it actually obscures its real meaning the more it observes this standard, *i.e.* the *clearer* it is to the average reader. A poem that is potentially superior to the average standard of comprehension and which, disregarding it, fulfils all its potentialities, makes its real meaning clearer and clearer, as it retreats from this average, *i.e.* as it becomes more and more obscure to the average reader. The trouble is not with the reader or with the poem but with the government of criticism by the sales-principle, which must make an average standard of public taste allowing for the most backward reader of each of the three reading classes corresponding with the three different degrees of popular education. If a variable standard of comprehension were admitted, the poem would have the privilege of developing itself to the degree of clearness corresponding with the degree of comprehension in the reader most above the average. As the poet himself would thus be allowed as a possible reader of his own poem, it would be encouraged to attain its maximum, not its minimum, of real clearness; and the word *obscure* would disappear from the vocabulary of criticism except to denote the obscurity of particular references. *Bad* would be the only possible critical term by which a poem could be categorically dismissed: at the present time, regardless of the possible classification of a poem as *good* or *bad* according to the standards it suggests, it is enough for the critic to call a poem *obscure* to relieve himself of the obligation of giving a real criticism of it.

Here is an example, in the first eighteen lines of what might be called a modernist poem, of the 'obscurity' which would probably cause it to be put aside by the critic after he had allowed it the customary two-minute reading (for if the poet has obeyed all the rules, this is long enough to give a rough idea of what the poem is all about and that is all that is generally wanted). Or if by chance the critic is 'advanced', serving such a limited public that his criticism is mere literary snobbery, he may pretend to understand it and dislike it equally, because he does not understand it; or, if he does, he may dislike it all the same because it is 'too simple' (a common charge against the 'obscure' poem when its obscurity is seen to have been only excessive clearness).

> The rugged black of anger
> Has an uncertain smile-border.
> The transition from one kind to another
> May be love between neighbour and neighbour;
> Or natural death; or discontinuance
> Because so small is space,
> The extent of kind must be expressed otherwise;
> Or loss of kind when proof of no uniqueness
> Strikes the broadening edge and discourages.
> Therefore and therefore all things have experience
> Of ending and of meeting
> And of ending, that much being
> As grows faint of self and withers
> When more is the intenser self
> That is another or nothing.
> And therefore smiles, when least smiling –
> The gift of nature to necessity
> When relenting grows involuntary.[1]

The reaction, then, will be either one of 'blank incomprehension' or, since the critic-reader recognizes a few long words and a certain atmosphere created by the poet's 'saying what he means', one of antagonism due to the impression that the poem gives of being didactic. The reaction of blank incomprehension will be commonest. 'What, in so many words', the critic-reader will ask, 'is this all about?' Now, to tell what a poem is all about in 'so many words' is to reduce the poem to so many words, to leave out all that the reader cannot at the moment understand in order to give him the satisfaction of feeling that he is understanding it. If it were possible to give the complete force of a poem in a prose summary, then there would be no excuse for writing the poem: the 'so many words' are, to the last punctuation-mark, the poem itself. Where such a prose summary does render the poem in its entirety, except for rhymes and other external dressings, the poem cannot have been a complete one; and indeed a great deal of what passes for poetry is the rewriting of the prose summary of a hypothetical poem in poetical language. Before further discussing this particular poem, let us quote the beginning of a ballad by Mr Ezra Pound in illustration of the prose-idea poeticalized:

THE BALLAD OF THE GOODLY FERE*

(Simon Zelotes speaketh it somewhile after the Crucifixion)

Ha' we lost the goodliest fere o' all
    For the priests and the gallows tree?
Aye, lover he was of brawny men
    O' ships and the open sea.

When they came wi' a host to take Our Man
    His smile was good to see,
'First let these go!' quo' our Goodly Fere,
    'Or I'll see ye damned,' says he.

Aye, he sent us out through the crossed high spears,
    And the scorn of his laugh rang free,
'Why took ye not me when I walked about
    Alone in the town?' says he.

Oh, we drank his 'Hale' in the good red wine
    When we last made company,
No capon priest was the Goodly Fere
    But a man o' men was he.

I ha' seen him drive a hundred men
    Wi' a bundle o' cords swung free
When they took the high and holy house
    For their pawn and treasury...[2]

---

* Mate or companion.

Stripped of its imitated antiqueness, the substance of all this could be given simply as follows: 'It would be false to identify the Christ of the sentimentalists with the Christ of the Gospels. So far from being a meek or effeminate character He strikes us as a very *manly* man, and His disciples, fishermen and others, must have reverenced Him for His manly qualities as much as for His spiritual teaching. His action in driving the money-changers from the Temple with a scourge of cords is a proof of this. So is His courageous action when confronted by the soldiers of the High Priest sent to arrest Him – He mockingly enquired why they had not dared arrest Him previously when He walked about freely in the city of Jerusalem, and consented to offer no resistance only if His disciples were allowed to escape. The Last Supper was surely a very different scene from the Church Sacrament derived from it, where a full-fed priest condescendingly officiates; it was a banquet of friends of which the Dearest Friend was Our Saviour.' Here we see that the poeticalization has in fact weakened the historical argument. By using the ballad setting Mr Pound has made the fishermen of Galilee into North-country sailors of the Patrick Spens tradition and given them sentiments more proper to the left wing of the YMCA.

The extravagant use of metaphor and simile in poetry is thus seen to be governed by the necessity of making a poem of this sort equal the prose summary which really is dictating it. This practice is founded on two fallacies, one of which follows from the other: the first, that the poet is not saying what he means but something *like* what he means in prettier language than he uses to himself about it; the second, from which the first is deduced, that the ideas of truth in which poetry deals are not agreeable in themselves but that a distinction is to be made by the poet between what is pretty and not pretty, poetical and not poetical. When, therefore, bare, undressed ideas are found in poetry instead of the rhetorical devices by which poets try to 'put over' their ideas, such poetry is naturally accused of being didactic. Another way of saying this is that the poet has cut off all his communications. As a matter of fact all that has happened is that he has made the poem out of the poem itself: its final form is identical in terms with its preliminary form in the poet's mind, uncorrupted by hints to the reader, familiar asides to make it less terrifying, and flattering conceits to enliven, to entertain and to display the poet's virtuosity. But it is almost impossible for a poet who does really mean what he says to make the critic-reader believe that he does: the more he means what he says and the more earnest he is to make this clear, the more he will be thought to be concealing his meaning in clever evasions called 'obscurity'.

If, then, the author of the lines beginning 'The rugged black of anger' were asked to explain their meaning, the only proper reply would be to repeat the lines, perhaps with greater emphasis: by which, presumably, they would only become more obscure. If the poet were pressed to employ some familiar metaphor or simile to explain them, then he would have to prefix his remarks with some such insult: 'At your request I shall make my poem into a bad imitation of itself. I shall, in fact, call this version *your* poem, the more yours the sillier it grows. But you must promise not to deceive yourself that this is what the poem means. It is rather what it does not mean.' This method of understanding a poem may be called Smoking Out The Meaning. To consider how the meaning may be smoked out here let us put these lines into the first metaphor that occurs to us. Indeed it is not wholly impossible that the first two lines may conceal an incidental satire on the popular poetical sentiment:

> Look around and you will find
> Every cloud is silver-lined,
> The sun still shines
> Although the sky's a grey one.
> It's a short life but a gay one.

If such is the interpretation suggested by the first two lines, then they are being treated as the prose idea from which the real poem, apparently unwritten, is derived. That is, the ordinary translation system of poetry, thus:

(I)

A	B	C
Poet's prose idea	*Poem*	*Reader's prose summary*
1.	1.	1.
2.	2.	2.
3.	3.	3.
4.	4.	4.

is assumed to have been reversed, thus:

(II)

A	B	C
Poem (suppressed)	*Prose idea as poem*	*Reader's poetical summary*
1.	1.	1.
2.	2.	3.
3.	3.	3.
4.	4.	4.

The truth is that there is no fundamental difference between these two systems. The same principle that $1 = 1 = 1$ prevails (*i.e.* that prose ideas have their exact equivalents in poetry, and many of them to one idea); though in a different order, we find the same categories representing the stages of the poem from creation to criticism. And the fact that the reader finds it necessary to make a poetical rather than a more strictly prose

summary in (II) would really make no appreciable difference in his enjoy-
ment of the poem if it were really written as set forth in (II). For the
element of strangeness and excitement would perhaps be added to his
enjoyment if the ordinary system were reversed: the novelty would at least
last for a few poems of this sort, as it lasted for the first year or two of the
recent *Vers Libre* movement, a dead movement which tried to coué poetry
back into health by depriving it of its crutches. But if the lines in question
were not the prose idea as poem – B of (II) – that is, the prose idea in a
slightly poetical form which the reader had to amplify along suggested
poetical lines, a discrepancy would appear between the poem as it stands
and the reader's poetical summary of it, should he find it possible to make
one: we should have not two equivalent meanings but one meaning and
another gratuitous meaning derived from it. B1 would not equal C1, but
C1 would merely be X1, one of the many possible derived meanings of B1,
but not the real meaning. B and C of (II) would therefore read:

B	C
1.	X 1
2.	X 2
3.	X 3
4.	X 4

X1-2-3-4 being but a digression from B, B then would not be the prose
idea as poem, but the poem itself. If, as such, without the addition of any
associations not provided in the poem, or of collateral interpretations, it
could reveal an internal consistency strengthened at every point in its
development and free of the necessity of external application, that is,
complete without criticism – if it could do this, it would have established
an insurmountable difference between prose ideas and poetic ideas, prose
facts and poetic facts. This difference would mean the independence of
poetic facts, as real facts, from any prose or poetical explanation in the
terms of practical workaday reality which would make them seem unreal,
or poetical facts.

  If we assume that the first two lines here do not mean what they say,
and accept the silver-lined cloud explanation, we find that we are brought
into a sentimental personal atmosphere in which *anger* is anger as felt by
someone, or bad-luck seen as the anger of providence or fate, and in which
smile-border is either personal happiness or good luck. Any such interpre-
tation of *anger* and *smile-border*, indeed, would involve us in some such
sympathetic history of the poem. But if we consult the poem itself we find,
after the first two lines, that any possible parallelism with an interpreta-
tion of this sort ends: *anger* means just anger, *smile-border* just smile-
border. So much so do they mean just what they are that the rest of the
poem is developed from their being just what they are: *anger*, anger ; *smile-
border*, the smiling border of anger which apparently separates it from

some other kind, or concept, whose border separating it from anger might equally be called an 'anger-border'. What are we to do, then, since the poem really seems to mean what it says? All we can do is to let it interpret itself, without introducing any new associations or, if possible, any new words.

> The rugged black of anger
> Has an uncertain smile-border.
> The transition from one kind to another,
> As from anger, rugged black,
> To what lies across its smile-border,
> May be love between neighbour and neighbour
> (Love between neighbouring kind and kind);
> Or natural death (death of one,
> Though not of the other); or discontinuance
> (Discontinuance of kind,
> As anger no more anger)
> Because so small is space
> (So small the space for kind and kind and kind),
> The extent of kind must be expressed otherwise
> (The extent of kind beyond its border
> Is end of kind, because space is so small
> There is not room enough for all
> Kinds: anger *angrier* has to be
> Expressed otherwise than by anger,
> So by an uncertain smile-border);

This will serve as a sufficient illustration of the method of letting the poem interpret itself. It was done without introducing any words not actually belonging to the poem, without throwing any of the poem away as superfluous padding and without having recourse to a prose version: the poem interpreted is practically itself repeated to three times its own length. It may be objected that it is still not entirely clear, but not that it is not *any* clearer, that it could not be made clearer still by an increase in length proportionate to the need of the reader in question. For instance, if the reader is puzzled by the sixth of the original lines and cannot at the first reading persuade himself that *Because so small is space* really means *Because so small is space*, yet sees that it can mean nothing else, he can repeat to himself:

> Because so small is space,
> Because so small is space,

until he is convinced; or, perhaps,

> Because space is so small,
> Because space is so small,

an inversion which the poet would surely mind less than the use of a prose summary, such as a philosophical reading: 'Because so small is Space or the Universe or the Human Mind, not allowing Ideas to reach their full development but crowding them into cramped quarters so that they have a hard time keeping their independence and are often even completely extinguished.'

The important thing that would be revealed by a wide application of this method to the reading of poems that really mean what they say (for obviously it could not be applied to poems that do not) would be that much of the so-called obscurity of poems was created by the laziness of the plain reader, who wishes to hurry through poetry as quickly as he does through prose, not realizing that he is dealing with a kind of thought which, though it may have the speed of prose to the poet, he must follow with a slowness proportionate to how much he is not a poet. Indeed, with a just realization of this proportion it should be possible for the plain reader to read a very difficult poem without even adding any repetitional lines. Increasing the time-length of reading is one way of getting out of the prose and into the poetic state of mind, of developing a capacity for minuteness, for seeing all there is to see at a given point and for taking it all with one as one goes along. We have forgotten, however, that the plain reader, while he does not object to the poetic state of mind in the poet, has a fear of cultivating it in himself. This is why he prefers the prose summary to the poem and to see the poem, as it began in the poet's mind, as a genial prose idea free of those terrors which the poet is supposed to keep to himself or carefully disguise. Part of the reader's reaction to what he calls the obscurity of certain poems is really his nervous embarrassment at feeling himself left alone with the meaning of the poem itself.

But whatever may be the cause of the reader's embarrassment with the poem, the important fact is, from the point of view of the poem and the poet, that the 'making' poet does not write because of the demand of the reader to be fed with poetry but because certain poems demand to be written and the poet is 'somebody who is obsessed by Making'. Once the poems are 'made', his personal activity ceases in them. They begin a life of their own toward which he has no responsibility of advertising or selling: that they reach the reader at all is an accident, an affair entirely between them and the reader. This, by the way, is not what used to be meant by 'art for art's sake'. 'Art for art's sake' was as if a cook should say, 'I am employed as a cook, I know, but I am such a superior cook that what I cook is not to be eaten, it is a purely esoteric culinary mystery.' The modernist poet will not adopt this attitude at all, because he will not start with the sense of being an artist in an official, public-service sense.

The purpose of printing in book-form poetry construed in this private sense is not to convert it into a selling product but merely to give it an identity separate from the author's; and the disinterested anxiety of poets to get their work printed must be attributed partly to this desire to see it as a separate life. It is practically impossible for a poet to read his own poetry intelligently unless separated from him in some way. The easiest and most obvious way is to have it set down in print, since his own handwriting is like a physical part of himself: the printed page acts as a mirror. This explains the mystery of Shakespeare's failure to have his plays uniformly printed in his lifetime: they had become sufficiently externalized by being presented on the stage. But the process of externalization must be seen to have two aspects: externalization for the sake of a legitimate vanity in the poet, a curiosity in him about his own poems; and externalization as a poet's duty toward his poem. When both of these aspects are balanced, the poem has an outward and an inward sincerity. When externalization, or formalizing, has only what we may call the *printing* aspect, which has only to do with the poem as something made by the poet and read by the reader – a theatrical 'showing off' on the part of the poet; when it means only this and has no *creative* aspect, then the more facile the poem is as a printed piece the more insincere it is as a private, independent poem-person.

In a great deal of traditional poetry the problem of externalizing his work is an easy one for the poet because there is a whole apparatus of conventions at his service ready to give it a formal literary independence of him. But as such conventions (stanza, rhyme, poetical punctuation, etc.) are really the conventions of the printing, not of the making, of poetry, this independence is only an artificial one. Of course there undoubtedly are really independent poems written in traditional forms, for which such conventions have only meant an additional guarantee of their individuality. But as these conventions give an artificial appearance of independence to poems, they are a constant temptation to people who are not poets to write things that look like poems and to poets themselves to be lazy, because the finality of traditional verse-forms can make an incomplete poem seem complete ('incomplete' meaning, of course, 'not thoroughly separated from the poet'). Poetry like this, then, principally composed of literary conventions, is bound sooner or later to show its shabbiness; and attempts to smarten it up again only change the old conventions for new ones instead of striking at the underlying fallacy, that it is completeness of method that turns out good poems, or technical indefatigability, rather than an indefatigable obsession for making until the poem is made.

For if the poet has poems in him they will get themselves made regardless of the poet's method of setting them down. No technical method, whatever its merits, can extract poems where there are no poems: a method can *seem* to make, it cannot *make*. The Imagists, for example, did not make new poems, only a new kind of stanza which seemed to them more real than traditional stanza-forms because it was new. When Mr cummings says that his 'poems are competing with locomotives and roses' he means that they were made as real entities, whether mechanical or natural. He does not claim to have a sure method to be used over and over again in making more and more poems, but to be irresistibly besieged by poems of even contradictory natures and of contradictory principles of growth, each with its own separate method of being made. All that the methodist poet boasts, however, is a trick for producing things that resemble locomotives or roses. In constantly repeating his method in poems he is only saying over and over again that two times two is four. The making poet, on the other hand, has no method, but a faculty for allowing things to invent themselves. As he cannot then write a poem unless there is one to write and is consequently incapable of repeating himself, he is declaring, with each new poem, a new truth, a complete truth, even a contradictory truth. He is allowing two times two (or truth) to become all it is possible for it to be, since truth cannot be reduced to a fixed mathematical law any more than poetry to a fixed literary method: two times two, like poetry, may be everything and anything.

CHAPTER VII

Modernist Poetry and Civilization

THE vulgar meaning of modernism, especially when the word is employed as a term of critical condemnation or by poets themselves as a literary affectation, is modern-ness, a keeping-up in poetry with the pace of civilization and intellectual history. It is thus used by the reader or critic who makes a sentimental association of poetry with the past, and perhaps with a particular period of the past, as an epithet for 'new' poetry which seems irreverent of the general tradition; and, in the other extreme, it is deliberately adopted by individual poets and movements as a contemporary programme. Poetry in this light becomes a matter of temperamental politics, with a conservative flank opposed to a radical flank; and an imaginary battle ensues in which the main issue is lost sight of: may a poet write as a poet or must he write as a period? For modernism, in this perverted sense, likewise becomes a critical tyranny, increasing contemporary mannerisms in poetry instead of freeing the poet of obligation to conform to any particular set of literary theories. There is, indeed, a genuine modernism, which is not a part of a 'modernist' programme but a natural personal manner and attitude in the poet to his work, and which accepts the denomination 'modernist' because it prefers this to other denominations; also because there is a conspicuous force operating at great odds to free the *poem* of many of the traditional habits which prevented it from achieving its full significance. Keeping in mind this conspicuous force, more excuse can be found for 'modernist' as applied to the poem than to the poet; as *poems* is a more accurate, less prejudiced term for *poetry* (a vague and sentimental idea in relation to which *poet* is a more vague and sentimental idea still). But even into this more genuine aspect of poetic modernism creep some of the prejudices of perverted modernism – into its criticism especially. It has, for example, an intolerance toward contemporary poetry which confesses no programme, a suspicion, more properly, of poetry which does not seem to profess a literary cause; and a self-protective sympathy for manifestations of modernism in the past – the present vogue of eighteenth-century poetry is largely inspired by its quaintness, which, however affected, was in its day an up-to-dateness.

For no matter how restrained, how impersonal a literary attitude may be, it is difficult for it to resist the temptation to convert and to receive converts; and modernist poetry, whatever its purity, is especially in danger of succumbing to this temptation to convert, because it is much attacked, and to receive converts, because there are always literary loose-ends anxious to acquire character and standing by attaching themselves to a cause.

The sense of modernism is further perverted by the existence of a middle position between the conservative flank and the radical flank – the intelligent, plain-man point of view. This middle view, this middle population, we might say, is the prop and advocate of civilization; and the idea of civilization as a steady human progress does not exclude the idea of a modernist, *historically* forward poetry. A possible rapprochement exists, therefore, between this middle population, to whom poetry is just one of the many instruments of progress, and that type of contemporary poetical writing which advertises itself by its historical progressiveness. It is diffi-cult, in attempting to make clear some of the aspects of genuine poetic modernism, to avoid appealing to the progressiveness of this middle population, that is, making poetry a historical branch of civilization, and to avoid likewise the appearance of condoning that perverted modernism which takes advantage of a false idea of 'advance' to justify feeble eccen-tricity. The real task is, in fact, not to explain modernism in poetry but to separate false modernism, or faith in history, from genuine modernism, or faith in the immediate, the *new* doings of poems (or poets or poetry) as not necessarily derived from history. Modernist poetry as such should mean no more than fresh poetry, more poetry, poetry based on honest invention rather than on conscientious imitation of the time-spirit.

But honest invention and affectation of originality can both be confused in the single term 'modernism'. Francis Thompson, in his essay on Coleridge, complained that

> the charge of affectation has been hurled in turn at the outset of their careers against Coleridge, Wordsworth, Shelley, Keats, Tennyson and Browning. Wordsworth wrote simple diction and his simplicity was termed affected; Shelley gorgeous diction and his gorgeousness was affected; Keats rich diction and his richness was affected; Tennyson cunning diction and his cunning was affected; Browning rugged diction and his ruggedness was affected. Why Coleridge was called affected passes the wit of man, except it be that he did not write like Pope or the elegant Mr Rogers – or, indeed, that all crit-ical tradition would be outraged if a mere recent poet were not labelled with the epithetic made and provided for him by wise critical precedent.

Now Thompson, who was writing to defend his own poems against the charge, was a somewhat affected writer himself, and it suited him to hint that the very fact that a poet is called 'affected' or 'modernist' is a proof of his genuineness; he did not, therefore, stop to enquire how many of these charges of affectation were justified at the outset of the careers of the poets concerned. As a matter of fact, Shelley is the only one of them who can be fairly exculpated of the charge, because the only one who was free of the authorship ambition: his political and philosophical enthusiasms, which were, however, real, absorbed what professional literary enthusiasm he may have had to begin with. Wordsworth's early simplicity *was* affected:

> A simple child, dear brother Jim,
> That lightly draws its breath
> And feels its life in every limb,
> What should it know of death?
>
> I met a little cottage Girl;
> She was eight years old, she said.
> Her hair was thick with many a curl
> That clustered round her head.[1]

Keats' early richness *was* affected:

> here is cream
> Deepening to richness from a snowy gleam;
> Sweeter than that nurse Amalthea skimmed
> For the boy Jupiter; and here, undimmed
> By any touch, a bunch of blooming plums
> Ready to melt between an infant's gums,
> And here is manna pick'd from Syrian trees,
> In starlight, by the three Hesperides.[2]

Tennyson's early cunning *was* affected:

> The streams through many a lilied row
> Down-carolling to the crisped sea,
> Low tinkled with a bell-like flow
> Atween the blossoms 'We are free'.[3]

Browning's early ruggedness *was* affected:

> And on that young round cheek of thine
> I make them recognise the tinge,
> As when of the costly scarlet wine
> They drip so much as will impinge
> And spread in a thinnest scale afloat
> One thick gold drop from the olive's coat
> Over a silver plate whose sheen
> Still through the mixture shall be seen.[4]

The history of these affectations is the history of the various social requirements made of poetry by the middle position, by the intelligent plain man who is religiously devoted to the idea of human uplift; and of the conforming by poets themselves to popular notions held about the place of poetry in this uplift. Poetry is seen first of all as supplying an elegance and refinement which must of necessity be neglected in practical experience. Common affairs are not genteel; and so poetry has generally been expected to feed an upper class hunger in man for nobility: poetry is the high polish of civilization. The next general demand thus made on poetry is that it should be romantically imbued with progressiveness, that it should act as a superior touter for civilization. To this demand Tennyson devoted his maturity in the *Princess* and other verse tracts. This particular, assigned function of poetry is only a development of the old idea of the poet as the regular tribal prophet; that Tennyson could foresee air warfare in 'navies grappling in the central blue' and the League of Nations in 'The Parliament of Man, the Federation of the World' undoubtedly contributed to his success with the middle reader. Following this is the demand for poetry as a sign of intellectual advancement, as distinct from social or political advancement: poetry as deep and deeper thinking. Browning is an excellent example of the poet who appreciated the popular weakness for profundity. He fed this vanity successfully, without bringing it low; seeming to be profound without really being profound, keeping the necessary illusion by various technical devices such as unnecessarily protracted sentences and an over-clipped grammar.

Poetry, consequently, is made into a constantly expanding institution, embodying from period to period all the rapidly developing specialized forms of knowledge, enlarging itself by broadening the definition of poetry to include psychology, applied theories of music and painting, philosophy, physical science and so on. The poet himself feels obliged to appear as a sage; as Tennyson, when he became Poet Laureate, conscientiously sent himself to school again and made and kept to a weekly curriculum of studies, including science, foreign languages, mathematics, philosophy. Not only is the nature of the poet, in this view, expected to change in a scheme of constant and minute adjustment to history, but the nature of poetry itself is supposed to undergo historical evolution: keeping up with the times is a sign of its good behaviour and its worthiness to be incorporated among the material evidences of progress.

Such an opinion of poetry is based on a view of civilization as modernist, as continuously developing in the direction of an absolute and perfect end – which it obviously is not. The poet who considers himself a modernist because he is successfully keeping up with his date is, however unaware he is of so being and whatever his antagonism to Tennyson, merely an earnest Tennysonian. A strong distinction must be drawn between poetry as something developing through civilization and as something developing organically by itself – not a minor branch of human endeavour but a complete and separate form of energy which is neither more nor less in the twentieth century AD than in the tenth century BC, nor a different kind of energy now from what it was in Homeric times, but merely lodged in different, or *other*, persons. Civilization develops only in the sense that one thing follows another, not in the sense that things get progressively better or more harmonious because they follow. Poetry does develop in the sense that it is contemporaneous with civilization, but for this reason it has even to protect itself from civilization, to resist, to a certain extent, contemporaneous influences, since there is no merit in modernism for the sake of modernism, and since civilization must, in self-defence, believe in modernism for the sake of modernism. It is therefore always important to distinguish between what is historically new in poetry because the poet is contemporary with a civilization of a certain kind, and what is intrinsically new in poetry because the poet is a new and original individual, something more than a mere servant and interpreter of civilization.

A great deal of poetry written today, in fact, must be understood as a reaction against the demands made on it by civilized society, an unfortunate waste of energy in defiance that is often trivial and insincere. Reaction against civilization in a dogmatic sense is found in nearly all modernist poets, from affected modernists to more or less genuine modernists. It has, indeed, been one of the refinements of contemporary poetry to react against the refinements of civilization which poetry has generally been expected to cultivate. Even such a sentimentalist as Rupert Brooke mentioned love and sea-sickness in the same breath:

> The damned ship lurched and slithered. Quiet and quick
> > My cold gorge rose; the long sea rolled; I knew
> I must think hard of something, or be sick;
> > And could think hard of only one thing – *you*!
> … Do I forget you? Retchings twist and tie me,
> > Old meat, good meals, brown gobbets, up I throw.
> Do I remember? Acrid return and slimy,
> > The sobs and slobber of a last year's woe …[5]

The War provoked in poetry both genuine and affected examples of reaction against heroics. These lines of Wilfred Owen's describe with painful literalness a man dying from poison-gas:

> … If in some smothering dreams, you too could pace
> Behind the wagon that we flung him in
> And watch the white eyes writhing in his face,
> His hanging face, like a devil's sick of sin,
> If you could hear, at every jolt, the blood

> Come gargling from the froth-corrupted lungs
> Bitten as the cud
> Of vile, incurable sores on innocent tongues ...[6]

Or we find close juxtapositions of elegance and vulgarity in the same poem, the poet's low-brow satire of his own elegance. This is a familiar device in the poetry of T.S. Eliot, as:

> The hot water at ten.
> And if it rains, a closed car at four.
> And we shall play a game of chess,
> Pressing lidless eyes and waiting for a knock
>   upon the door.

which is fine writing, immediately followed by:

> When Lil's husband got demobbed, I said –
> I didn't mince my words, I said to her myself,
> HURRY UP PLEASE IT'S TIME
> Now Albert's coming back, make yourself a bit smart.
> He'll want to know what you done with that money he gave you
> To get yourself some teeth.[7]

To the demand for romantic progressiveness there is a reaction of utterly hopeless and unpurposed pessimism, as in Miss Nancy Cunard's *Parallax*, an imitation of T.S. Eliot:

> In the rooms
> A sombre carpet broods, stagnates beneath deliberate steps.
> Here drag a foot, there a foot, drop sighs, look round for nothing,
>   shiver.
>
> Sunday creeps in silence
> Under suspended smoke
> And curdles defiant in unreal sleep.
> The gas-fire puffs, consumes, ticks out its minor chords –
> And at the door
> I guess the arrested knuckles of the one-time friend
> One foot on the stair delaying, that turns again.

To the demand for deep thinking the reaction is a frivolousness like Mr Wallace Stevens':

> La – la! The cat is in the violets
> And the awnings are let down.
> The cat should not be where she is
> And the awnings are too brown,
> Emphatically so.[8]

The reaction to the demand that poetry shall combine all arts and sciences into a master-art is an excuse for poetry devoted to the praise of either silliness or simpleness, as in Mr Witter Bynner's:

> I'm a-building my house
>   On a mountain so high,
> A good place to wait
>   For my love to come by.
>
> Go 'way now, all of you,
>   Leave me alone
> On the peacefullest mountain
>   Ever was known.

or A.E.'s:

> Cloistered amid these austere rocks,
> A brooding seer, I watched an hour
> Close to the earth, lost to all else,
> The marvel of a tiny flower.[9]

To all of these demands and to this last demand particularly, there exists also a more complex reaction. Much contemporary poetry not only snaps its fingers at civilization; it further elaborates its superior attitude toward it by proving that it can not only keep up with civilization but even get ahead of it. For civilization grows so vain that it does, in effect, tell poetry that it cannot keep up with it, that it must disappear in the old sense of an interpretation and mirror of life. Cock-a-hoop scientists like Mr J.B.S. Haldane write that 'not until our poets are once more drawn from the educated classes (I speak as a scientist), will they appeal to the average man by showing him the beauty in his own life'. There are poets who take this challenge seriously and even resume Tennyson's curriculum where he left off. Alfred Noyes, although neither mature nor serious, has written a long narrative poem *The Torch Bearers* to celebrate the progress of science from its beginnings to its present days. Patronizing of modern musical theory appears in the poetry of W.J. Turner, of modern painting theory in that of Edith Sitwell and Sacheverell Sitwell, of psychological theory in that of Herbert Read and Archibald Macleish, of modern sex-engrossment in that of D.H. Lawrence, of philosophical theory in that of Conrad Aiken and T.S. Eliot, of encyclopedic learning in that of Marianne Moore, T.S. Eliot – and so on and so on. This reaction inspires not only an emulative display of modernist learning and subjects, but also a cultivation of fine-writing to prove that this generation can beat the most cunning Elizabethan, Romantic Revivalist or Victorian at his own game. The task it sets itself is to be advanced and yet elegant: mere low-browness being considered too primitive a reaction. The following is an example of Sacheverell Sitwell's fine-writing. He is doing what John Fletcher might be doing were he alive now: taking liberties with blank verse and imagery under the influence of modern painting and music, while still remaining recognizably a late-Elizabethan dramatist:

> Who can have trod, before, this field of fire
> The huge floor of ocean, unfoamed, shining,
> Lit with loud stars and mellow harvest moon?
> The sea-nymphs swimming by the galleon's side
> Have never shone, golden, in its wake before:
> Like winds they play among the corn's gold tide
> Loosing those windy locks, or down they dive
> Through amber furrows lifted by the keel,
> Past starlight, crackling to the sad shell note
> Of scalèd Tritons in deep water depths.

Mr Sitwell's modernism appears in such lines as the second and fifth, which the Elizabethans or Jacobeans, great as were the liberties they took with blank verse (far greater than those taken by the eighteenth century or the Victorians) could not have written for a gentle lyrical passage. They would have put instead:

> The húgy flóor of ócean foámless shíning

and

> Have ne'ér shone gólden ín its wáke befóre.

The first of these lines of Mr Sitwell's must be read:

> The húge flóor of ócean (pause) unfoámed (pause) shíning

and the next

> Have néver shóne (pause) gólden (pause) in its wáke befóre.

Here the influence of modern music reveals itself in the readiness with which the monotony of the metrical pattern is varied. It is rarely, indeed, in a poem of modernist blank verse that so few variations are introduced as in this passage. The pictorial element is also modern. 'The loud stars', 'the corn's gold tide', the nymphs diving 'crackling' down, are not Elizabethan conceits but verbal equivalents for a modern picture in which the size and shape of the stars, the cornfield aspect of the sea, the sharpness of the water-flurry where the nymphs dive would be anti-realistically repre-sented to suggest just these figures. Fletcher would have written 'bright stars' and

> Like winds that wanton in the yellow corn,
> So do they wanton in this golden tide

and

> shivering the sad shell note

and so on.

These lines of T.S. Eliot's further illustrate the tendency in contempo-
rary poetry to outdo the past in elaborate and elegant writing; that is, to
flout conservative literary elegance rather than elegance in general. They
are an improvement on all previous treatments of a favourite refined topic
– perfumes:

> In vials of ivory and coloured glass
> Unstoppered, lurked her strange synthetic perfumes,
> Unguent, powdered or liquid – troubled, confused
> And drowned the sense in odours; stirred by the air
> That freshened from the window, these ascended
> In fattening the prolonged candle-flames,
> Flung their smoke into the laquearia,
> Stirring the pattern on the coppered ceiling.
> Huge sea-wood fed with copper
> Burned green and orange, framed by the coloured stone
> In which sad light a carvèd dolphin swam.[10]

How pale indeed is Keats beside him:

> Of wealthy lustre was the banquet-room
> Fill'd with pervading brilliance and perfume:
> Before each lucid pannel fuming stood
> A censer fed with myrrh and spiced wood,
> Each by a sacred tripod held aloft,
> Whose slender feet wide-swerved upon the soft
> Wool-woofèd carpets: fifty wreaths of smoke
> From fifty censers their light voyage took
> To the high roof, still mimick'd as they rose
> Along the mirror'd walls by twin-clouds odourous.
>
> (from *Lamia*).

The combined pressure of romantic progressiveness, intellectual
advancement, knowledge-expansion and change-processes against which
contemporary poetry has tried to protect itself by showing that it can bear
this pressure and still survive, has driven it to make a tremendous and
sometimes a strained effort at overmatching its age. In many instances,
loaded with learned vanities and sophistications, it does not, it must be
confessed, succeed in keeping its head above water. Much of this enlarge-
ment has been accomplished by incorporating in poetry the modern
science of anthropology, which is really a new synthetic mythology
composed of many mythologies. Not content with Tritons and Galleons

and neo–Keatsian or neo–Elizabethan writing, many, as Mr Eliot, for instance, have borrowed extensively from Sir James Frazer's comparative study of primitive myths.[11] When Sacheverell Sitwell writes of Alexander:

> He is dreaming what he planned and never conquered:
> Time, that summer afternoon, burns slow,
> And one more chance is given him
> On a battlefield, or warm, slow bank of flowers,
> While a reaper on the hillside kills his fair-haired prisoners …

the reference to fair-haired prisoners is not only to the cutting down of the yellow grain but also to the ancient harvest-field custom, related by Sir James Frazer, of binding fair-haired or red-haired men in the corn-straw and killing them ritually as representatives of the corn-god.

Literary internationalism – the incorporation of foreign tongues and atmospheres – is still another method of civilizing and enlarging poetry. French is perhaps the most common language introduced to this end, with Italian and Spanish closely following. Mr Eliot not only makes free use of French side by side with English; he has written poems entirely in French. An even greater enlargement is made by an abnormal cultivation of the classics, especially of the more remote classics. Some poets are able to maintain a sense of balance and dignity in this cultivation, if only because they are good scholars. But it can easily become absurd, as in the poetry of Mr Ezra Pound. In a single volume of his, *Lustra*, occur literary references to Greek, Latin, Spanish, Italian, Provençale and Chinese literature – some of these incorrectly given.[12] Mr Eliot, who is a more serious scholar, has references in *The Waste Land* to Greek, Latin, Spanish, Italian, French, German and Sanskrit. The English classics quoted or referred to are not now the stock-classics to which Victorian and post-Victorian poets paid tribute, not Chaucer, Spenser, Shakespeare, Milton, Burns, but others known only to the cognoscenti – Peele, Kyd, Lyly, the less familiar Shakespeare, Webster, Marvell, Dryden, Swift, Darley, Beddoes; making the succession of English poetry wear a more varied look. The same enlargement is made with the Greek, Latin, Italian and French poets.

Sympathy with low life and the use of the vocabulary of low life in modernist poetry, besides their simpler burlesque role, are both an earnest of romantic progressiveness and of literary refinement. For, if it would put aside previous literary affectations and yet not turn into a crude instrument of reaction, it must have elegances of its own; and among the few unexploited elegances left to poetry is an affectation of the vocabulary of low life. Wordsworth's theories on the use of the language of simple men were, in a conservative way, a similar counter-elegance. Modernist poets, however, surpass Wordsworth in literary slumming. Whereas Wordsworth wrote:

And now the same strong voice more near
Said cordially, 'My Friend, what cheer?
Rough doings these! as God's my judge,
The sky owes somebody a grudge!
We've had in half an hour or less
A twelve month's terror and distress!'[13]

T.S. Eliot writes, as already shown, unexpurgated and unsentimental-
ized cockney, and e.e. cummings:

> ... some
> guys talk big
> about Lundun Burlin an gay Paree an
> some guys claims der never was
> nutn like Nooer Leans Shikahgo Sain
> Looey Noo York an San Fran dictaphones
> wireless subways vacuum
> cleaners pianolas funnygraphs skyscrapers an safety razors
>
> sall right in its way kiddo
> but as fer I gimme de good ole daze ...[14]

In this way much modernist poetry, in attempting to justify itself to
civilization, which is always the civilization of the average intelligent
person, succeeds so well that it is rejected by him as *too* advanced; when it
turns to a smaller audience or to no audience at all, consoling itself with its
advancement. For as the average intelligent person has no real sympathy
with low life except from vague humanitarian principles, so he is only
interested in civilization as a sentimental idea; he does not want to think
harder or work harder; he does not want to advance, but to be flatteringly
reminded that he belongs to the twentieth century. Nor does he have, or
want to have, new or different feelings. The poet formally devoted to
modernism, on the other hand, generally has or affects historically new
feelings about things. And so the space between the general reader and the
poet who is responding to the demands of this imaginary client becomes
wider and wider.

Take, as a single instance of this breach, the conception of Destiny. To
the Greek dramatists it was the strongest of the gods, the dark power
behind the thrones of Olympus. To the poets of the Romantic Revival it
was the greatest and blindest motive power; it transcended Love, Religion
and Knowledge. But Miss Sitwell can write today (or perhaps yesterday):

> Now from the countrysides where people know
> That Destiny is wingless and bemired
> With feathers dirty as a hen's too tired
> To fly – [15]

Then follows a reference to Darkness, one of the grandest of tradition-
ally poetical concepts:

> – where old pig-snouted Darkness grovels
> For life's mired rags among the broken hovels –

The general reader, however, will be out of sympathy with this:
Destiny to him is not as oppressive as it was to Euripides or Byron, but it
is still a force to be reckoned with, though he only calls it 'Luck' or 'Joss';
and Darkness is still respected in spite of the electric illuminations of
Science.

Of some contemporary poets 'modernist' is used merely to describe a
certain independence in them, without definitely associating them with
modernism as a literary cause: though content to stay in the main stream
of poetry, they make judicious splashes to show that they are aware of the
date. This has been the tactical position adopted by some poets whose
modernism consists in an aloof moderateness or sensibleness in all direc-
tions – a studied inaction – and by others who have had neither the
courage nor the capacity to go the whole way with modernism and yet
have not wished to be left behind. In the first class belong such poets as
Siegfried Sassoon and Robert Frost. Mr Frost's nature-poems are unaf-
fected nature-poems and, with the exception of a few of Frank Prewett's,
perhaps the only real, that is, unliterary, ones since Clare's.[16] (Edmund
Blunden's show accurate observation but grow more and more literary.)
The following is from Mr Frost's *Runaway*, describing a foal afraid of his
first sight of snow. The faint modernism of this poem consists in its
complete casualness and matter-of-factness:

> Once when the snow of the year was beginning to fall
> We stopped by a mountain pasture to say 'Whose colt?'
> A little Morgan had one forefoot on the wall,
> The other curled at his breast. He dipped his head
> And snorted at us. And then he had to bolt ...
> And now he comes again with a clatter of stone
> And mounts the wall again with whited eyes
> And all his tail that isn't hair up straight.
> He shudders his coat as if to throw off flies ...

Mr Sassoon, who has, like Mr Frost, never troubled to keep up with
literary fashions and who, when he occasionally yields to the temptation of
poeticalness, adopts the manner of a generation ago, writes as follows
about a Founder's Feast held in one of the greater Colleges at Cambridge
University shortly after the War ended. The poem carries on the indigna-
tion of his war poems against the General Staff. Modernism in Mr
Sassoon is an intelligent, satiric reaction to contemporary political and
social Bluffs; it is not a literary policy – which is why, in fact, professed

literary modernists patronize him:

> ... Gowns, rose and scarlet in flamingo ranks,
> Adorned the dais that shone with ancient silver;
> And guests of honour gazed far down the Hall
> With precognition of returning thanks.
> There beamed the urbanest Law-lord on the Bench,
> Debating with the Provost (ceremonious
> In flushed degrees of vintage scholarship)
> The politics of Plato – and the French
>
> But on the Provost's left, in gold and blue
> Sat ... O my God! ... great Major-General Bluff
> Enough enough enough enough enough![17]

In the second class belong poets like Mr Yeats who, observing that his old poetical robes have worn rather shabby, acquires a new outfit. But the old romantic weaknesses are not so easily discarded: even when he writes of 'Lois Fuller's Chinese Dancers' – a high-brow Vaudeville turn – instead of Eire and the ancient ways, And the Red Rose upon the Rood of Time.

Such are the shifts to which poets have been driven in trying to cope with civilization and in rejecting or keeping up with, from an imagined necessity of action, the social requirements that seem to be laid upon poetry. In the resulting confusion one thing at least is clear, that in modernist poetry, however it has been weakened or perverted by its race with civilization, is to be found the best and undoubtedly the most enduring contemporary poetry. This is not because historical modernism is in itself an excellence, but because the best poets happen to be modernists: whether they are deliberately so or not, they can be called modernist if only because they are good, and because what is good always seems advanced.

Modernist, indeed, should describe a quality in poetry which has nothing to do with the date or with responding to civilization. Poetry to which *modernist* in this sense could be fully applied would derive its excellence neither from its reacting against civilization, by satiric or actual primitivism; nor from its proved ability to keep up with or keep ahead of civilization. It would not, however, ignore its contemporaneous universe, for the reason that it would not be stupid and that it would have a sense of humour – the most intelligent attitude toward history is not to take one's own date too seriously. There would occur evidences of time in such poetry; but always its modernism would lie in its independence, in its relying on none of the traditional devices of poetry-making in the past nor on any of the artificial effects to be got by using the atmosphere of contemporary life and knowledge to startle or to give reality. If, in such poetry, a topical institution or person or object should occur, it would be only because it made an image more accurately suited to the particular requirements of the poem than another less recent one. Most of all, such poetry would be characterized by a lack of strain, by an intelligent ease. Not only would its references have a simplicity and naturalness no matter how difficult, that is, no matter how highly developed aside from references, such poetry was – not only would it not have to rely on references; it would not, either, have to rely on modern short-story material, such as Mr Pound, for example, has incorporated in one of his poems:

> Like a skein of loose silk blown against a wall
> She walks by the railing of a path in Kensington Gardens,
> And she is dying piece-meal
>   of a sort of emotional anaemia[18]

It would not have to rely on such material because it would have something to say that had nothing to do with reporting contemporary life or with vying with the progress of intelligence.

And even poetry that is *modernist* only in the historical sense – even Ezra Pound's or Vachel Lindsay's – accomplishes at least this: by its enlarging process it has widened the limits of reference, diction and construction in poetry; by extending the poet's curriculum it has also extended his acceptable scope. So that poetry that is modernist only in the personal sense has some chance of attention, its frowardness being taken for historical modernism.

Many common symbols of civilization, in any case, are bound to be absorbed naturally by poetry, although at the beginning they cannot but be used with self-consciousness. The naturalness with which some new invention or scientific discovery may be uttered in poetry depends on its recentness. There is even a definite time-limit before such a 'new' thing becomes a common object and before which it is affected to write of it in poetry except rarely and then with deliberate affectation. This time-limit varies, of course, with the nature of the oddity – with the train, for example, the period was about seventy years. During this period of human acclimatization the oddity gradually loses the capital letter and the italics with which it was perhaps originally written; its name comes to be pronounced without any sense of strangeness or second-thought. It gradually approaches a stage, in fact, when it is nearly quaint; and it is just in this stage when it is most natural.

The train has passed from a stage of complete strangeness to one of complete familiarity. Wordsworth was one of the first poets to notice the train, but as a curiosity rather than as a common object and on the theory that poetry should take recognition of modern scientific development. Although his view was that poetry was conferring favour on the scientists in recognizing their products, it will be seen from the following lines that he admitted minutely and specifically the various requirements which civilization puts upon poetry: material progressiveness, literal prophecy, intellectual advancements, 'future change', and, finally, elegance, which he achieves by calling Steamboats, Viaducts, Railways otherwise than by their own names ('Motions and Means', 'Nature's lawful offspring'). But he mentions them in the title:

STEAMBOATS, VIADUCTS, AND RAILWAYS

Motions and Means, on land and sea at war
With old poetic feeling, not for this
Shall ye, by Poets even, be judged amiss!
Nor shall your presence, howsoe'er it mar
The loveliness of Nature, prove a bar
To the Mind's gaining that prophetic sense
Of future change, that point of vision, whence
May be discovered what in soul ye are.

In spite of all that beauty may disown
In your harsh features, Nature doth embrace
Her lawful offspring in Man's art; and Time,
Pleased with your triumphs o'er his brother Space,
Accepts from your bold hands the proffered crown
Of hope, and smiles on you with cheer sublime.[19]

Tennyson was forced to accept the train, but he handled it gingerly. *Lady Godiva* has this short prelude to show his broadmindedness; but it is only a foil to the romantic story:

I waited for the train at Coventry;
I hung with grooms and porters on the bridge,
To watch the three tall spires; and there I shaped
The city's ancient legend into this: –

In '*Mechanophilus* – in the time of the first railways' he frankly romanticizes:

Now first we stand and understand,
And sunder false from true,
And handle boldly with the hand,
    And see and shape and do.

Dash back that ocean with a pier,
    Strow yonder mountain flat,
A railway there, a tunnel here,
    Mix we this Zone with that ...

As we surpass our fathers' skill,
    Our sons will shame our own;
A thousand things are hidden still
    And not a hundred known ...

Browning was rather more courageous; he first introduced the train as a commonplace into poetry, but through the back door, in what was known as serio-comic verse. The lines are from *Christmas-Eve and Easter-Day*:

> A tune was born in my head last week
> Out of the thump-thump and shriek-shriek
> Of the train, as I came by it, up from Manchester;
> And when, next week, I take it back again,
> My head will sing to the engine's clack again
> While it only makes my neighbour's haunches stir.

By the use of rhymes like 'back again' and 'engines clack again', 'Manchester' and 'haunches stir', he is saying in effect that a train is no proper subject for true poetical feelings; that as it is a part of modern life we must include it in our poems but in the low style proper to it. Emily Dickinson was perhaps the first to confess to a feeling of personal affection for the train as such:

> I love to see it lap the miles,
> And lick the valleys up,
> And pause to feed itself at tanks;
> And then prodigious, step
> Around a pile of mountains
> And, supercilious, peer
> In shanties by the sides of roads ...
>
> And neigh like Boanerges;
> Then, punctual as a star,
> Stop – docile and omnipotent –
> At its own stable door.[20]

To John Davidson it was an appealing creature, too, although more terrible; in no way comic. His *Song of the Train* begins:

> A monster taught
> To come to hand
> Amain,
> As swift as thought
> Across the land
> The train.
> ... O'er bosky dens
> By marsh and mead,
> Forest and fens
> Embodied speed
> Is clanked and hurled ...[21]

In a poem of Mr Robert Nichols we find the train treated with more modern nonchalance. *The Express: Hereford to London* begins:

> On sways the tilting train:
> We feel the carriage bluffly sideways blown,
> We see the chill shower brighten on the pane,
> We hear the high wind through the lantern moan,
> We three borne ever through the wind and rain,
> We three who meet here not to meet again,
> We three poor faring fools who sit alone.

But toward the end there is a romantic lapse to excuse the liberties taken:

> But the giant Train begins a confident song
> 'Why be so meek, so proud, when both are wrong.'

Sacheverell Sitwell can write even more casually of the train. For romantic lapses like the following in *At Breakfast:*

> A railway engine ran across the field
> Galloping like a swift horse down the rails.
> As it came quicker the window-panes rattled,
> The roof shook side to side: all its beams trembled,
> Thundering hoofs were upon us – glass chariots.

are not even real lapses like Mr Nichols' but a half-satiric 'Look: modernist though I am, I can still be romantic about old-fashioned romantic subjects like the railway train'. It is now not a 'monster' but a charming early-Victorian *objet de vertu* under a glass dome. We find Miss Marianne Moore describing expanding bookcases and books printed on India paper in a serious poem, without self-consciousness:

> the vast indestructible necropolis
> of composite Yawman-Erbe separable units;
> the steel, the oak, the glass, the Poor Richard publications
> containing the public secrets of efficiency
> on 'paper so thin that one thousand four hundred and twenty
> pages make one inch'.[22]

Without self-consciousness? Perhaps that is too much to say when so short a space of years separate poetry of this sort from the once-advanced poetry of, say, Richard Le Gallienne, a 'decadent' of the nineties still alive and at present living in the same city as Miss Moore, like her a literary critic; a city where there must be large backward sections of the reading public to whom Mr Le Gallienne is still an advanced writer because he has, perhaps, written familiarly of the Devil and the sweets of sin.

But is it necessary for the poet to come to the point, after a long history of gradually acclimatizing his verse to what were once considered unpoetical subjects, where he can, with Miss Moore, bring himself to insert four-

teen unrevised and consecutive words straight from a newspaper adver-
tisement into his poem, and put them into quotation marks as well?
Though a feat of poetic self-martyrdom, doubtless, and perhaps the
logical conclusion of giving civilization what it wants – verse actually
interpretative of what is called 'the poetry of modern business' – it is bad
for both poetry and business: the quotation would have been much more
effective left in the original setting to compose the daily synthetic adver-
tisement-poem of the morning newspaper.

True modernist poetry can appear equally at all stages of historical
development from Wordsworth to Miss Moore. And it does appear when
the poet forgets what is the correct literary conduct demanded of him in
relation to contemporary institutions (with civilization speaking through
criticism) and can write a poem having the power of survival in spite of its
disregarding these demands; a poem of purity – of a certain old-fash-
ionedness even, but not an old-fashionedness of reaction against the time
to archaism, or of retreat to nature and the primitive passions. All poetry
that deserves to endure is at once old-fashioned and modernist. How
much of modernist poetry is merely up-to-date conduct-poetry, the
poetry of conversion to the last-minute salvationism of civilization, and
how much is poetry in need of no conversion, but working out its own
salvation by itself, is a difficult question to settle offhand. The proportions
vary with individuals. With Mr Pound the former sort predominates
greatly, one would say; with cummings, though he is more 'daring' than
Mr Pound, there is much less of this than at first sight appears; with Mr
Archibald Macleish, an ambitious imitator of cummings, much more.

The great danger in any discussion of modernist poetry which may reach
the plain reader is that in pointing out how many of its qualities are inspired
by necessity, sincerity or truthfulness, these qualities may endear them-
selves to him not because of necessity, sincerity or truthfulness but only
because he can understand them as up-to-date; the danger, in fact, that
the plain reader may fall in love with the up-to-dateness of this poetry. In
this case, with modernist poetry seen and applauded as a part of the move-
ment of civilization, the demands made upon it as such would become
intensified. A world of plain readers hungering for up-to-date poetry
would turn poetry into one of the gross industries. There is such a great
gap between Victorian poetry and the poetry of just before the War, and
again between this poetry and advanced modern poetry, that the converted
plain reader might fail to see that the theories of 1860 or 1910 or 1927 have
nothing to do with the essential goodness of poetry, though much to do
with its up-to-dateness. Would not, it may be asked, a hunger for essential
goodness in poetry also turn it into one of the gross industries? Perhaps;
on the other hand perhaps not, since the reader's capacity for essential
goodness is to his capacity for up-to-dateness as the capacity for writing
essentially good poetry to the capacity for writing up-to-date poetry.

CHAPTER VIII

Variety in Modernist Poetry

THE plain reader whose introduction to poetry is generally not through personal compulsion or curiosity but through the systematic require-ments of his education, naturally associates it with the utilitarian point of view, which must dominate any formal educational process. If the school-system has happened to be old-fashioned and has used poetry merely as a means of teaching grammar, or as so many lines to be learned by heart as a disciplinary task or penalty, the reaction to poetry is negative: the reader either discounts poetry for ever as a dreary pedagogical invention or he can perhaps rediscover it as something so different from the classroom exercise as to be unaffected by the unpleasant associations attached to it as such. A 'liberal school-system' does not however leave alone poetry as poetry. It attempts to interest the child in the 'values' of poetry; the child's reaction to this method will therefore be a positive one: he will subscribe to these values and accept poetry through them, or he will not subscribe to these values but reject poetry through them. 'Beauty' is the term of approval which the schoolmaster applies to the 'values' of poetry; char-acter-formation is their expressed practical end, or if not character-forma-tion, at least a wholesome relief from its ardours.

The elder system, which on the whole was preferable, has been gener-ally superseded by the new both in England and America: the official report on 'The Teaching of English in England' (1919) lays great stress on the folly of the teacher in 'throwing away' an important 'weapon', if he refuses to win his pupils over to him by making the literature lesson inter-esting, particularly through poetry. Particularly through Shakespeare. The report, in reply to an objection that 'Shakespeare is over the heads of the children', approves a professor-witness who replied 'He is over all our heads'; as though that made it any better. One of the stock essay-subjects in the schools is 'The Uses of Poetry'; and when the essays come up to be 'corrected' and the humanistic teacher prepares a composite specimen-essay on the subject, the 'uses' are found to be as follows:

1. Poetry gives the reader joy.
2. Poetry gives relief to sorrow, pain or weariness.

3. Poetry teaches the reader to love the Good.
4. Poetry is the concentrated wisdom of former ages.
5. Poetry teaches other-worldliness.

and so on to the final summing-up:

> Poetry's uses may be expressed in a single phrase: Spiritual Elevation.

All poetry, that is, tends toward the same general tone and the same general purpose.

Now it is unimportant to decide whether education since the time of Aristotle has been responsible for the spread of this view of poetry; or whether it is the great numerical predominance of poets who have professed it from a policy of self-protection, and have written most of their poetry to support it, over poets who have either dissented or refused to commit themselves, that has been responsible. The fact remains that this has been the officially accepted academic view and the view of orthodox criticisms: even a self-proclaimed dissenter like Poe defined the end of poetry as spiritual elevation. Poetry in every Classical period has been formed according to this principle. The mass-impressiveness of Classical poetry is, indeed, largely due to its uniformity. And though we know from historical reconstructions that even between romantics like Byron, Wordsworth, Keats, Coleridge and Shelley there was about as much personal dissimilarity as could possibly be found between contemporary poets, yet the lip-service that each of these paid to this creed of the uses of poetry induced for the most part a corresponding pen-service. The emphasis that the educational system lays on personal and literary similarities in poets makes it still more difficult to appraise them separately. Here are descriptive passages by six more or less contemporary writers, typical classroom passages:

the hoar

And aery Alps towards the North appeared
Through mist, an heaven-sustaining bulwark reared
Between the East and West, and half the sky
Was roofed with clouds of rich emblazonry
Dark purple at the Zenith, which still grew
Down the steep West into a wondrous hue
Brighter than burning gold, even to the rent
Where the swift sun yet paused in his descent
Among the many folded hills ...

o–o–o–o–o–o–o–o

It was no marvel – from my very birth

My soul was drunk with love – which did pervade
And mingle with whate'er I saw on earth.
Of objects all inanimate I made
Idols, and out of wild and lonely flowers
And rocks, whereby they grew, a paradise.

0–0–0–0–0–0–0–0

Woodlark may sink from sandy fern – the Sun may hear his lay;
Runnels may kiss the grass on shelves and shallows clear,
But their low voices are not heard, though come on travels drear;
Blood-red the Sun may set behind black mountain peaks;
Blue tides may sluice and drench their time in caves and weedy
                                                                                   creeks.

0–0–0–0–0–0–0–0

Mournfully breaks the north wave on thy shore,
        Silent Iona, and the mocking blast
                Sweeps sternly o'er thy relics of the past,
        The stricken cross, the desecrated tomb
Of abbots and barbarian kings of yore ...

0–0–0–0–0–0–0–0

Since risen from ocean, ocean to defy
Appeared the Crag of Ailsa, ne'er did morn
With gleaming lights more gracefully adorn
His sides, or wreathe with mist his forehead high
Now, faintly darkening with the sun's eclipse,
Still is he seen, in lone sublimity.

0–0–0–0–0–0–0–0

I stood on Brocken's sovran height, and saw
Woods crowding upon woods, hills over hills,
A surging scene, and only limited
By the blue distance. Heavily my way
Downward I dragged through fir groves evermore.[1]

Actually these pieces are by Shelley, Byron, Keats, Tupper, Wordsworth
and Coleridge, in that order: but what reader could off-hand ascribe them
correctly? Who would not give the first to Keats, the second to
Wordsworth and stumble over the last four?

This extraordinary sameness in poets of such entirely different
personal character is due principally to the limitations which 'spiritual
elevation' in the academic sense imposes: these poets only wrote authentic
poetry when off their guard. The sameness is accentuated by the national-

istic element: every poet wrote as an Englishman first, bound by his very use of the language to a policy of increasing the national heritage of song rather than to the development of a strictly personal idiom. He also wrote as a member of a class, the governing class. One of the last surviving rewards of the poet as a privileged member of the community was that, whatever his birth, by writing acceptable poetry he became a gentleman; even in the narrowly aristocratic eighteeth century this tradition obtained. (Even today, when literary culture is the only gentility possible to affect.)

Stephen Duck, the 'Thresher Poet', whose works pleased George II's Queen, was officially confirmed in his gentility by being presented with a country-living as a clergyman. Burns was, for a while at least, given the freedom of smart Edinburgh society and allowed to write familiar epistles to members of the aristocracy. Poetical ideas and poetical technique – the substance of poetical education, in fact – have always been class-institutions, and poets born from the labouring or shop-keeping classes have with very few exceptions tried to elevate themselves by borrowing ideas and techniques to the enjoyment of which they were not born. Even revolutionary ideas are, by a paradox, upper-class ideas, a rebound from excesses of poetical refinement. Burns' romantic sympathy with the French Revolution in its earlier stages could be read as a sign of natural breeding, the gentlemanly radicalism of the literary *jeunesse*. The social gap between the crofters and the gentry was, moreover, not so wide a one in Scotland as in England; and Burns soon learned the trick of drawing-room writing. Keats, not being, like Burns or John Clare, an obvious example of peasant genius, or an aristocrat like Shelley, always had difficulty in discovering his temperamental biases. The son of a tradesman, he could not afford to be politically as radical as those inferior and superior to him in class; though he went with Leigh Hunt as far as he thought it safe. Blake was also a radical: one of the few Englishmen who dared walk about in London wearing a cap of Liberty. But he is a very rare instance of a poet who could afford not to affect a class-technique: for he was on intimate terms with the angels and wrote like an angel rather than like a gentleman. His radicalism was part of his religion and not a sentimentality as Wordsworth's early radicalism was. If a man has complete identity with his convictions, then he is tough about them, he is not sentimental; if not, then his convictions are a sentimental weakness however strongly he feels about them. The Romantic Revivalists were all spoiled as revolutionaries by their gentility. Blake was in no sense a Romantic Revivalist. He was a seer, or a poet. He despised the gentry in religion, literature and painting equally. That is why there is little or nothing of Blake's mature work that could be confused with that of any contemporary or previous writer. He did not forfeit his personality by submitting to any conventional medium; and he did not complain of the neglect of his poems by the greater reading public.

The sameness of poetry is likewise accentuated rather than diminished by the spirit of competition. Once there is a tacit or written critical agreement as to the historical form proper to the poetry of any period, all the poets of fashion or 'taste' vie with each other in approximating to the perfect period manner. In the eighteenth century such major poets as Pope and Shenstone were only to be distinguished from such minor ones as Ambrose Philips and Richard Graves by being more willing to polish away every vestige of personal eccentricity from their work. Period-monotony is further increased by imitation of the most successful 'period' poets. In the last century there were successively dozens of imitation Moores, Byrons, Wordsworths, Tennysons, Brownings, Swinburnes and Wildes; and dozens more who tried to synthesize the methods of these several inventors of slightly different styles. Among these, as we have seen, the several inventors themselves, who were all in search of a single period style.

All such monotony sprang from the necessity of having socially secure convictions. Poetry was to poets of the school-room tradition the instrument, the illustration of their convictions, whether (to take examples only from the nineteenth century) patriotic as with Campbell, moral as with Tupper, religious as with Aubrey de Vere, 'philosophical' as with Wordsworth and Whitman, social as with Moore, 'artistic' as with Poe and the pre-Raphaelites. Even the decadents at the end of last century were decadent from conviction rather than from wilfulness or inertia. Decadence introduced no variety. It merely substituted self-satisfied pessimism for self-satisfied optimism; and one nationalism for another by moving the poetical centre from London to Paris.

When Decadence decayed and was succeeded by the spurious healthiness of the country-rambler, the beer-drinker and the earlier patriotic soldier-poet, and this in turn broke down, the spirit of scepticism began seriously to invade poetry. It had found expression before in the poems of Thomas Hardy and A.E. Housman; but with certain important conservative reservations in the former, while in the latter it was confused with the shy or aggressive anti-religiousness of the 1890s. Modern scepticism was of a different order. The conscious bravado of anti-social or anti-idealistic writing disappeared. The poet did not feel cut off from his fellow-men by the loss of his more bigoted convictions, for he could assume that an increasingly large section of the educated classes was in agreement with him. At the time of the Romantic Revival, though the debaucheries of Byron could be sympathetically discounted because of his rank, a confessed atheist like Shelley was not admitted into polite society: it was assumed that every reader at least professed allegiance to Christianity, however lax his private life. The modernist poet assumes that his readers owe no trite emotional allegiance to any religious or social or national institution, even that they have emerged from the combative stages of mere 'doubt' or 'naughtiness' and are organizing their lives more intellectually; that to them the consistent and humane atheism of Shelley, or the consistent and humane saintliness of Traherne or Blake is preferable to the vulgarly incongruous lives of Byron and Wilde, as reflected in their poetry. The schoolroom may still remain the citadel of convictions; and Byron and Wilde may be morally whitewashed because their poetry abounds in old-fashioned convictions. But the modernist poet does not write for the schoolroom: if for anything at all, for the university.

This refinement of conviction, this maturing of social purposiveness, contributes more than any other cause to the raising of the barriers of poetical monotony. The poet may admit spiritual elevation as one possible personal 'tone' of poetry and spiritual depression as another; or an evenness of spiritual temper or a rapid alternation between depression and exaltation – the poeticizing of bathos and anticlimax – as further alternatives. But poetry ceases to be the maintenance of a single idealistic tone; it has a less obvious, a more complicated consistency. It is a broader intellectual exercise than before; even at its most pedantic it is still an intellectual exercise.

The old world of poetry, however, is going on at the same time; the old institutions are still officially and indeed numerically predominant; though it is not too much to say that no single poet of any real distinction since the death of Charles Doughty believes fervently in them or even pays them homage. The lack of narrow schoolroom purposiveness shown by modernist poets is actually as offensive to the survivors of the aggressively ungodly school and their followers as to the true believers: the anthologies and poets' corners in public periodicals are strictly censored both against abstruseness of conviction and against ungodliness. The public that enjoys the simple ruralities of W.H. Davies':

> A Rainbow and a Cuckoo! Lord!
> How rich and great the times are now!

is unaware that he has written even such naughty lines as:

> Lord, I say nothing; I profess
> No faith in thee nor Christ thy Son:

in which he mildly idealizes Christ the Man, as opposed to Christ the God; still less of his modernism, which is a genuine modernism, though of rare occurrence in his recent work, as in the poem beginning:

> I took my oath I would enquire
> 　　Without affection, hate or wrath
> Into the death of Ada Wright.
> 　　So help me God, I took that oath

and describing without reticence or sentimentality how the coroner's jury condoned a child-murder, how the mother gave evidence:

> It was a love-child, she explained,
>   And laughed for our intelligence.[2]

and how the emaciated corpse, that had but one eye shut and the other half-open, 'seemed a knowing little child'. Though Mr Davies consented to omit this poem from his *Collected Poems*, he wrote it, nevertheless; a poem that could not possibly have been written even at the end of last century.

The raising of the barriers of monotony by modernism has encouraged imitative or feeble poets, who in the eighteenth century would have been happy in formal submission to them, to adventure into all the new fields now opened to them with great audacity of subject and form. Some of these poets are more self-confident than others, and hence call more attention to themselves; and the confusion of the modern poetic scene is increased by the failure of even the specialized poetry-reading public to distinguish genuine poetry like a not inconsiderable part of Messrs Eliot, cummings and Miss Sitwell from the spurious individuality of, say, Dr William Carlos Williams. It is possible at once to recognize a writer like Mr Harold Acton as a Sitwellite by his borrowed stage-properties, or Miss Cunard as an Eliotite in the same way. But Dr Carlos Williams is not quite so clumsy. This is from a poem, *Struggle of Wings:*

> ... the string from the windowshade
> has a noose at the bottom, a noose? or
> a ring – bound with white cord, knotted
> around the circumference designedly in a design
>   And all there is is won

> And it is Inness on the meadows and fruit is
> yellow ripening in windows every minute
> growing brighter in the bulblight by the
> cabbages and spuds –
>   And all there is is won

> What are black 4 AM's after all but black
> 4 AM's like anything else: a tree,
> a fork, a leaf, a pane of glass – ?
>   And all there is is won

> A relic of old decency; a very personal friend
>   And all there is is won

> *Envoi*
> Pic, your crows feed at your windowsill
> Asso, try and get near mine ...
>   And all there is is won[3]

This is obvious charlatanry: a synthetic modernist poetry composed of ingredients plainly imitative of those that go to make up the poems of more genuine writers, and yet not too closely resembling them. There is a mystic refrain such as T.S. Eliot has used, typographic nonconformity as in e.e. cummings, a reference to modern painting – the divided word *Picasso*, which also suggests the verbal disintegration which appears more completely in James Joyce. Possibly the crows occur in an actual picture: possibly they refer to the black 4 AM's. There is also the up-to-date mannerism of marking the poem 'Incomplete' and publishing it with lacunae shown by dots enclosed in parentheses. There is a passing satiric reference to Philosophy in 'Inness on the meadows', called attention to by the modernist diction of 'bulblight' and 'spuds'. The pretended subject is the random thoughts that occur to a poet half awake and half asleep at 4 AM. The realistic window cord gives the reader a false confidence that 'And all there is is won' has some sense; whereas it is an unrelated phrase suggesting those that occur without discoverable sense in dreams. The poem continues:

> Out of such drab trash as this
> by a metamorphosis
> bright as wallpaper or crayon
> or where the sun casts ray on ray on
> flowers in a dish, weave, weave
> for Poesy a gaudy sleeve
> a scarf, a cap and find him gloves
> white as the backs of Turtledoves ...

This last, dangerously near enough to Edith Sitwell in the third line and in the last three lines, is an assumption of poetic awareness within the poem of the poem itself – another modernist mannerism. The 'drab trash' is carefully collected – in imitation of T.S. Eliot – to set off the 'fine writing' that follows. Not only Edith Sitwell but, in the rest of the poem, Milton's nativity hymn, a popular song and a reference to oleochromes contribute. Dr Williams' early poetic travels are outlined on the dust-cover of his *Sour Grapes:*

> The surer and sounder but not the less unusual handling of free verse by a contributor to the original Imagist anthology and a later member of the so-called 'Others' school, who has already made a distinct place for himself in contemporary poetry.

his more recent ones in the first paragraph of a chapter of his *In the American Grain*:

> Picasso (turning to look back, with a smile), Braque (brown cotton), Gertrude Stein (opening the doors of a cabinet of MSS), Tzara

(grinning), André Germain (blocking the door), Van der Pyl (speaking of St Cloud) ... the Prince of Dahomi, Clive Bell (dressed); ... James and Nora Joyce (in a taxi at the Place de l'Étoile); McAlmon, Antheil, Bryher, H.D. and dear Ezra (Pound) who took me to talk with Léger; and finally Adrienne Monnier – these were my six weeks in Paris.

To such a poetry and such an atmosphere who would not prefer an unassuming authentic piece of contemporary writing no more 'new' than 'old'? Say, Mr Prewett's:

> Seeing my love but lately come
>   And unexpecting she should be found
> I trembled, I was dumb
>   And fell upon the ground;
> Her only thus in distance to see
>   Was to me pain so profound
> I fell down in an agony ...[4]

Freelance modernists do not make 'individuality' their object: their object is to write each poem in the most fitting way. But the sum of their work has individuality because of their natural variousness; like the individuality of the handwriting of all independent-minded men or women, however clearly and conventionally they form their actual letters. The only legitimate use of the word 'style' in poetry is as the personal handwriting in which it is written; if it can be easily imitated or defined as a formula it should be immediately suspect to the poets themselves. To professional modernists individuality is the earnest of a varied social purposiveness. To pseudo-modernists individuality is the earnest of a narrow literary purposiveness. In this they are not dissimilar from those eighteenth-century poets whose sole object was to write correctly, to conform to the manner of the period. In practice this conforming individualism means an imitation, studiously concealed, merely of the eccentricities of poetry that is really individual.

'Groups' may spring up in the old style around any poet; but in general the freelance modernist who had by accident become popular or notorious and still retained a sense of personal dignity would shrink from being made a *cher maître* as a grotesque position for him to occupy in a literary scene that he can only take casually. Indeed, as soon as any imitation is made of his work, and his style by imitation becomes a formula of mannerisms, he may be even inclined to change them to preserve his integrity. It is not, as Mr Philip Guedalla suggests, that there is no English equivalent for *cher maître*, but merely that the modern English poet good enough to be one does not take his poetry like that. A certain sifting and grading of personalities and groups, however, does occur where modernism is a professional conscience rather than a personal trait: the modernist poetry-producing world has the look of a complicated hierarchy. The complication is increased by the efforts of professional modernists to enrol freelance modernists in their socially purposive movement, and of pseudo-modernists to enrol themselves in it by literary forgery.

In every modernist group the members are aware who is the Queen Bee and who are the drones of the *schwärmerei*. Eventually the parasitical members ambitious to become Queen Bees will desert to other hives and to other modes. They make a quick-change from one group to another, acquiring as they go a patchwork synthetic style that they hope to impose on general readers and critics as a large-scale exercise of originality, a contemporary grand manner. The aspirant has a much more difficult problem to face in the new poetic order than in the old. In the old it was sufficient for him to write well. Now he must not only write well, he must be original. A desperate hunt for originality ensues in which aspirants are driven for inspiration to foreign literatures, to old French, to eighteenth-century quaintness, to Spanish, to Demotic Greek, to mediaeval Latin, to Chinese or Javanese or Aztec; to various low dialects – Bowery, White-chapel, Chicago, journalese; to ancient religious writers, particularly the Early Fathers and Buddhists, and so on.

The contemporary poetic scene, then, appears to the interested but perplexed reader a chaotic conglomerate of freelance originality or group originality; a restless multitude of types, imitation of types, antithesis and synthesis of types. Variety is the most characteristic general feature of contemporary poetry, and variety means quantity: it not only encourages poets themselves to experiment freely, it encourages a great many people who are not poets in literary competition. Although it was comparatively easier in periods where a single poetical type prevailed for people who were not poets to write poetry, there are undoubtedly more people who are not poets writing poetry at the present time than ever before, though proportionately fewer find publishers. Even when one has cut out of critical consideration the quantities of backward verse directly imitative of Keats or Tennyson or Oscar Wilde or Swinburne or Francis Thompson or Whitman; of ordinary adolescent verse of distinguishable male and female varieties; there still remains an enormous quantity of miscellaneous verse to be sorted. Criticism (even advanced criticism), reared for centuries on the faith of the technical and philosophical consistency of poetry (a faith continuously derived and revised from Aristotle), cannot cope with poetry in quantity; as it could a hundred years ago, when the possible varieties of poetical composition were countable on the fingers and the most daring were either imitations of Chaucer, Ossian or Spenser, or affectations of country simplicity or of childishness. Criticism in the simplest literary sense has never been able to recognize who are the authentic contemporary poets and how much of each poet is authentic.

Today, having either fallen in arrear of its age or dashed ahead of its age into vague philosophical formulas, it is not even as sure as it once was who are the innovators of any particular type, and who are the copyists, or to what extent striking resemblances are attributable to unconscious contemporary sympathy; or, in the case of imitations of the Chinese or Japanese or American Indian, how close these imitations are to their originals.

The following are lines from the work of two poets, Donald Davidson and John Crowe Ransom, between whom a fairly conscious contemporary sympathy exists, without callow imitation on either side.

> Here's one Phineas
> Out for a walk,
> Tired of skulls
> And bones that talk ...
>
> There's a palimpsest
> In a puff of spring,
> But Phineas looks
> At the blossoming,
> Transfigures road
> Into new corpuscles,
> Elucidates bush
> With a bound of muscles.[5]

and

> Now what can he want,
> The vagrant, the lout,
> Who leers in the parson's face,
> Lolls with tongue out?
>
> Nothing that you have,
> Men with a motor car;
> God keep you your high hats
> And fine things you are!
>
> With a knot in his bosom
> And a bee in his brains,
> He goes full of pictures
> Around the flat lanes.

Even supposing a reader or a critic were able to make a just valuation of an existent sympathy between two particular contemporary poets: how is he to make a satisfactory definition of the relation between the work of either of these two poets, or both, and that of a poet in an entirely different walk of modernism, the work, for example, of Mr Osbert Sitwell? The following is from Mr Sitwell's *English Gothic:*

The souls of bishops, shut in stone
By masons, rest in quietude
As flies in amber. They atone
Each buzzing long-dead platitude.

Above, where flutter angel-wings
Caught in the organ's rolling loom,
Hang in the air, like jugglers' rings,
Dim quatrefoils of coloured gloom.

Tall arches rise to imitate
The jaws of Jonah's whale. Up flows
The chant. Thin spinsters sibilate
Beneath-a full-blown Gothic rose.[6]

Could the reader or critic be expected to have the courage or presence
of mind to say that mere contemporaneousness was an insufficient basis
for making critical comparisons between poets; that Mr Sitwell and Mr
Ransom or Mr Sitwell and Mr Davidson were so separated by locality,
nationality and formative tradition as to belong, so to speak, to entirely
different 'periods'? Suppose that, the problem of Mr Sitwell, Mr Ransom
and Mr Davidson having been settled, a new element of confusion were
introduced by quoting from Mr T.S. Eliot's 'Mr Eliot's Sunday Service'
the following lines as being perplexingly similar to Mr Sitwell's *English
Gothic:*

A painter of the Umbrian school
Designed upon a gesso ground
The nimbus of the Baptized God.
The wilderness is cracked and browned

But through the water pale and thin
Still shine the unoffending feet
And there above the painter set
The Father and the Paraclete

. . . . .

The sable presbyters approach
The avenue of penitence;
The young are red and pustular
Clutching piaculative pence.

Suppose, it being possible to determine from the date of publication of
the volumes in which these poems appeared the date of their writing and
the degrees of intimacy between these two poets at the time of their
respective writings – suppose these poems are set down as an example of

contemporary sympathy? Especially as Mr Eliot is a transplanted American now for a long time acclimatized to literary England? What, however, is to be said when we come upon lines in Mr Eliot's work which do not show him writing in a certain way out of contemporary sympathy with Mr Osbert Sitwell, but writing simply and originally as Mr Eliot? As in the following lines:

> Webster was much possessed by death
> And saw the skull beneath the skin;
> And breastless creatures underground
> Leaned backward with a lipless grin ...
>
> Donne, I suppose, was such another
> Who found no substitute for sense;
> To seize and clutch and penetrate,
> Expert beyond experience ...[7]

Suppose we say, then, that Mr Eliot is himself. He may, as a transplanted American, have moments of contemporary sympathy with modernist English poets, but he is, in the main, uniquely himself. But what if we are suddenly confronted, in the work of an American poet, Allen Tate, who has not been transplanted, with lines like the following from a poem called 'Non Omnis Moriar':

> I ask you: Has the Singer sung
> The drear quintessence of the Song?
> John Ford knew more than I of death –
> John Ford to death has passed along.
>
> I ask you: Has the Singer said
> Wherefore his spirit is not dust?
> Marlowe went muttering to death
> When he had done with song and lust.[8]

As the volume in which Mr Eliot's poem appeared was published in 1920 and as Mr Tate's poem was not printed until 1922 and then in a magazine, Mr Eliot must be accorded priority rights in the manner in which both poems are written. Yet we know directly from Mr Tate that he was writing in this manner long before he was aware that Mr Eliot was also writing in this manner. Since to an American poet who has not been transplanted an American poet transplanted to England is as good as an English poet, the complicated situation now reads something like this: between Mr Osbert Sitwell, an English poet and Mr T.S. Eliot, an American poet transplanted to England, there exists a contemporary sympathy, stronger on Mr Eliot's side because he is the transplanted one; but Mr Eliot's contemporary sympathies with modernist English poets, shall we say, are only incidental in his work – he is, in the main, inimitably himself; yet not entirely so, for other poets have contemporary sympathies with him, which he cannot help, but which nevertheless detract from his inimitability; in fact, at least one American poet has had a contemporary sympathy with him as a modernist English poet (of whom he was not, at a time when the sympathy was strong, aware), not as a transplanted American poet or a resident American poet with whom a contemporary sympathy might have existed without detracting from the inimitability of either; finally, the situation is further complicated by the fact that a certain contemporary sympathy did exist at the time of the poem 'Non Omnis Moriar', between Mr Tate and Mr Davidson and Mr Ransom, without, as it later appeared, detracting from the inimitability of any one of these in relation to any other – which makes an unconscious accidental contemporary sympathy more significant than a sympathy derived from conscious personal association. So the circle is tied, and so it might be tied over and over again in contemporary poetry without making the situation read more clearly.

It might, however, be made clearer than it is if bigoted inefficiency of criticism were replaced by an intelligent policy of laissez-faire; which would allow that a variety of modes may exist side by side in a period, having strong or slight dissimilarities and strong or slight correspondences with one another; that sometimes the dissimilarities can be explained as conscious disaffections or as the unconscious result of dissimilar personal background; that sometimes the correspondences can be explained as conscious affections or affectations or as the unconscious results of similar personal associations, a personal association being at times nothing more definite than a certain literary slant two poets may have caught from some common source of infection – Mr Tate, without having read Wordsworth or his imitators, might as easily have caught the Wordsworth germ as the Eliot germ, had he happened to be constitutionally subject to infection from it.

The situation would be clearer still if many dissimilarities were left as unexplainable, except as facts of absolute personal eccentricity; and if many correspondences were left as unexplainable, except as facts of mysterious personal coincidence not to be accounted for in terms of causality or of excessive openness to infection from without. Some obvious correspondences must be explained, if only because they are easily explained, and because poetry in which too obvious correspondences occur is part of the clutter in the poetry of any time that can be immediately cleared away. The following complete poems are all by different authors:

> The beech-leaves are silver
> For lack of the tree's blood.

At your kiss my lips
Become like the autumn beech-leaves.

0–0–0–0–0–0–0–0

An old willow with hollow branches
Slowly swayed his few high bright tendrils
And sang:

Love is a young green willow
Shimmering at the bare wood's edge.

0–0–0–0–0–0–0–0

As cool as the pale wet leaves of lily-of-the-valley
She lay beside me in the dawn.

0–0–0–0–0–0–0–0

Among twenty snowy mountains
The only moving thing
Was the eye of the black bird[9]

Richard Aldington, William Carlos Williams, Ezra Pound and Wallace Stevens are the so-called authors of these poems. These might pass as legitimate instances of correspondence and not be suspect as parasitical inter-imitativeness, were any of the poems in themselves of separate poetic importance; were not all of these poems, and many more like them, closely dependent on one another – were they private individuals and not members of an institution; and were not the Imagist school, to which all of these poets at one time or another belonged, a notoriously self-advertising institution. These things being so, we are provoked to ask questions that we need not ask in the case of legitimate instances of correspondence. Such as: who was the inventor of the style of the first two pieces, Mr Aldington or Mr Williams? or yet H.D. or F.S. Flint? Is not Mr Williams at least suspect for his later obvious imitation of T.S. Eliot, e.e. cummings, Edith Sitwell? Is not Mr Aldington at least suspect as the husband of H.D.? In the two last pieces who is responsible for the form? Who first thought of imitating the Japanese *hokku* form? Or rather who first thought of imitating the French imitations of the *hokku* form? Did Mr Aldington suggest a slightly shorter poem to Mr Stevens or Mr Pound or did Mr Pound suggest a slightly longer poem to Mr Aldington, etc., or did Mr Pound and Mr Stevens and Mr Aldington and Mr Williams decide, as mutual pairs, to work as a school team, or did Mr Williams and Mr Stevens and Mr Aldington and Mr Pound pair off, as being by nation-ality more pairable – Mr Pound, a transplanted American, counting as either English or French, as the need may be? ... These are questions to concern the curious dustman, but not the plain reader, least of all the critic. The reader, even the critic, does not have to trouble to plot out a literary chart, to develop a carefully graded technical vocabulary. All that either of them needs is a simple and instinctive recognition of the real, which is easily discovered if all other personal or critical questions are brushed aside as irrelevant.

When modernist poetry or what, not so long ago, passed for modernist poetry, can reach the stage where the following:

PAPYRUS

Spring ...
Too long ...
Gongula ...[10]

is seriously offered as a poem, there is some justification for the plain reader and orthodox critic who are frightened away from anything which may be labelled 'modernist' either in terms of condemnation or approbation. Who or what is Gongula? Is it a name of a person? of a town? of a musical instrument? Or is it the obsolete botanical word meaning 'spores'? Or is it a mistake for Gongora, the Spanish poet from whom the word 'gongorism' is formed, meaning 'an affected elegance of style, also called "cultism"?' And why 'Papyrus'? Is the poem a fragment from a real papyrus? Or from an imaginary one? Or is it the poet's thoughts about either a real or imaginary fragment? Or about spring too long because of the gongula of the papyrus-reeds? Rather than answer any of these questions and be driven to the shame-faced bluff of making much out of little, the common-sense reader retires to surer ground. Better, he thinks, presumably, that ten authentic poets should be left for posterity to discover than that one charlatan should be allowed to steal into the Temple of Fame. The plain reader objects to the idea of charlatanry in poetry more than he objects to the idea of stupidity, excess of learnedness, or honest inferiority: charlatanry being dishonest superiority. As the usual type of unorthodox critic is generally so superior himself that he either tolerates charlatanry because it is superior or snubs it because it is not superior enough; and as the usual type of orthodox critic is more equipped with prejudices than the plain reader, if only because his position forces him to know quantitatively more, and as he therefore has a less reliable instinct than the plain reader for determining what is genuine and what is not; the plain reader bears the full burden of challenging and unmasking charlatanry. The critic, of whatever type, is always over-cautious because his professional vanity is at stake in his judgement. The plain reader, because he is of a disorganized, unprofessional and unassisted majority, and therefore more easily imposed upon if too ingenuous, is only over-suspicious.

So cautious and suspicious, in fact, is the whole reading population, the critics and the readers, that a poet like Isaac Rosenberg, for instance, a young English Jew who was killed in France and whose poems were posthumously published, can pass them by altogether. Isaac Rosenberg was one of the few poets who might have served as a fair challenge to sham modernism. He had, one would say, everything to recommend him. His verse was irregular but not too irregular; his meaning was difficult but not too difficult; his references were not far-fetched; he knew his Bible well – a great recommendation to any public; and he died young and in battle. But he was not celebrated and for this reason: that the two editors of his posthumous volume, Mr Bottomley and Mr Binyon, both 'safe' poets, introduced him merely as a poet of promise killed in defence of his country: 'the immaturities of style and taste are apparent on the surface'. The critics in England by 1922 had ceased to blow the trumpet over young poets of promise killed in the War – the reaction against war-poetry had set in. In America, however, because he was a Jew he was used as a pawn in literary politics; but his vogue was short-lived. The real reason why he was generally overlooked was that, in spite of falling into the friendship of the early Georgian Group and accepting their criticism of his work through loneliness, he was not classifiable as a member of a group, or yet, because of his quietness, as a sensational individual type. The following is a passage from his play *Moses*. A young Hebrew is speaking of Moses himself:

> Yesterday as I lay nigh dead with toil
> Underneath the hurtling crane oiled with our blood
> Thinking to end all and let the crane crush me
> He came by and bore me into the shade:
> O, what a furnace roaring in his blood
> Thawed my congealed sinews and tingled my own
> Raging through me like a strong cordial.
> He spoke! Since yesterday
> Am I not larger grown?
> I've seen men hugely shapen in soul,
> Of such unhuman shaggy male turbulence
> They tower in foam miles from our neck-strained sight,
> And to their shop only heroes come;
> But all were cripples to this speed
> Constrained to the stables of flesh.
> I say there is a famine in ripe harvest
> When hungry giants come as guests:
> Come knead the hills and ocean into food,
> There is none for him.
> The streaming vigours of his blood erupting
> From his halt tongue are like an anger thrust

Out of a madman's piteous craving for
A monstrous baulked perfection.[11]

Such work as this had to pass as 'promise'; work better than this will undoubtedly have to pass for a time entirely unnoticed; because variety itself, especially when it becomes a social programme, tends to harden into defined types, or groups, of variety. For an individual poet to achieve the smallest popular reputation today he must, indeed, have a certain 'groupish' quality, or, to put it differently, he must suggest a style capable of being imitated; or he must be a brilliant group-member or imitator. Otherwise he is likely, as one of the consequences of the diversification of poetic activity, to be lost to the literary news-sheets of every critical colour and not even to occur as a subject of the plain reader's suspicion or of the critic's caution: to exist, in fact, only unto himself. Which is not, if the poet appreciates the privilege of privacy, so bad a fate as it sounds. Never, indeed, has it been possible for a poet to remain unknown with so little discredit and dishonour as at the present time. The prima donna reputation acquired by Mr Humbert Wolfe with work of the most crudely histrionic and imitative brilliance (his original comma-effects in *Kensington Gardens* began it) should not only comfort the obscure poet but drive him further into his obscurity.

CHAPTER IX

The Humorous Element in Modernist Poetry

THE motto to Mr Hemingway's modernist novel *The Sun Also Rises* is: '"You are all a lost generation" – Gertrude Stein, in conversation.' The title ('The sun also ariseth') is taken from Ecclesiastes, from the passage in which occurs the better-known text: 'Vanity of vanities, saith the Preacher, vanity of vanities; all is vanity.' This is the conclusion of the greater number of the modernist poets, though not a counsel of altogether unrelieved gloom. Miss Sitwell's chief message, if she may be said to have one, is the endless, minute triviality of life. Mr Eliot's *Waste Land is* prefixed by a Latin motto which relates how the Cumaean Sibyl, when asked by the acolytes what her wishes were, replied (exhausted by her prophetic visions) 'I wish to die'. But in general, although the total effect of modernist poetry on the reader may be depressing because it does not shine with those convictions and grandeurs which have made poetry in the past a beacon of seldom-failing optimism, the modernist poet himself is gay – if drearily gay – under the triviality of life or the philosophy of gloom to which he may be committed. The vanity of the world seen without other-worldly compensation does, in fact, demand a wilful cheerfulness in the poet. And it is this gloomy cheerfulness, if anything, which produces an effect of gloom on the reader; and perhaps rightly, if the reader's temperament is not thus complicated. The temper of this generation, however, is not to be confused with the temper of two other previous lost generations, the generation of Byron and the generation of the Nineties. The first was gloomy because gloom gave a tone of romantic defeat to fanciful ideals that could not be seriously lived up to; the next was gloomy because gloom gave a tone of romantic defeat to a fanciful want of ideals. The poet of the Nineties could either get over his gloominess by becoming successful, or by becoming a blindly devout Catholic; or he could blow out his brains. The present lost generation does not feel its lack of ideals as sinfulness, but rather as sophistication. It does not love itself, but it does not hate itself. It does not think much of life, but neither does it think much of death. It is a cynically common-sense generation which would not, for example, consider dying for the freedom of a small enslaved nation or for literary fame, for that matter. The gloom, then, that it seems to cast does not come from self-pity or emotional prostration; but even from its painful wittiness, as extreme common-sense is always witty. The intellectuality of the humour of this generation may indeed be responsible for the impression of gloom it gives – its passion to show that common-sense is not common, that it is, in fact, not of the substance of happy platitudes but of hard wit.

Because it is a common-sense generation, it must claim experience, it must have tried everything. Because it emphasises the wit in common-sense rather than the common-sense in wit, and because wit is cynical, it is a cynical generation; yet not a sentimental generation, because of its common-sense; nor a pessimistic generation, because pessimism is sentimental. It has tried everything and like Ecclesiastes found it lacking. But it has reached a degree of sophistication which is a stage beyond that of Thomas Hardy or Anatole France. It is not interested in denouncing. It cannot be bothered any more about the failure of Heaven to answer prayers, or the hypocrisy of the 'unco guid', or the inconstancy of lovers and fortune. It declares, more definitely, a drastic alteration in traditional values; but without the violence characteristic of minds that have reached this stage by more emotional paths. It is a generation opposed to stress; and to go on living is always easier than to die. Above all things, it is interested in self-preservation. It is therefore an intensely serious generation in its way, whose wilful cheerfulness is often mistaken for drunken frivolousness: a generation that the War came upon at its most impressionable stage and taught the necessity for a self-protective scepticism of the stability of all human relationships, particularly of all national and religious institutions, of all existing moral codes, of all sentimental formulas for future harmony. From the War it also learned a scale of emotional excitement and depression with which no subsequent variations can compete; yet the scale was too nervously destructive to be wished for again. The disillusion of the War has been completed by the Peace, by the continuation of the old regime patched up with political Fascism, by the same atmosphere of suspense that prevailed from 1911 to the outbreak of nationalistic war and now again gathering around further nationalistic and civil wars.

The other set of experiences beside the War that have most impressed this generation might be called knowledge-experiences. It has witnessed, as well as a variegation, a fresh synthesis of intellectual interests. It must not only revise traditional values; it must appreciate new ones. That is, as a generation writing in the limelight of modernism it has an over-developed historical sense and professional self-consciousness. It is mentally uncomfortable – shrewd, nervous, suspicious of itself. It rejects philosophy and religion in the old drivelling romantic sense, but would welcome an intellectual system – a permanently accessible mental cocktail – that would be a stiff, sane, steadying combination of both. It cares so much that in all matters where the plain reader is accustomed to meet with earnest conviction of one kind or another in the poet, it is hysterically, gruesomely 'I-don't-care-ish'. It is like a person between life and death: everything that would ordinarily seem serious to him now seems a tragic joke. This nervousness, this superior sort of stage-fright, is aggravated by the fact that in the new synthesis of values – even in the system that he is attempting to realize for himself – the historically-minded modernist poet is uncertain whether there is any excuse for the existence of poets at all. He finds himself in a defensive position; and in sympathy with his position; but also with the system that has put him in this position. So he brazens out the dilemma by making cruel jokes at his own expense – jokes which he expects no one to see or not to be laughed at if seen.

The modernist poet, then, as a type (and a type can, of course, contradict itself in its individuals) may be said to possess a peculiar and a recognizable intellectual slant; or, if we feel 'intellectual' to imply too bland a sort of seriousness, we may say that the modernist has such and such a technique of opinion in his poetry. He does not commit himself wholeheartedly to any obvious conviction. He does not, on the other hand, waste himself in obvious attack. When any choice of faith, action or habit is held to belong to the lower, less developed processes of reasoning, the making of a choice is a vulgarism. It is a point of intellectual pride with him to refrain from making utilitarian choices: his choices are in the more serious realm of speculation. His aversion to indulging in feelings merely because they are temporarily pleasant to him or to others, or because they are the feelings expected of him as a poet, or because they best show off his talents, or because they are easy and obvious feelings to have – this emotional abstinence amounts to a severe asceticism, as one modernist poet has himself put it. But asceticism is an easily parodied position and the modernist poet is aware of this. He is also aware, because he is a hard-headed, common-sense creature, that asceticism is in practice impossible. So he has common-sense even about his common-sense, which has led him to this asceticism: he is able to do what no generation of poets before him has been able to do – to make fun of himself when he is at his most serious.

The poet's self-mockery is that feature of modernist poetry most likely to puzzle the reader or the critic who has not properly appraised the poet's intellectual slant. A poem which is a joke at the poet's expense can obviously not be sympathized with as it should be unless the reader sees it as in some respects a joke against himself too. Obviously he cannot do this unless he is at least capable of discovering in the poem clues to the poet's wit and its direction: the reader himself must have wit. The probable failure of wit in the reader, whether plain reader or critic, removes from the poet that measure of *address* which an audience imposes. Relieved of the obligations of address the modernist poem frequently leaps from formal clownishness to unrestrained burlesque. The closing lines of a poem, *Winter Remembered*, by John Crowe Ransom illustrates that formal clownishness which is the poet's role when he intentionally keeps himself within reach of his audience's sentiment:

> Dear Love, these fingers that had known your touch,
> And tied our separate forces first together,
> Were ten poor idiot fingers not worth much,
> Ten frozen parsnips hanging in the weather.

Mr Ransom, therefore, though a modernist in his disrespect to himself, leans rather toward the sentimental tradition of irony. He insists upon the wit of his reader; he makes an appeal which it is impossible that the reader shall overlook: if the reader be slow in discovering the clues to the poet's clownishness, the poet forces his clownishness in a way that the reader cannot mistake. It is as if a performing clown had made a deep but delicate joke against himself which the audience had missed. Bound to have his audience appreciate his mood, the clown slaps himself very hard and makes a long face. The audience now sees the joke and laughs. But the clown was obliged to brutalize his joke in order to soften his audience to him. It is a question whether irony, as a means of self-mockery, does not fail, in overstepping the disrespect which the poet wishes to do himself. For it adds a pathetic element, a tearfulness, which rarely is entirely sincere.

In the main, however, the modernist clown, feeling a want in his audience, turns his back on it and performs his ritual of antics without benefit of applause. As he is not out to make anyone laugh and cry in the same breath, and as his audience is not likely to respond unless he exerts himself to do this, he relieves himself of the burden of an audience. It is for this reason that we find in modernist poetry so many examples of *pure* burlesque, not in the trapeze tradition, but in the tearless, heartless tradition of the early Italian comedy. Miss Sitwell, as much as any modernist poet, belongs to this tradition:

> The wind's bastinado
> Whipt on the calico
> Skin of the Macaroon
> And the black Picaroon
> Beneath the galloon
> Of the midnight sky.
> Came the great Soldan
> In his sedan
> Floating his fan, –
> Saw what the sly
> Shadow's cocoon

In the barracoon
Held. Out they fly.
'This melon,
Sir Mammon,
Comes out of Babylon:
Buy for a patacoon –
Sir, you must buy!'[1]

So far, so good. The poem is a fantasia, a sort of a mime-show, and the antic figures are expressed by obsolete romance words like Macaroon (a clown) Picaroon (a rogue) galloon (rich embroidery) barracoon (convict-prison) patacoon (Spanish dollar). The clown and rogue come out from the shadow of the prison dressed in their white calico pierrot costumes (see the cover of Sacheverell Sitwell's *Thirteenth Caesar*) and offer a fruit to the great Soldan: as two old-style poets might offer their works to the great Public.

Said il Magnifico
Pulling a fico, –
With a stoccado
And a gambado
Making a wry
Face: 'This corraceous
Round orchidaceous
Laceous porraceous
Fruit is a lie!
It is my friend King Pharaoh's head
That nodding blew out of the Pyramid ...'

In effect, the Soldan, snapping his fingers (pulling a fico) with a stoc-cado (a lunge as in fencing) and a gambado (gambol) said – but by this time Miss Sitwell, who has been going very fast, has left her audience far behind: they have either deserted her, or are a dozen lines behind fumbling in the dictionary. So at this point she whips up her horse and goes faster than she knows herself. Even the dictionary sense, at this speed, falls to pieces and the words themselves turn into clowns. It no longer matters that 'orchidaceous' means 'belonging to the orchid family' or that 'porraceous' means 'belonging to the leek family' or that (unless Miss Sitwell has a bigger dictionary than ours) 'laceous' and 'corraceous' are mere nonsense-words. For by this time nothing matters and nothing makes sense, not even what the great Soldan says. Indeed the boisterous collapse is so sudden and so complete that 'laceous' and 'corraceous' may be deliberate misspellings to indicate the state of merry disintegration that the poem has reached. The principal observation to be made about this performance is, perhaps, that it has two separate aspects, a theatrical aspect and a poetic aspect. The first is the poem as a visible gesture which either is or is not a signal to the reader's wit. If it is, the reader may perceive the poetic aspect according to his capacity or leisure. The theatrical aspect at any rate remains and, if the eye is quick, includes the poetic aspect. For it is possible that a sensitive audience which did not catch all her words, so to speak, might by the excellence of Miss Sitwell's pantomime follow with perfect understanding her light-hearted gallop to despair and self-stultification. If it could not, then be assured Miss Sitwell would *not* slap herself in the face.

Limitations in the sense of humour of the critic-reader have thus the effect of making the modernist poem more and more difficult. For, the poet tells himself, if the reading public is bound anyhow to be a limited one, the poem may as well take advantage of its isolation by using references and associations which are as far out of the ordinary critic's reach as the modernist sense of humour. When, for example, Edith and Sacheverell Sitwell both introduce a Captain Fracasse into their poems as a symbol of the comic opera sword-and-cape hero, they are going too far for the average English reader and critic who is perhaps entirely unaware of Gautier's romance of that name or of Catulle Mendes' comic opera drawn from it, but would immediately recognize a character corresponding to Fracasse in English literature. Fracasse is used because French comic opera heroes have an eccentric quality not to be matched quite accurately in the English Classics; but he would undoubtedly not have been used if a freer commerce in humour existed between the reader and the poet. Again, when Miss Sitwell writes of:

> winding
> Roads whose dust seems gilded binding
>
> Made for 'Paul et Virginie' –
> (so flimsy-tough those roads are), see
>
> The panniered donkey pass ...

the reference is to a pastoral by Bernardin de Saint-Pierre, an old-fashioned French nursery classic. It is a sentimental record of true love in the picturesquely savage Isle of Mauritius, a mixed flimsiness and toughness of story with which we may imagine the format of Miss Sitwell's schoolroom copy to have been analogous – heavy gilt binding and the usual flimsy French paper. This is a little more than a family joke, but certainly not a popular one.

A poem by Mr Eliot may be quoted in full as an example of how limited the humorous appeal of modernist verse may become. The extreme particularity of some of the references may be called the teasing element of modernist wit. Here is our poor understanding of the poem. We do not pretend to be wise to all the jokes in Mr Eliot's poem; undoubtedly the pertinaceous and joke-shrewd reader will be able to carry the scent further; and of course Mr Eliot himself could, if pressed, make everything clear:

BURBANK WITH A BAEDEKER:
BLEISTEIN WITH A CIGAR.

Tra-la-la-la-la-la-laire – nil nisi divinum stabile est; caetera fumus – the gondola stopped, the old palace was there, how charming its grey and pink – goats and monkeys with such hair too! – so the countess passed on until she came through the little park, where Niobe presented her with a casket, and so departed.

Burbank crossed a little bridge
    Descending at a small hotel;
Princess Volupine arrived,
    They were together, and he fell.

Defunctive music under sea
    Passed seaward with the passing bell
Slowly: the God Hercules
    Had left him, that had loved him well

The horses, under the axle-tree
    Beat up the dawn from Istria
With even feet. Her shuttered barge
    Burned on the water all the day.

This is evidently modern Venice visited by two tourists, one an American, who may or may not be called Burbank on account of Burbank the botanist, the other a caricature-Jew. The Latin quotation means: 'Nothing is lasting unless it is divine: the rest is smoke.' The rest of the introduction, with the exception of 'with such hair too' out of Browning, may be by Ruskin or by some obscure diarist or by Mr Eliot himself: we cannot be bothered to discover whom. The best that we can do for it is to apply it to the poem. The old palace is one of the many show-places on the Grand Canal: the one possibly where Lord Byron's intrigue with the Countess Guiccoli took place. The goats and monkeys may be part of the zoo that Lord Byron kept there and later conveyed to Pisa; but also may symbolise lechery. Not only are monkeys permanent features, like gargoyles, of Venetian palaces; but monkeys play a symbolic part in the *Merchant of Venice*, and the *Merchant of Venice* is a suppressed *motif*, shaping the poem from behind the scenes, so to speak. Jessica, it will be remembered, turned her back on Jewry, took up with Christians and immediately bought a monkey. The little parks are features of these

Venetian palaces. Niobe is the Greek emblem of sorrow; her children were slain as a punishment for her pride in them. The casket is a memorial of Niobe's sympathy with Venice, whose pride has also been brought low. Princess Volupine evidently represents the degenerate aristocratic romanticism of Venice: she has an intrigue with Burbank who stands for the element of sentiment in modern civilization – a sort of symbolical 'decent chap'. 'Defunctive music' is from Shakespeare's *Phoenix and Turtle*. The last line of the first stanza, like the last two of the second and the first two of the third, is possibly also a quotation, but here again we leave pedigrees to more reference-proud critics than ourselves. Burbank's power leaves him. (The God Hercules is the Latin god of strength and also the guardian of money.) The third stanza marks an increase from the second in the mock-grandeur of the writing: at this point it seems to fall in love with itself and threatens to become serious. This in turn demands the sudden bathetic drop of the fourth stanza. The manner of the third stanza accounts for the especial artificiality of the symbols used: their grandiosity and the obscurity of their source throw a cloud over their precise significance. The horses under the axle-tree may be the horses of the sun under the axle-tree of heaven; but they may also suggest the little heraldic horses fixed at the side of every Venetian gondola, which may be said to be under the axle-tree of the gondola, *i.e.* the oar. So this may be a conceit that amounts to calling the sun a sky-gondola rather than a chariot. Or it may not. Istria lies east from Venice on the road to Vienna. Princess Volupine's shuttered barge burns significantly on the water all day, a sign that she is now closeted with someone else. There is an echo here from *Antony and Cleopatra*:

> The barge she sat in, like a burnished throne,
> Burned on the water ...!

At this point the other half of the cast enters the poem: Bleistein the Jew. Burbank walks through Venice with a Baedeker, that is, with a melancholy respect for the past. Bleistein, on the contrary, walks through Venice with a cigar, a symbol of vulgar and ignorant self-enjoyment. The name Bleistein itself is a caricature of the common Goldstein or 'Goldstone': it means 'Leadstone'.

> But this or such was Bleistein's way:
>   A saggy bending of the knees
> And elbows, with the palms turned out,
>   Chicago Semite Viennese.
>
> A lustreless protrusive eye
>   Stares from the protozoic slime
> At a perspective of Canaletto.
>   The smoky candle end of time

Declines. On the Rialto once.
   The rats are underneath the piles.
The jew is underneath the lot.
   Money in furs. The boatman smiles,

Burbank sees the strength and wealth of Venice departed, the remnants of
her glory enjoyed by an upstart Chicago Jew who probably started life as a
tailor's apprentice in Galicia (whose origin is Austria, whither Hercules
first went from Venice in 1814). Canaletto was a painter of the eighteenth
century whose aristocratic pictures of Venice are a long way from
Bleistein's kind. The smoky candle end recalls the Latin motto: 'the rest is
smoke.' Burbank pictures sorrowfully the Rialto of other days. The rats
are underneath the piles now, and the Jew (the eternal Shylock) is the rat
of rats. The jew (Jew is written with a small initial letter like rat) is appar-
ently a rat because he has made money and because for some reason Jewish
wealth, as opposed to Gentile wealth, has a mystical connection with the
decline of Venice. This may not be Burbank's private opinion or even Mr
Eliot's. It at any rate expresses for Mr Burbank and Mr Eliot the way
Venice at present feels or should feel about the modern Jew strutting
through its streets. 'Money in furs' refers not only to the fact that the fur
trade is largely in Jewish hands and that this is how Bleistein probably
made his money, but also to some proverbial witticism, perhaps, about the
ability of a Jew to make money even out of rats' skins, out of the instru-
ments of decay, that is. The smiling boatman, who has for centuries seen
everything, stands as an ironic fate between Bleistein and Princess
Volupine.

   Princess Volupine extends
      A meagre, blue-nailed, pthisic hand
   To climb the waterstair. Lights, lights,
      She entertains Sir Ferdinand

   Klein. Who clipped the lion's wings
      And flea'd his rump and pared his claws?
   Thought Burbank, meditating on
      Time's ruins, and the seven laws.

   Venice in the person of Princess Volupine (is this another French
comic-opera character; or a coined word compounded of the Latin for
'pleasure', *Voluptas*, and the name of a play of Ben Jonson's *Volpone, the
Fox*; or a character from one of the obscurer dramatists of the *Mermaid
Series*? We confess we do not care) has now descended so low that, no
longer content with Byronic intrigues with civilization, she actually
admits the Jew (in the person of Sir Ferdinand Klein, an English
financier) to her embraces. Sir Ferdinand's name is an epitome of
contempt and pathetic comedy: the Jew, having made money, has likewise

conquered and corrupted English society; his noble Christian name is stolen from the very country which most persecuted him (now also in decay); his family name means 'little' and is, appropriately enough, from the German (there is no sentimental condolence with the Germans because, presumably, they do not suffer from this peculiarly Mediterranean type of decay). So, in the person of Sir Ferdinand Klein, Bleistein succeeds where Burbank fails; the implication being that the Jew is not an individual but an eternal symbol, each Jew always being the entire race. 'Lights, lights!' is a Shakespearianism further evoking the *Merchant of Venice* atmosphere. The lion is the winged lion of St Mark, the patron saint of Venice; but also, in a secondary sense, the British lion, whose wings have been clipped by the Jew. What the seven laws are in the Venetian context will probably be found in Baedeker or the Classical Dictionary or the *Merchant of Venice* (where rats, the Rialto and pet monkeys also occur).

This is not, of course, popular writing. It is aristocratic writing, and its jokes are exclusive; but only exclusive if the reader has no capacity or interest for sharing in them: the Baedeker is common to all men, so are the Classical Dictionary and La Rousse. The jokes are against modern civilization, against money, against classicism, against romanticism, against Mr Eliot himself as a tourist in Venice with a Baedeker. One of the privileges of the comedian is to have prejudices without being held morally accountable for them; and the modernist poet is inclined to take full advantage of this privilege, to have caprices without being obliged to render a dull, rationalistic account of them. The anti-Jewish prejudice, for instance, occurs frequently in modernist poetry, and the anti-American prejudice also. It is part of the comedy that a Jew or an American may equally have these prejudices.

Although written in a mood of intellectual severity, modernist poetry retains the clown's privilege of having irrational prejudices in favour of a few things as well as against a few things. It assumes, indeed, the humorous championship of things that the last centuries have either hated, neglected or mishandled. Toward poetical items that have been worn out by spiritual elevation, such as motherhood, childhood, nature, national pride, the soul, fame, freedom and perfection, it maintains a policy of disinterested neutrality; not because of a prejudice against motherhood, nature, etc., but because of a feeling that they have had their day and that it is now the turn of other things like obscenity, lodging-house life, pedantry, vulgarity, frivolousness, failure, drunkenness, and so on, to be put into the scales. This is out of a desire not for sensationalism but for emotional equilibrium. The generation to which the modernist poet belongs is, as we have said, an exceedingly common-sense, 'sensible' generation, to which most things are equally poetic because equally commonplace.

The only way that traditional poetry could treat drink, for example, was either with sentimental gaiety, as in Shakespeare's:

> Let the canakin clink,
> And let the canakin clink!
>   A soldier's a man
>   And life's but a span,
> So let the canakin clink![2]

or with irony, as in Gay's song from *The Mohocks:*

> Come fill up the glass!
> Round, round, let it pass,
> Till our reason be lost in our wine:
> Leave conscience's rules
> To women and fools,
> *This* only can make us divine.

or with loathing for its fatal fascination as in Lefanu's *Drunkard's address to a Bottle of Whiskey:*

> Oh terrible darling,
> How have you sought me,
> Enchanted, and caught me,
> See, now, where you've brought me
> To sleep by the road-side, and dress out in rags.

Drunkenness, as a poetical subject, was either comic or disgusting. Comic, as in George Colman's *Toby Tosspot*: when the drunken man on his way home at midnight saw a notice on a street-door 'Please Ring the Bell', and did so vigorously out of mere friendliness. Disgusting, as in Mr Masefield's *Everlasting Mercy:*

> 'Look on him, there,' she says, 'look on him
> And smell the stinking gin upon him,
> The lowest sot, the drunk'nest liar,
> The dirtiest dog in all the shire.'[3]

The modernist poet, however, does not have, properly speaking, 'poetical' subjects, since most subjects are to him commonplaces. So that when the fact of drunkenness gets into poetry, the poem does not explain how the poet feels about drunkenness but, in a callous, precise way, what drunkenness is. If, therefore, the poem is a 'comic' poem, it is not so because the poet thinks drunkenness a comic subject but because it happens, as a shrewd mental condition, to share in his wit. So Mr cummings:

> death is more than
> certain a hundred these
> sounds crowds odours it
> is in a hurry
> beyond that any this
> taxi smile or angle we do
>
> not sell and buy
> things so necessary as
> is death and unlike shirts
> neckties trousers
> we cannot wear it out
>
> no sir which is why
> granted who discovered
> America ether the movies
> may claim general importance
>
> to me to you nothing is
> what particularly
> matters hence in a
>
> little sunlight and less
> moonlight ourselves against the worms
>
> hate laugh shimmy[4]

The wit of drunkenness can easily be deciphered from this taxi-and-gin shorthand. Drunkenness is a mental dare-devilry; one of the few conditions, indeed, in which it is not disgraceful to be sentimental. The last thing drunkenness takes notice of is drink; and it is not sufficiently understood that a person in drunkenness is not drunk, but only very serious and therefore very hilarious or very gloomy. Mr cummings' most serious poems, for example, are drunken poems; except his love poems – but these, perhaps, may also be classified as drunken poems. Therefore Mr cummings does not here say: 'Death is more than certain, fellow drunkards. Out of every hundred people born a hundred die', and proceed, as in *Down Among the Dead Men*:

> Then come, let us drink it while we have breath,
> For there's no drinking after death!

He clips his grammar, increases his speed and goes on with the argument, and does not stop until he has reached the conclusion that all there is left to do under the circumstances is to 'hate, laugh, shimmy' – and speculate. For in drunkenness, it appears, one's mind is not less but more clear than usual. It holds more, it thinks faster, it sees and understands everything; it is even like the taxi which, we gather, is assisting the poet in his poetic argument. So death triumphs, it is not left behind by the taxi (no sir!) together with the shops, the crowds and our rake's fast thoughts. Nothing matters, therefore, (and here our rake turns, perhaps, to the other occupant of the taxi) except a little bragging sunshine to show the worms we don't care and to hate, laugh, shimmy. And so Death does not triumph. Thus reads an old comic subject in 1926.

The haughty intellectual slant of the modernist poet involves him in a bright game of spite against the middle classes, which are responsible for the front of solemn good-breeding and politeness that poetry acquired in the last century. He combines upper-class impeccability and lower-class rough-neckedness into a disdainful modernist recklessness on the road. The stalest joke of comic song (but not of poetry) is the mother-in-law. Miss Sitwell's *Fantasia for Mouth Organ* dashingly takes the mother-in-law joke and sends it round the world to India, the North Pole and South Pole, the land of the red-skins, the land of the humming birds and the equatorial isles where the savages sank upon one knee –

> For when they saw
> My mother-in-law
> They decided not to tackle
> Me!
> She is tough as the armorian
> Leather that the saurian
> Sun spreads over the
> Sea –
> So she saved my life
> Did the mother of my wife
> Who is more than a mother to
> Me![5]

The humorous element in poetry, it is seen, has undergone a complete reversal and become part of the mechanism of fine writing; Miss Sitwell's mother-in-law poem, for instance, is not offered as a comic poem. Even what appears to be an obvious comic satire of Victorianism in many of her poems is, in reality, a spiteful championship of a former comic subject – Victorianism as a bourgeois comic subject was long ago worn out. The humorous element here lies in the spice which a much abused institution acquires when restored by impudent artifice to connoisseur sentiment. A sophisticated partiality for Victorianism is at any rate one of the disingenuously irrational prejudices in which the three Sitwells indulge themselves. The Queen becomes a rather robustious and slangy old lady telling Lady Venus just where to get off.

> 'For the minx,'
>   Said she,

'And the drinks,
You can see,
Are hot as any hottentot and not the goods for me!'

Victorian fashions evoke literary enthusiasm:

Rose Castles
Those bustles
Beneath parasols seen!
Fat blondine pearls
Rondine curls
Seem.

Even Victorian rococo architecture and interior decoration become semi-humorously aetherialized: Balmoral's towers, its pitch-pine floors and special tartan, the Crystal Palace, the Albert Memorial and the horse-hair settees of Buckingham Palace.

On the other hand this serious poem of Miss Marianne Moore's:

Openly, yes
with the naturalness
    of the hippopotamus or the alligator
    when it climbs out on the bank to experience the

Sun, I do these
things which I do, which please
    no one but myself. Now I breathe and now I am sub-
    merged; the blemishes stand up and shout when the object

in view was a
renaissance; shall I say
    the contrary? the sediment of the river which
    encrusts my joints, makes me very grey but I am used ...

or the many serious pieces of Mr cummings written in comic vernacular, bring the full circle round to the professionally comic vein of traditional poetry. A poem by J.W. Morris, a writer of the American Sixties, should be brought face to face with Miss Moore's poem to mark the reversal that serious and comic elements have undergone in poetry. It is called 'Collusion between a Alegaiter and a Water-Snaik'. The scene is 'Guatimaly'. It should be read as a parody of 'unpoetical' poetry, even perhaps as a prophetic parody. The following lines from it in fact might have been written by Mr cummings were he a traditional poet of the Sixties, satirizing Miss Moore, a modernist poet of the 1920s.

Evidently a good chance for a water snaik
Of the large specie, which soon appeared
Into the horison, near the bank where repos'd

Calmly in slepe the Alegaiter before spoken of
About 60 feet was his length (not the 'gaiter')
And he was aperiently a well-proportioned snaik.

When he was all ashore he glared upon
The island with approval but was soon
'Astonished with the view and lost to wonder'

(from Watts)

(For jest then he began to see the Alegaiter)
Being a natural enemy of his'n he worked hisself
Into a fury, also a ni position.
Before the Alegaiter well could ope
His eye (in other words perceive his danger)
The Snaik had enveloped his body just 19
Times with 'foalds voluminous and vast'

(from Milton)

… But soon by grate force the tail was, bit complete-
Ly off …

   The mental agility required of the poet who wishes to reconcile poetry to modernism and modernism to poetry gives him an exaggerated nimbleness that one modernist poet may have had in mind when speaking of the 'athleticism' of this generation. Much of his superfluous energy is consumed in an ostentatious display – sometimes childish but in general harmless – of the Protean powers of poetry. The badge of the modernist poet might well be the one that the Stanley family gave to the Isle of Man – three legs conjoined at the middle and the motto 'Wherever you throw it, it will stand'. For, though by his technical flexibility he may seem to be continually standing on his head, by his common-sense he inclines to be all legs; and however extreme the comedy – however wilful his caprices, however grotesque the contrasts between innocence and obscenity or brutality and preciousness – it is a point of intellectual vanity in him to laugh last, to be found on his feet when the performance is over. He completes and in a sense contradicts his clownishness by revealing that even clownishness is a joke: that it is a joke to be writing poetry, a joke to be writing modernist poetry. By this token he belongs to the most serious generation of poets that has ever written; with the final self-protective corollary, of course, that it is also a joke to be serious.

   Sometimes, however, the modernist poet in his grotesque pantomime is very nearly tempted, out of virtuosity, to leave himself standing on his head. The following is a passage from *Causerie*, a poem by Mr Allen Tate. It is a rambling midnight pillow-cogitation on the vulgarization and mechanization of the language of Homer, Catullus, Shakespeare and Rousseau. The poem is otherwise historically interesting as a psychological synthesis of the manners of his contemporaries, among them T.S.

Eliot, e.e. cummings, John Crowe Ransom, Marianne Moore, and at least one other poet:

> Hermes decorates
> A cornice on the Third National Bank. Vocabulary
> Becomes confusion, decoration a blight, the Parthenon
> In Tennessee stucco, art for the sake of death. Now
> (the bedpost receding in stillness) you brush your teeth
> 'Hitting on all thirty-two'; scholarship pares
> The nails of Catullus, sniffs his sheets, restores
> His 'passionate underwear'; morality disciplines the other
> Person; snakes speak the idiom of Rousseau; Prospero
> Serves Humanity in steam-heated universities, three
> Thousand dollars a year; – for simplicity is obscene
> Sunlight topples indignant from the hill.
> In every railway station everywhere, every lover
> Waits for his train. He cannot hear. The smoke
> Thickens. Ticket in hand he pumps his body
> Toward lower six, for one more terse ineffable trip,
> His very eyeballs fixed in disarticulation. The berth
> Is clean; no elephants, vultures, mice, or spiders
> Distract him from nonentity; for his metaphors are dead.
> *Notescatque magis mortuus atque magis,*
> *Nec tenuem texens sublimis aranea telam ...*

The motto to the poem is from an American newspaper:

> ... party on the stage of the Earl Carrol Theatre on February 23. At this party Joyce Hawley, a chorus-girl, bathed in the nude in a bathtub filled with alleged wine.

The comic technique is devoted to a contrast between Imperial America and Imperial Rome in general conversational style. The mind, in being democratized, runs the theme, has grown large, complicated, vulgar and dead. The poet's clownishness consists in swift and showy acrobatic turns from present-day vulgar sophistication to the comparative simplicity of classical manners and from classical civilization on the other hand to twentieth-century vocabularistic vulgarity. A snobbish prejudice in favour of classical phrasing is the special privilege in which this poet indulges himself. The Latin verse from Catullus reads: 'And may he when dead grow more and more famous, nor may the spider spinning its fine thread from above ... (make a web upon the forgotten name of Allius).' The quotation, somewhat forced in its application we must confess, is from an elegy on the death of Allius, a friend who has helped Catullus in his intrigues by providing him and his Lesbia with a rendezvous at the house of a mistress of his own: for which Catullus thanks him in all frankness and simplicity. The vultures occur in this poem of Catullus': and 'hitting on all thirty-two' – an advertisement for a toothpaste – is probably an ironic comment in the style of Catullus' ironic comment on the fine teeth of his friend Egnatius. Prospero is the symbol of learning, which did not become, until advanced times, humanitarian and democratic, commercialized and vulgar. The element of humour in this poem is not entirely sincere because the prejudice is somewhat too dogmatic, the poet failing to identify himself with both subjects of the contrast. He was not willing, that is, to be the complete clown and has thus very nearly left himself on his head.

The bourgeois character of common convictions and of human progress in the popular sense does indeed inspire in the modernist generation a temperamental antagonism to old-fashioned democratic civilization. In pseudo-modernist types this antagonism is inclined to manifest itself in a social, political or literary gospel of pessimism. Genuine professional modernism inclines rather toward the two extremes of radicalism and conservatism, or aristocraticness and rough-neckedness; not so much out of militant opposition to bourgeois liberalism as out of peripatetic avoidance of a crowded thoroughfare – bourgeois liberalism, being a position of compromise between all extremes, is the breeding place of settled, personally secure convictions. At the extremes instead of convictions there is a border-sense, a well-poised mental hysteria, a direct exposure to time: there is the far-driven boundary line of humour: there is, in both, the callous haughtiness of indifference to danger, of a more acute technique of self-preservation. The mind, human nature, poetry, are at their best when they combine the elements of both roughness and gentleness; and this is not a politician's trick or a philosopher's trick or a sentimentalist's trick, but a clown's trick.

The only flaw in humour of the modernist poet is his failure to include the bourgeois in his intellectual scale. It is, we might say, the only turn missing in his clownish repertory. Indeed James Joyce has suggested that Shakespeare's greatness lay in his power to play the bourgeois impersonally, but as a bourgeois, without having a bourgeois dummy to kick or yet slapping his own face:

> And the sense of property, Stephen said. He drew Shylock out of his own long pocket. The son of a maltjobber and moneylender he was himself a cornjobber and moneylender with ten tods of corn hoarded in the famine riots ... He sued a fellow-player for the price of a few bags of malt and exacted his pound of flesh in interest for every money lent. How else could Aubrey's ostler and callboy get rich quick?[6]

Death, a common bourgeois conviction, is the only progressive liberal subject which the modernist poet sometimes treats without prejudice.

One contemporary poet actually writes of it:

> This I admit, death is terrible to me,
> To no man more so naturally,
> And I have disenthralled my natural terror
> Of every comfortable philosopher
> Or tall dark doctor of Divinity.
> Death stands again in his true rank and order.[7]

But even with Death the modernist poet is in the main not quite at his clownish best because of his awareness of its bourgeois applications: it is very difficult to deal with Death and, considering its history, not treat it as a religious conviction – to treat it as a dead-earnest joke. A similar difficulty exists with Love, the twin bourgeois conviction to Death. In Love even the most modernist of modernist poets is bourgeois. He is narrowly idealistic and therefore incapable, except in rare cases, of making it another dead-earnest joke: The clown in this feat is afraid of not landing on his legs. The most he trusts himself to is a few ribald high jumps.

CHAPTER X

Conclusion

SO far our sympathy with modernist poetry has been contemporary
sympathy. We have been writing as it were from the middle of the modern-
ist movement in order to justify it if possible against criticism which was
not proper to it, which belonged to the preceding stage in poetry-making
and which should have passed as the stage passed. It is now possible to
reach a position where the modernist movement itself can be looked at
with historical (as opposed to contemporary) sympathy as a stage in poetry
that is to pass in turn, or may have already passed, leaving behind only
such work as did not belong too much to history. The apparent contradic-
tions that will occur in this chapter and seem to gainsay the emphatic
sympathy of former chapters will be found to be caused by this super-
seding of contemporary sympathy by historical sympathy. As nothing can
remain contemporary for very long, we were obliged to assume this posi-
tion if our criticism was to stand before rather than behind its subject.

In discussing the difficulties which exist between contemporary poetry
and the contemporary reader, it is necessary to discuss also the difficulties
which the contemporary poet has had to face if he has wished to write as a
contemporary – to be included in the generation to which by birth and
personal sympathy he historically belongs. As the poet, if a true poet, is
one by nature and not by effort, he must be seen writing as unconsciously
as regards time as his ordinary reader lives. For one remembers the date
only by compulsion; no one really feels older today than he felt yesterday.
The relation of a poet's poetry to Poetry as a whole and to the time in
which it is written is the problem of criticism; and if this problem becomes
part of the making of a poem, it adds to the unconscious consciousness of
the poet when he is in the act of composition an alien element, a *conscious*
consciousness which we may call the 'historical effort'. In reading poetry
in which this alien element appears one must indeed make the same
historical effort if the full intention of the poem is to be appreciated.
Therefore the plain reader is likely to prefer to modernist poetry poetry of
a past period, in which the historical effort, wherever it has been present,
has been absorbed or neutralized by the automatic passing of the period
into history.

The greatest difficulty is obviously to define 'poetry as a whole' from the point of view of a *temporary* personal consciousness – that of the poet or reader – attempting to connect itself with a long-term impersonal consciousness, an evolving professional sense. Yet it is easier to do this now than formerly, since poetry, which was once an all-embracing human activity, has been narrowed down by the specialization of other general activities, such as religion and the arts and sciences, into a technical branch of culture of the most limited kind. It has been changed from a 'humanity' into an 'art'; it has attempted to discipline itself with a professionalized criticism which was not needed in the time of the balladists or in primitive societies where poetry went hand in hand with magical religion. Modern civilization seems to demand that the poet should justify himself not only by writing poems but furthermore by proving with each poem the contemporary legitimacy of poetry itself – the professional authority of the term 'poet' in fact. And though in a few rare cases the poet may succeed even now in writing by nature without historical or professional effort, he is in general too conscious of the forced professionalization of poetry to be able to avoid justifying himself and his work professionally, that is, critically, as a point of honour. Yet if he does admit poetry to be only one of the specialized, professionalized activities of his period, like music, painting, radiology, aerostatics, the cinema, modern tennis or morbid psychology, he must see it as a very small patch on the time-chart, a mere dot; because society allows less and less space for poetry in its organization. The only way that this dot on the time-chart can provide itself with artificial dignity and space is through historical depth; if its significance in a particular period is no greater than the size of a dot on the period's time-chart, then to make itself an authoritative expression of this period it must extend this dot into the past, it must make a historical straight line of it. Poetry becomes the tradition of poetry.

The tradition of poetry, or rather of the art of poetry, then, is the formal organisation which the modernist poet finds himself serving as an affiliated member. He must not only have a personal capacity for poetry; that is merely an apprentice certificate. He must also have a master's sense of the historical experience of poetry – of its past functions and usefulness, its present fitness and possibilities. He must have a science of the 'values' of poetry, a scale of bad and good, false and true, ephemeral and lasting; a theory of the tradition of poetry in which successive period-poetries are historically judged either favourably or unfavourably and in which his own period-poetry is carefully adjusted to satisfy the values which the tradition is believed to be continuously evolving. As this tradition is seen as a logical historical development, these values, in their most recent statement, are considered, if observed, sufficient to produce the proper poetic expression of the age. So the poet has no longer to make adjustment to his social environment, as the hero-celebrating bard of the *Beowulf* time or the religious poet of ancient Egypt had, but critical adjustments to a special tradition of poetic values; and to his own period only an indirect adjustment through the past, the past seen as the poetry of the past narrowing down to the poetry of the present.

The modernist poet therefore has an exaggerated preoccupation with criticism. He has a professional conscience forced on him by the encroachments and pressure of new period activities; and this is understandable. When the prestige of any organization is curtailed – the army or navy for example – a greater internal discipline, morality and study of tactics results, a greater sophistication and up-to-date-ness. In poetry this discipline means the avoidance of all the wrongly-conceived habits and tactics of the past: poetry becomes so sophisticated that it seems to know at last how it should be written and written at the very moment. The more definitely activities like religion, science, psychology and philosophy, which once existed in poetry as loose sentiment, are specialized and confined to their proper departmental technique, the more pure and sharp the technique of poetry itself seems bound to become. It ceases to be civilized in the sense of becoming more and more cultured with loose sentiment; everything in it is particular and strict. It is, indeed, as if poetry were beginning as at the beginning; using all its civilized sophistications to inaugurate a carefully calculated, censored primitiveness.

This new primitive stage, however, has been implied rather than reached in contemporary poetry. There is an increased strictness and experimenting in the construction of the poem, and an increased consciousness of what a poem should not be. But, so far, critical self-consciousness has been only a negative element in the making of poetry. It might seem that the atmosphere it has created would at least make it easier for those who are poets by nature to write well, by removing the temptation to write badly. But on the contrary it hampers them with the consideration of all the poets who have ever written or may be writing or may ever write – not only in the English language but in all languages of the world under every possible social organisation. It invents a communal poetic mind which sits over the individual poet whenever he writes; it binds him with the necessity of writing correctly in extension of the tradition, the world-tradition of poetry; and so makes poetry internally an even narrower period activity than it is forced to be by outside influences. In consequence the modernist generation is already over before its time, having counted itself out and swallowed itself up by its very efficiency – a true 'lost generation'. Already, its most 'correct' writers, such as T.S. Eliot, have become classics over the heads of the plain reader, having solved the problem of taste, or period-fashion, so strictly and accurately by themselves and having been so critically severe with themselves beforehand, that their 'acceptance' by contemporary or future plain readers has been made superfluous. Creation and critical judgement being made one act, a work has no future history with readers; it is ended when it is ended.

There has been, we see, a short and very concentrated period of carefully disciplined and self-conscious poetry. It has been followed by a pause in which no poetry of any certainty is appearing at all, an embarrassed pause after an arduous and erudite stock-taking. The next stage is not clear. But it is not impossible that there will be a resumption of less eccentric, less strained, more critically unconscious poetry, purified however by this experience of historical effort. In the period just passing no new era was begun. A climax was merely reached in criticism by a combination of sophistication and a desire for a new enlightened primitiveness. Wherever attempts at sheer newness in poetry were made they merely ended in dead movements. Yet the new feeling in criticism did achieve something. It is true in the more extreme cases that by turning into a critical philosophization of itself, poetry ceased to be poetry: it became poetically introspective philosophy. But this was perhaps necessary before poetry could be normal without being vulgar, and deal naturally with truth without being trite.

The abstract nature of poetry in this time became more important than the poetic nature of the poet; the poet tried to write something better than poetry, that is, the poetry of poetry. This laboratory phase, this complex interrelation of metaphysics and psychology blighted the creative processes wherever it was the predominant influence in the actual moments of writing. Compare the highly organized nature of Mr Eliot's criticism in its present stage with the gradual disintegration of his poetry since *The Waste Land*. The poem, indeed, gained a certain degree of freedom by the weakening of the personal relationship between it and its creator, but this freedom was, on the other hand, compromised by the forced relation of the poem to the historical period to which it accidentally belonged. The time-element was made the foundation of composition, and any poem which could not be related to its period could not be said to have any immediate critical value, and critical value was the only value by which poetry could become current. The only virtue in this critical tyranny has been to make the world in general more conscious of poetry in a specialized sense and more conversant with its processes and problems.

Briefly, the developments which account for the historical effort which has characterized the period are these. Poetry in the past had found it expedient to accept barbaric philosophical or religious 'ideas' and to cast itself within the limits imposed by them. They were barbaric ideas because they were large but definite; infinite, yet fixed by the way that they fixed man; crude and unshaded but incontestable – such as the barbaric idea of God as compared with the civilized idea of God (who is contestable if only in small points, while in barbaric God there are no small points). A barbaric view or order depends on the underlying conception of a crude, undifferentiated, infinite, all-contemporaneous time, and of a humanity co-existent with this time, a humanity consoli-dated as a mass and not composed of individuals. But when the idea of humanity as a consolidated mass was discredited by the Renaissance, the idea of gross contemporaneousness – of barbaric time – also fell to pieces. Gross time was superseded by relative time – the sense of many times going on at once; as we talk of the suburbs being five years behind the town, of the country being ten years behind the suburbs, of the colonies being ten years behind the country, of the primitive community in Africa being a thousand years behind the colonies; of an inventor being fifty years ahead of commercial recognition. Living, in fact, in different communities of time, or more than this, in different personalities of time, means the same degree of freedom that living in barbaric time does. The poet in the first case need make no historical effort because he has such perfect control over time; he need make none in the second case because time has such perfect control over him. Intense differentiation of time is romanticism, strict uniformity and stabilization of time is classicism. And it would be thought, considering that these distinctions, however contra-dictory in appearance, did not affect the poetry-making faculties in the poet himself, but only the look of poetry as a whole, that criticism could go on using them without prejudice; as verbal conveniences, for example, for describing the general character of all poetry-making during a particular period – chaotic and individualistic, or orderly and severely conventional-ized, as the case might be.

But when poetry began to lose caste among other cultural activities by its diversification of professional method and manners, modernist criti-cism found it convenient to attack this apparent lack of professional coher-ence as romantic, to insist on the traditional character of Poetry as an *art*, to reintroduce barbaric (or 'classical') time by emphasizing the element of contemporaneousness in composition. When all other activities, particu-larly those classified as scientific, were developing carefully relative time-senses, poetry now attempted to stabilize itself by reverting to an absolute time-sense. A relative time-sense in poetry was critically condemned as vulgar, unprofessional, extravagant, because much that was vulgar, falsely poetic and personally extravagant could in fact smuggle itself into poetry under the guise of relativity. It seemed to criticism hopeless and silly to attempt to repair the dignity of poetry by demanding greater personal integrity in the poet. The only practicable remedy seemed to be the decla-ration of an absolute which should bring about immediate – if artificial – order and uniformity. For this, however, an intellectual time-effort was necessary in workmanship which stultified or deformed this workman-ship. The absoluteness or barbarism of the modern poet was an unhappy strained product of sophistications.

It is one thing to observe historically that at such and such a period an idea of humanity, time and art, each consolidated as a mass, prevailed, and that a peculiarly fixed kind of perfection, as in Egyptian art, appeared in this period. But it is another thing to try to give such an idea of consolidation artificially to poetry: that it is creating not poetry but historical criticism. Such an attempt to submerge all separate poetic faculties in a single professional communism would by its simplicity be naturally pleasing to criticism; but the more simple in theory, the more complicated in practice. In a natural classical period the elaborate complexity of the personal poetic faculty – at any time nearly insoluble – becomes soluble because the demands made on it for conformity are superficial, formal, ritualistic. The poetic faculty does not only have to betray its complexity in an artificially classical period. The poetic faculty itself is called upon to invent the rituals by which it is to become formalized; to do the impossible, in other words – to invent simplicity with complexity. Which explains why there is more eccentric variety in this modernist classicism than ever appeared in romanticism. The early nineteenth-century poets wrote so similarly principally because, in spite of their individualistic propensities and their private purposes or passions, they were historically one in reacting against the same sort of classicism, and were never, moreover, able to get beyond serving this reaction; modernism, in the early nineteenth century, meant reaction. Modernism in the early twentieth century has also meant reaction, a reaction against reaction, setting itself the impossible task of individually but not individualistically creating a new classicism – a classicism founded on a philosophical theory which each poet was bound to interpret differently because he was not, so to speak, classically born.

The habit of philosophy is to observe and from observations to order conduct; to generalize from particulars and to simplify its generalities, in search of a code of perfection: and thus to minimize the reality of variation, digression, error in order to arrive at a single barbaric whole. Pure philosophy is thus always classical in spirit. When the relativist idea of personality began to break down classical social formality, pure philosophy grew more and more feeble. Philosophy could either devote itself to attacking caprice (it could fight the battle of classicism against romanticism), or it could become romantic – that is, it could allow itself to decay. This in the main is what it did, any other alternatives being generally too obscure, unhistorical and eccentric to be attractive. The chance, however, eventually came to philosophy of reviving its old authority as the science of sciences against the encroachment of modern differentiation and specialization, in a prospective alliance with poetry, which originally had first-class and general significance as the undifferentiated art of arts in a barbaric order. Poetry itself, dissatisfied with the position to which it had been reduced by the romantic nineteenth century – a position in which it seemed to be allowed to exist only by the humour and grace of science – was, of course, favourably inclined to such an alliance. And so began the new classicism.

This alliance, in the beginning only a sentimental one, needed to be legalized by some tame philosopher, some Aristotle of modernism who would make the new barbarism respectable and provide it with a coherent argument and a vocabulary. Such a person was found in T.E. Hulme,[1] who was killed in 1917 before he had developed a well-defined system of aesthetics; who had, however, left enough fragments to be accepted as gospel by a generation starved for suitable philosophico-literary dogma. Hulme was, naturally, a man disappointed with philosophy since the Renaissance. It was no longer 'pure'; and, searching for a way to purify it, he stumbled on the need which art – painting or sculpture or poetry – had to be philosophically organized and corrected. His concept of the absolute (the search for the absolute is the chief concern, as we have seen, of 'pure' philosophy) derided any idea of relativity: it emphasized the general principle of poetic co-ordination; but the general principle rather than the form in which co-ordination should take place. It is significant that the few poems Hulme wrote himself fall under the period classification popular in his time, Imagism. In his desire to coordinate and correctly generalize, Hulme fell into the familiar philosophical confusion – the confusion of analogy. Art, for instance, is a philosophical term invented for the convenience of classification, not a term that poetry would naturally invent for itself, though painting and sculpture, on the other hand, might. To the philosopher, however, the most accurate term is the most general rather than the most particular, and so to Hulme a common co-ordination of the 'arts' of painting, sculpture and poetry seemed possible and necessary. The fundamental fallacy in such an attempted co-ordination appears with the difficulty which poetry has to face in entering a new artificially barbaric era. In painting and sculpture neither colour nor stone had been intrinsically affected by the romantic works in which they had been used. To escape the Renaissance, painting and sculpture merely had to revert to barbaric modes – negroid, Oceanic, Aztec, Egyptian, Chinese, archaic Greek – creating modern forms as if in primitive times; forms primitive, obedient to the conventions which they accepted, therefore final, absolute, 'abstract'. But poetry could not seemingly submit itself to an *as if*, because its expressive medium, language, had been intrinsically affected not only by the works in which it had been used but also by all the non-poetic uses of which language is capable. This difference between poetry and more regular arts points to a variance in poetry and suggests the probable falsity of all philosophical generalizations on art. The falsity is the falsity of analogy; yet analogy is the strongest philosophical instrument of co-ordination. Since poetry as an art is not sufficiently regular, not sufficiently professional, it is to become so by being made more sculptural or pictorial, by having grafted on it the values and methods of more professional arts.

Language, therefore, had to be reorganized, used as if afresh, cleansed of its experience: to be as 'pure' and 'abstract' as colour or stone. Words had to be reduced to their least historical value; the purer they could be made, the more eternally immediate and present they would be; they could express the absolute at the same time as they expressed the age. Or this was at any rate the logical effect of scientific barbarism if taken literally.

Gertrude Stein is perhaps the only artisan of language who has ever succeeded in practising scientific barbarism literally. Her words are primitive in the sense that they are bare, immobile, mathematically placed, abstract: so primitive indeed that the theorists of the new barbarism have repudiated her work as a romantic vulgar barbarism, expressing the personal crudeness of a mechanical age rather than a refined historical effort to restore a lost absolute to a community of co-ordinated poets. Mr Eliot has said of her work that

> it is not improving, it is not amusing, it is not interesting, it is not good for one's mind. But its rhythms have a peculiar hypnotic power not met with before. It has a kinship with the saxophone. If this is the future then the future is, as it very likely is, of the barbarians. But this is the future in which we ought not to be interested.

Mr Eliot was for the moment speaking for civilization. He was obliged to do this because it seemed suddenly impossible to reconcile the philosophy of the new barbarism with the historical state of the poetic mind and with the professional dignity of poetry which the new barbarism was invented to restore: a sincere attempt to do so was at once crude and obscure like the work of Miss Stein. Except for such whole-hog literalness as hers, professional modernist poetry has lacked the co-ordination which professional modernist criticism implies: and this contradiction between criticism and workmanship makes it incoherent. It has been too busy being civilized, varied, intellectual – too socially and poetically energetic – to take advantage of the privileged consistency of the new barbarism.

Criticism has been so busy talking about criticism (criticism has been so philosophical, that is) that it has had little either relevant or helpful to say about poetry itself – not poetry as a philosophical abstraction but as *poems* and as the poets, who are potential poems. Though objecting to the romantic disorganization in which there are 'beauties' instead of beauty, it has nevertheless had no absolute canon of beauty to offer to the classical poetry it has wished to inspire, but only an undifferentiated satire of beauties and a counsel to suppress the obvious because the obvious is often romantically, personally and therefore sentimentally beautiful. It has insisted that a fixed dogmatic abstract beauty is the only possible system for poetic perfection and yet has had nothing better to offer than a few elementary suggestions and clues such as that 'golden lad' is a beautiful classical phrase and 'golden youth' a beautiful romantic phrase (Hulme).

'The thing has got so bad now', wrote Hulme, 'that a poem which is all dry and hard, a properly Classical poem, would not be considered poetry at all. They cannot see that accurate description is a legitimate object of verse.'[2]

Hulme was asking a forward-looking twentieth-century generation to arm itself against romanticism, an early nineteenth-century bogey, or against the Renaissance bogey itself. He wanted to oppose a sophisticated levity to the idiot-headed seriousness of romanticism, a classical fancy to a romantic imagination; but in practice the opposition was of a heavy, rigid, originally dull seriousness to a rather ingenuous sometimes successful often droll though perhaps eventually dull seriousness. 'Wonder must cease to be wonder', Hulme complained: but in the beginning while there is wonder there is always the chance of a surprise success in romanticism. In classicism, which sets out with a very limited, certain intention, there is never the chance of success in this sense. If romantic freakishness generally quiets down to triteness and is for this reason dull, classical freakishness is fixed and eternal from the outset; and thus eternally dull.

The most serious flaw in poetic modernism has been its attachment to originality. The modernist poet has not been able to forsake originality however directly it might contradict the classical idea of discipline; and the effect of discipline has therefore only been to make originality more original. As originality increased and as modernist poetry consequently became more and more romantic, the contradiction between it and modernist criticism was intensified. Criticism became more dogmatic and unreal, poetry more eccentric and chaotic. Classicism and originality could only be reconciled in the invention of an original type, were this possible, of a form entirely new, peculiar, particular, uncommon, and yet universal, general, common; when once invented, as old as the hills. But obviously the invention of an original type in personal embodiments can get no further than an earnest caricature of the ordinary, as in Joyce's Leopold Blum [*sic*], or T.S. Eliot's Prufrock and other low types; no further certainly in mechanical embodiments. Originality becomes an attack on a degenerated ordinary.

The problem was further complicated by the insistence (as in Hulme) on the 'direct communication' by which originality was to make itself effective; direct communication referring to an immediate ideal intelligibility. But since language had been tainted by false experiences, much of the energy of this originality had to be devoted to an attack on the ordinary language of communication; and direct communication, like the original type, could get no further than an earnest caricature of ordinary language. This is from Mr Eliot's most recent stage:

DUSTY: Do you know London well, Mr Krumpacker?
KLIPSTEIN: No, we have never been here before.

KRUMPACKER: We hit this town last night for the first time.
KLIPSTEIN : And I certainly hope it won't be the last time.
DORIS: You like London, Mr Klipstein?
KRUMPACKER: Do we like London? Do we like London!
    Do we like London!! Eh, what Klip?
KLIPSTEIN : Say, Miss – er – uh! London's swell.
    We like London fine.
KRUMPACKER: Perfectly slick.
DUSTY: Why don't you come and live here then?[3]

But caricature is romantic. Miss Edith Sitwell's poetry is perhaps the clearest instance of the romantic caricature of language that critical classicism is obliged to take under its wing.

Another aspect of the same general flaw is the incompatibility of the 'things' which were supposed to be revealed in the direct communication ('things' in which apparently the first principle inheres) with the talent of the artist to see things 'as no one else sees them'. The barbaric absolute, the divine source of things, wherever it has prevailed naturally, has always been marked by a penetrating obviousness. The pyramids are penetratingly obvious, so much so that they nearly make the absolute synonymous with obviousness.

But a belief in the fundamental obviousness or absoluteness of 'things' is inconsistent with a belief in an eccentricity in things which the artist is supposed to reveal: and a belief in the fundamental obviousness or ordinariness of a mass humanity, adhering personally to the same absolute to which 'things' adhere, is inconsistent with a belief in the creative originality which is to reveal the eccentricity latent in obviousness to this mass humanity equipped only to seize the obvious. The only possible way for creative originality to be consistent with mass humanity is by some mystical process in which the artist is chosen as the inspired instrument of mass-ordinariness to reveal 'things' which he sees as no one else sees because everything is so obvious and everyone so ordinary that one does not ordinarily 'see' the obviousness and ordinariness unless one is possessed of creative originality.

While such a philosophical tangle was forcing modernist poets into an unwitting romanticism, Gertrude Stein went on – and kept going on for twenty years – quietly, patiently and successfully practising an authentic barbarism; quite by herself and without encouragement. Her only fault, from the practical point of view, was that she took primitiveness too literally, so literally that she made herself incomprehensible to the exponents of primitivism – to everyone for that matter. She exercised perfect discipline over her creative faculties and she was able to do this because she was completely without originality. Everybody being unable to understand her thought that this was because she was too original or was trying hard to be original. But she was only divinely inspired in ordinariness: her creative originality, that is, was original only because it was so grossly, so humanly, all-inclusively ordinary. She used language automatically to record pure ultimate obviousness. She made it capable of direct communication not by caricaturing contemporary language – attacking decadence with decadence – but by purging it completely of its false experiences. None of the words Miss Stein uses ever had experience. They are no older than the use she makes of them, and she has been herself no older than her age conceived barbarically.

> Put it there in there where they have it
> Put it there in there there and they halve it
> Put it there in there there and they have it
> Put it there in there there and they halve it

These words have had no history, and the design that Miss Stein has made of them is literally 'abstract' and mathematical because they are commonplace words without any hidden etymology; they are mechanical and not eccentric. If they possess originality it is that of mass-automatism.

Miss Stein in her *Composition as Explanation* has written:

> Nothing changes from generation to generation except the thing seen, and that makes a composition.[4]

Her admission that there are generations does not contradict her belief in an unvarying first principle. Time does not vary, only the sense of time.

> Automatically with the acceptance of the time-sense comes the recognition of the beauty, and once the beauty is accepted the beauty never fails anyone.

Beauty has no history, according to Miss Stein, nor has time: only the time-sense has history. When the time-sense acclaims a beauty that was not at first recognized, the finality of this beauty is at once established; it is as though it had never been denied. All beauty is equally final. The reason why the time-sense if realized reveals the finality or classicalness of beauty, is that it is the feeling of beginning, of primitiveness and freshness which is each age's or each generation's version of time.

> Beginning again and again and again explaining composition and time is a natural thing. It is understood by this time that everything is the same except composition and time, composition and the time of the composition and the time in the composition.

Originality of vision, then, is invented, she holds, not by the artist but by the collective time-sense. The artist does not see things 'as no one else sees them'. He sees those objective 'things' by which the age repeatedly verifies and represents the absolute. He sees concretely and expressibly what everyone else possessed of the time-sense has an unexpressed intuition of: the time-sense may not be generally and particularly universal; but this does not mean that the artist's vision, even his originality of vision, is less collective or less universal.

> The composition is the thing seen by everyone living in the living they are doing, they are the composing of the composition that at the time they are living is the composition of the time in which they are living. It is that that makes living a thing they are doing. Nothing else is different, of that almost anyone can be certain. The time when and the time of and the time in that composition is the natural phenomena of that composition and of that perhaps everyone can be certain.

All this Gertrude Stein has understood and executed logically because of the perfect simplicity of her mind. Believing implicitly in an absolute, she has not been bothered to doubt the bodily presence of a first principle in her own time. Since she is alive and everybody around her seems to be alive, of course there is an acting first principle, there is composition. This first principle provides a theme for composition because there is time, and everybody, and the beginning again and again and again, and composition. In her primitive good-humour she has not found it necessary to trouble about defining the theme. The theme is to be inferred from the composition. The composition is clear because the language means nothing but what it means through her using of it. The composition is final because it is 'a more and more continuous present including more and more using of everything and continuing more and more beginning and beginning and beginning'. She creates this atmosphere of continuousness principally by her progressive use of the tenses of verbs, by intense and unflagging repetitiousness and an artificially assumed and regulated child-mentality: the child's time-sense is so vivid that an occurrence is always consecutive to itself, it goes on and on, it has been going on and on, it will be going on and on (a child does perhaps feel the passage of time, does to a certain extent feel itself older than it was yesterday because yesterday was already tomorrow even while it was yesterday).

This is from Miss Stein's *Saints in Season*:

> Saint –
> A Saint
> Saint and very well I thank you.
> Two in bed.
> Two in bed.
> Yes two in bed.
> They had eaten.
> Two in bed.

They had eaten.
Two in bed.

She says weaken.
If she said.
She said two in bed.
She said they had eaten.
She said yes two in bed.
She said weaken.

Do not acknowledge to me that seven are said that a Saint and
seven that it is said that a saint in seven that there is said to be
a saint in seven.

Now as to illuminations.

They are going to illuminate and everyone is to put into their
windows their most beautiful object and everyone will say and
the streets will be crowded everyone will say look at it.

They do say look at it.

To look at it. They will look at it. They will say look at it.

Repetition has the effect of breaking down the possible historical senses
still inherent in the words. So has the infantile jingle of rhyme and asso-
nance. So has the tense-changing of verbs, because restoring to them their
significance as a verbal mathematics of motion. Miss Stein's persistence in
her own continuousness is astonishing: this is how she wrote in 1926, and
in 1906. She has achieved a continuous present by always beginning again,
for this keeps everything different and everything the same. It creates
duration but makes it absolute by preventing anything from happening in
the duration.

And after that what changes what changes after that, after that what
changes and what changes after that and after that and what changes
and after that and what changes after that.

The composition has a theme because it has no theme. The words are a
self-pursuing, tail-swallowing series and are thus thoroughly abstract.
They achieve what Hulme called but could not properly envisage – not
being acquainted, it seems, with Miss Stein's work – a 'perpendicular', an
escape from the human horizontal plane. They contain no reference; no
meaning, no caricatures, no jokes, no despairs. They are ideally automatic,
creating one another. The only possible explanation of lines like the
following is that one word or combination of words creates the next.

Anyhow means furls furls with a chance chance with a change
change with as strong strong with as will will with as sign sign with

as west west with as most most with as in in with as by by with as
change change with as reason reason to be lest lest they did when
when they did for for they did there and then. Then does not cele-
brate the there and then.

This is repetition and continuousness and beginning again and again and
again.

Nothing that we have said here should be understood as disrespectful
to Gertrude Stein. She has had courage, clarity, sincerity, simplicity. She
has created a human mean in language, a mathematical equation of ordi-
nariness which leaves one with a tender respect for that changing and
unchanging slowness that is humanity and Gertrude Stein.

Miss Stein's sterilization of words until they are exhausted of history
and meaning must be distinguished from sophisticated abandonment of
meaning in the midst of a feverish pursuit of meaning, a blasé renounce-
ment of significance to confusion. The following from a poem by Mr
Sacheverell Sitwell is an instance of such a renouncement:

> Y.   '... a thundering motor
>   drumming its persistence on the giggling air.
>   Persistence, and I mean the everlasting life ...
>   And in fact the rolling drums should rattle in the square
>   before a thick curtain that no eye can pierce
>   And trumpets should sound out from all the square-set
>   towers ...
>   Persistence, I said – I mean the giggling air,
>   rather I should say I mean the giggling drums
>   or rolling drums: persistence – and I mean the ...'
> X   '... persistent air? ...'
> Y.   'No, no: Persistence, and I mean the giggling air;
>   I meant to talk about the everlasting life,
>   Until you muddled me and made me stop.'

Miss Stein's tidy processes must also be distinguished from the delib-
erate untidying of language to give it more meaning, more history, more
dramatic excitement, as in James Joyce's *Ulysses:*

> The Quaker librarian, quaking, tiptoed in, quake, his mask,
> quake, with haste, quake, quack
> Door closed. Cell. Day.
> They list. Three. They.
> I you he they
> Come, mess.[5]

This needs only to be accurately read in the rather complicated
context, to be tidied into its context, so to speak, to make obvious sense.

Even the following poem by e.e. cummings is neither pure nor abstract,
but realistic, wilfully linked to history.

> life hurl my
> yes, crumbles hand (ful released conarefetti) ev eryflitter, inga.
>
>   where
> mil (lions of aflickf) litter ing brightmillion ofS hurl; edindodg: ing
> whom are Eyes shy-dodge is bright cruMbshandful, quick-hurl
>   edinwho
> Is flittercrumbs, fluttercrimbs are floatfallin,g; allwhere:
> a: crimflitterinish, is arefloatsis ingfallall! mil, shy, milbrightlions
> my (hurl flicker handful
> in) dodging are shybrigHteyes is crum bs(alll)if, ey, Es*

It is an attempt to represent, in the manner of the early futurists, the
book of life torn into a million fragments as small as confetti, the bread of
life crumbled nervously under the disorganizing influence of shy bright
eyes, bright like the million stars. A most romantic theme and a most
romantic treatment, but Mr cummings was never apprenticed to the new
barbarism; he is a freebooter.

One way the modernist poet has of keeping romantically alive in this
classicism, whether or not he goes as far as Gertrude Stein's automatism,
is by carefully avoiding a theme. When Mr Allen Tate says, for instance,
in his introduction to Hart Crane's *White Buildings* that Mr Crane has not
yet found a theme to match his poetic vision, he is really explaining that
Mr Crane is preserving his vision from a theme, that his vision is reacting
romantically against contemporary classicism. Hart Crane's poems reveal
many of the qualities peculiar to enforced romantics: it is noticeable that
Mr Tate allies him with other enforced romantics – Poe, Rimbaud, Edith
Sitwell, T.S. Eliot, Wallace Stevens – though Mr Crane has sufficient
dignity to be able to dispense with such literary support. Much of the
intensity of his poetry – intensity often protracted into strain – is due to
the conflict between discipline and originality. The result is a compromise
in the mysticism of rhetoric:

> Bind us in time, O Seasons clear, and awe.
> O minstrel galleons of Carib fire,
> Bequeath us to no earthly shore until
> Is answered in the vortex of our grave
> The seal's wide spindrift gaze toward paradise.[6]

---

* It has been found impracticable in the printing of this poem to set it vertically
on the page, as it was originally printed – to suggest a downward fluttering
movement.

This romantic mysticism of rhetoric – romantic because discipline
merges with originality rather than originality with discipline – results in
a mysticism of geography, not to say of subjects. The movements of his
poems are the fluctuations of surfaces: they give a sea-sense of externality:
the moon, the sea, frost, tropical horizons, the monotony of continuous
exploration. Their direction is classical; that is, they tend to become
mechanical by a sort of ecstasy of technical excellence:

> O I have known metallic paradises
> Where cuckoos clucked to finches
> Above the deft catastrophes of drums.
> While titters hailed the groans of death
> Beneath gyrating awnings I have seen
> The incunabula of the divine grotesque.
> This music has a reassuring way.[7]

And here he would rest if he did not, in his restraint 'have extreame',
have what he calls 'fine collapses' –

> We can evade you and all else but the heart:
> What blame to us if the heart live on?[8]

By such fine collapses, composition just manages to escape with its life
– beginning again and again and again in spite of its posthumous
classicism.

Notes

Chapter I
1. This statement foreshadows the main body of argument in *A Pamphlet Against Anthologies*.
2. Louis Untermeyer's *Modern American Poetry* was first published in 1919, and went through several editions in the 1920s. This anthology is the target of criticism in *A Pamphlet*.
3. Georgianism and Imagism. These two early-century 'movements' are given greater scrutiny in Chapter V 'Modern Poetry and Dead Movements'. A number of Graves' poems were collected in Volumes III, IV and V of Edward Marsh's *Georgian Poetry*.
4. This poem is from e.e. cummings' collection *Tulips and Chimneys* (1923).
5. Remy de Gourmont (Riding and Graves misuse the acute accent) was an important link between French Symbolism and early Anglo-American modernism. Gourmont's prose and poetry had a significant influence on many modernist writers, including Ezra Pound (who translated Gourmont' s *Natural Philosophy of Love*), T.S. Eliot and Richard Aldington.
6. Rabindranath Tagore (1861–1941), Bengali poet and Nobel Prize winner (1913). His popularity was such that in 1925 he was included in the series of single-author volumes *The Augustan Books of Poetry*, edited by Edward Thompson. This series also included such 'popular' poets as Robert Bridges, Keats, Shelley, G.K. Chesterton, and Hilaire Belloc. Chesterton and Belloc are also mentioned here as 'influences' on the ironic 'Sunset Piece'. The related series *The Augustan Books of Modern Poetry* is mentioned in *A Pamphlet Against Anthologies*.
7. '… a time of popular though superficial education'. Riding and Graves are pointing to the generations of readers created in large part as a result of the changes to educational access brought about by the Elementary Education Act of 1870 and subsequent legislation.
8. The line is taken from Paul Valéry's 'Fragments du Narcisse', from *Charmes* (1922).
9. These lines are from Thomas Gray's poem 'The Bard. A Pindaric Ode'.
10. A reference to Rimbaud's poem of synaesthesia, 'Voyelles'.

Chapter II

1. These lines are from Paul Valéry's poem 'Ebauche d'un Serpent', from *Charmes*.

2. From Valéry, 'Fragments du Narcisse'.

3. These much-quoted lines are from Tennyson's *The Princess* (VII, third song). Riding and Graves slightly misquote – the line is properly "And murmuring of innumerable bees'.

4. The reference is to Valéry's *La Soirée avec Monsieur Teste* (1896).

5. Poe wrote about poetry and poetics in his essays 'The Poetic Principle' (1850), and 'The Philosophy of Composition' (1846), and his influence on Baudelaire, Mallarmé and Valéry was considerable. Poe's influence on the French is discussed by Laura Riding in her essay 'The Facts in the Case of Monsieur Poe', *Contemporaries and Snobs* (1928).

6. Hart Crane (1899–1932). Riding and Crane had been friends in New York. 'Passage' is from his collection *White Buildings* (1926).

7. The quotation is from the Second Book of Samuel, Chapter I, Verses 19 and 20.

8. Graves had in 1925 planned to collaborate with Eliot (at that time editor of *The Criterion*) on a book provisionally entitled 'Untraditional Elements in Poetry'. See Richard Perceval Graves, *Robert Graves. The Years with Laura 1926–40*, pp.23–24, and Paul O'Prey (ed.) *In Broken Images: Selected Letters of Robert Graves 1914–1946*, pp.161–2.

Chapter III

1. These lines are from cummings' poem 'because', *is 5* (1926).

2. This line is from cummings' poem 'the waddling', in *Tulips and Chimneys*. The line should properly read 'the/frivolous taximan p(ee)ps on his whistle'.

3. From 'weazened Irrefutable unastonished' (*is 5*).

4. The editorial and interpretative perspective on Shakespeare's Sonnets developed by Riding and Graves in this chapter has been the focus of much subsequent critical interest. For an extensive critique, and criticism, of their methodology and conclusions, see the 'Commentary' to Stephen Booth's *Shakespeare's Sonnets* (1977). For a very different evaluation of the importance of this chapter see Jonathan Bate, *The Genius of Shakespeare* (1997). Bate considers the Riding/Graves analysis and its place in the history of literary scholarship, particularly with reference to the revolutionary methods of Empsonian criticism.

Chapter IV

1. cummings' poem 'Among', from *is 5*.

2. Riding and Graves here paraphrase and quote from Robert Bridges' edition of the *Poems of Gerard Manley Hopkins* (1918). They later quote from Hopkins' sonnet beginning 'My own heart let me more have pity on …', and from Bridges' introduction.

3. Carl Sandburg (1878–1967), John Drinkwater (1882–1937), John Crowe Ransom (1888–1974). John Drinkwater was collected alongside Graves in *Georgian Poetry*. Laura Riding had been in contact with John Crowe Ransom and other 'Fugitive' poets in her American years shortly before the writing of this book.
4. Sandburg's poem 'Mamie' is from his collection *Chicago Poems* (1916).
5. 'Captain Carpenter' by John Crowe Ransom. This poem was published in *The Fugitive*, Vol III, No. 1 (February 1924).

Chapter V

1. These lines are from John Drinkwater's poem 'The Fires of God', from *Poems of Love and Earth* (1912).
2. Marianne Moore, 'To A Steam Roller'.
3. Marianne Moore, 'Poetry'. Moore was later to prefer a radically shorter version of this poem (Marianne Moore, *Complete Poems*, 1968).
4. Alan Seeger (1886–1916) Riding and Graves misspell his name, American poet of the First World War.
5. Rupert Brooke's earlier poems were included in Volumes One and Two of *Georgian Poetry* and his war poetry achieved widespread fame, especially through the posthumous wartime collection *1914 and Other Poems*.
6. The lines are from H.D.'s poem 'Night', in *Sea Garden* (1916).
7. The lines are from Emily Dickinson's poem 'Victory comes late'.
8. Two quotations from H.D.: from 'Pursuit' and 'Pygmalion'.

Chapter VI

1. The first two stanzas of 'The Rugged Black of Anger' by Laura Riding. There are several textual variations here from the text in the 1938 collection of Riding's poems. See also *The Poems of Laura Riding* (Carcanet, 1980).
2. The first stanzas of Ezra Pound's poem 'Ballad of the Goodly Fere', first collected in *Exultations* (1909). Graves' antipathy towards Pound is well documented.

Chapter VII

1. The first two stanzas of Wordsworth's 'We Are Seven'.
2. Lines from John Keats, *Endymion*, Book II, lines 446–453.
3. Lines from Tennyson's early poem 'We are Free'.
4. Lines from Robert Browning's 'The Flight of the Duchess'.
5. Lines from Rupert Brooke's poem 'A Channel Passage'.
6. From Wilfred Owen, 'Dulce et Decorum Est'. The last two lines of this excerpt are misquoted, and should read 'Obscene as cancer, bitter as the cud / Of vile, incurable sores on innocent tongues'. Graves had encountered Owen at Craiglockhart hospital during the war.
7. From *The Waste Land*, section II 'A Game of Chess'.
8. From Wallace Stevens' poem 'Mandolin and Liqueurs' (1923).

9. A.E. (George Russell), 'Magnificence', from *Voices of the Stones* (1925).

10. From Eliot's *The Waste Land*, section II 'A Game of Chess'. Riding and Graves misquote the line 'Stirring the pattern on the coffered ceiling'.

11. Sir James Frazer *The Golden Bough* (12 vols., 1890–1915). Eliot acknowledges his debt to Frazer in his 'Notes on *The Waste Land*': 'To another work of anthropology I am indebted profoundly; I mean *The Golden Bough* …'

12. Ezra Pound, *Lustra* (first published by Elkin Matthews in 1916). Graves in particular disliked what he viewed as Pound's poor scholarship, a view most clearly expressed in Graves' satirical essay 'Dr Syntax and Mr Pound'.

13. William Wordsworth, from 'The Waggoner', Canto First.

14. Lines from cummings' poem 'even if all desires things moments be', collected in *is 5*.

15. Lines from Edith Sitwell's poem 'The Sleeping Beauty' (Section XVI).

16. Siegfried Sassoon and Edmund Blunden were close friends of Graves. Blunden produced an important edition of John Clare's poetry in 1920. Graves wrote the introduction to Frank Prewett's *Collected Poems* in 1964.

17. From Sassoon's poem 'Founder's Feast'.

18. The first stanza of Ezra Pound's 'The Garden', from *Lustra* (1916).

19. 'Steamboats, Viaducts, and Railways' is one of Wordsworth's Itinerary poems of 1833, and was first published in *Yarrow Revisited, and Other Poems* (1835).

20. From Emily Dickinson's poem 'The Railway Train'.

21. John Davidson's 'Song of a Train', collected in *Ballads and Songs* (1894).

22. These lines are from Marianne Moore's poem 'People's Surroundings'.

Chapter VIII

1. The poems from which these extracts are taken are as follows: P.B. Shelley, 'Julian and Maddalo. A conversation'; Byron, 'The Lament of Tasso'; Keats, 'Lines Written in the Highlands after a Visit to Burns' Country'; Martin Farquhar Tupper (1810–1889), 'COLOMBA', from *Three Hundred Sonnets* (1860); Wordsworth, 'In the Frith of Clyde, Ailsa Crag (During an Eclipse of the Sun, July 17)'; Coleridge, 'Lines Written in the Album at Elbingerade, in the Hartz Forest'.

2. The quotations are variously from W.H. Davies, 'A Great Time', 'Christ, the Man', and 'The Inquest'. By 1928 the latter text is included in Davies' *Collected Poems* (1928).

3. William Carlos Williams first published the poem 'Struggle of wings' in *The Dial* in 1926. It was described at that stage as an 'incomplete poem', and one that Williams would later reprint with major emendations.

4. Lines from Frank Prewett's poem 'Seeing my Love but Lately Come', from *A Rural Scene* (1924).

5. The David Davidson poem 'Alla Stoccata', from which these lines are taken, was published in *The Fugitive*, Vol. II, No. 8.

6. Osbert Sitwell's 'English Gothic' is a section of the longer work *Friday Evening, Saturday Afternoon, and Songs for Sundays at Home and Abroad*.

7. Stanzas one and three of T.S. Eliot's 'Whispers of Immortality'.
8. Allen Tate was a regular contributor to *The Fugitive*, and a poet with whom Riding had a close relationship.
9. The lines are variously from: Richard Aldington, 'Epigrams', taken from *Images* (1915); William Carlos Williams, 'Epitaph', from *Sour Grapes* (1921); Ezra Pound, 'Alba', from *Lustra* (1916); Wallace Stevens, 'Thirteen Ways of Looking at a Blackbird', from *Harmonium* (1923).
10. Ezra Pound's 'Papyrus', from *Lustra* (1916).
11. Isaac Rosenberg (1890–1918). A selection of his poems and letters were introduced by Laurence Binyon in 1922. 'Moses: A Play 1916' is a verse drama.

Chapter IX

1. Edith Sitwell. This, and subsequent quotations, are from 'Façade' (1923).
2. Riding and Graves are approximating Iago's song from Act II of *Othello*.
3. John Gay (1685–1732). This is a song from Scene I of *The Mohocks*. A Tragi-Comical Farce (1712). Joseph Sheridan Le Fanu (1814–1873). *The Poems of Joseph Sheridan Le Fanu* (1896) were edited by Alfred Perceval Graves (Robert Graves' father). The full title of the poem from which the extract is taken is 'ABHAIN AU BHUIDEIL. Address of a Drunkard to a Bottle of Whiskey'. Riding and Graves miss out some punctuation marks:

    > 'Oh! terrible darling,
    > How have you sought me,
    > Enchanted, and caught me?
    > See, now, where you've brought me –
    > To sleep by the road-side, and dress out in rags'

    John Masefield. An extract from his long poem 'The Everlasting Mercy', postscripted 'Great Hampden 1911'.
4. This is cummings' poem 'death is more than' from *is 5*.
5. This and the following passage is from 'Façade'.
6. Taken from the Scylla and Charybdis section (9) of Joyce's *Ulysses*.
7. The 'contemporary poet' is of course Robert Graves himself. These are lines from his poem 'Pure Death'.

Chapter X

1. Riding writes at length on Hulme and Stein in *Contemporaries and Snobs*, and this concluding chapter draws on material used in Riding's essay. Stein's relationship with Riding and Graves was both personal and professional, and Stein was to publish *An Acquaintance with Description* with the Seizin Press in 1929.
2. The lines are quoted from Hulme's much-anthologised and widely influential 'Romanticism and Classicism' (published in *Speculations*, ed. Herbert Read, 1924). See also Patrick McGuinness' introduction to T.E. Hulme's *Selected Writings* (Carcanet, 1998).

3. T.S. Eliot, from *Sweeney Agonistes*, 'Fragment of a Prologue'.

4. Gertrude Stein's 'lecture' *Composition as Explanation* was published by the Hogarth Press in 1926.

5. This passage is again from the Scylla and Charybdis section of *Ulysses*. The cummings poem is from *is 5*, and, as the footnote indicates, the poem is originally printed sideways on the page.

6. Hart Crane, the fifth stanza of 'Voyages II', taken from his collection *White Buildings* (1926).

7. Hart Crane, from 'For the Marriage of Faustus and Helen', in *White Buildings*.

8. Hart Crane, from 'Chaplinesque', also in *White Buildings*.

LAURA RIDING and ROBERT GRAVES

A PAMPHLET
AGAINST ANTHOLOGIES

Contents

Foreword

AT the beginning of a previous work, *A Survey of Modernist Poetry*, we carefully described it as a word-by-word collaboration. We did this because it was obvious to us that the vulgarity of a certain type of English reviewer would be encouraged by the combined circumstances that the first author was a woman and that the second was a man whose name was perhaps better known to him than that of the first; and because we were interested to see how far this vulgarity would persist in spite of our statement.

We therefore take a statistical pleasure in listing the following papers which succumbed, through their reviewers, to this vulgarity:

1. The *Glasgow Herald*, which in one notice referred to the book as 'Mr Graves' book'; in another, thought it proper 'to give predominance to the male partner'.

2. *The South Wales Argus*, which also simplified the discussion by referring to the book as 'Mr Graves' book'.

3. *The Guardian*, the same.

4. *The Nottingham Journal*, which broke down after the formal opening sentence.

5. *The Liverpool Post*, which, 'to be chivalrous', decided that it must 'lay the blame on the masculine author'.

6. *The Gownsman* (the Cambridge undergraduate paper), which displayed a personal vulgarity possible only to adolescence and Cambridge united.

7. *The Oxford Magazine*, a donnish fortnightly, which, in contrast with the more representative Oxford undergraduate weeklies, followed the provincial example.

Shall we add, in anticipation of fresh statistical material, that this is also a word-by-word collaboration?

THE AUTHORS

CHAPTER I

The True Anthology and the Trade Anthology

IN every language and at all periods, loose poems or fragments of poems are found that cannot be formally classified among the collected works of any known author, or bound up with other anonymous material forming an historical unit for which a legendary author has been invented; or yet, because of their character and number, be given each the distinction of separate publication. Popular ballads, unless forming part of a single cycle, epigrams, epitaphs, squibs, stray lyrics and even longer poems that have irretrievably lost author and date, may be fittingly united in a volume of nonclassifiable verse; and this is always a legitimate use of the anthology.

The anthology of the days before cheap books were printed was justified as a secure portfolio for short poems that might otherwise have been lost: short poems in confederacy being as safe from loss as a drama or epic equalling their combined length. When at the beginning of the first century before Christ Meleager compiled his *Crown* of epigrammatic verse as a gift for one Diocles, 'weaving in the lilies of Anyte, the scarlet gopher of Antipater, the narcissus of Melanippides, the aromatic rush of Perseus, the young vine-branch of Simonides', and so on, he was doing a service both to Diocles and to the poems, which were fugitive pieces not obtainable at every public library or copying-school. Further, this compilation was made without prejudice to the longer poems by the authors represented in the anthology, or by other authors, which Diocles might obtain in manuscripts of formal length. Meleager added epigrams of his own to the *Crown*, but none written by any contemporary except those of his famous neighbour Antipater, and these probably for friendship's sake only; the poems of other contemporaries were left to their own fate. The *Crown* was an anthology in the sense that A.H. Bullen's *Lyrics from the Elizabethan Song Books* is an anthology: it was a collection of flowers, but from remote or not readily accessible gardens. But Meleager was a poet exercising an independent personal taste, Bullen a literary connoisseur. Although Diocles was informed at the end of the 'proem' that the garland was not merely a personal gift to him but a common gift to all lovers of poetry, this was rather a rhetorical flourish than an acknowledgement of responsibility to a poetry-consuming public, such as Bullen must have felt.

Diocles circulated the manuscript: it was copied and much admired. A hundred years later one Philippus added to it and brought it up to date, establishing it as a Classic, an authoritative collection of short poems of a certain character. Where Meleager had sensibly used a mere alphabetical arrangement of first lines, Philippus set the bad example to posterity of arranging the poems in subject-categories. By the time of the Antonines the use of anthologies seems to have been widespread; for instance, in the grave of a legionary of that period, in Egypt, a collection of regimental marching songs has been found. In the reign of the Emperor Justinian appeared Agathias, with the sinister surname 'Scholasticus', the first thoroughgoing example of what we may call the trade-anthologist. He made a collection of new epigrams modelled on the revised *Crown*, now more than a Classic, a required text-book: which signalled the end of the anthology as a casual portfolio of poems. It began with a servile panegyric of the Emperor, followed Philippus' vicious system of classification and included many contemporary exercises in the style of the early poems, even pseudo-dedicatory epigrams to the long-superseded Greek Gods. Agathias' anthology became a popular reciter for use in the intervals between the courses of banquets, and at the same time a *Models for Verse-writers*; for Classical Greek was now a merely literary language and any verse-writing for an occasion amatory, funerary or convivial looked to the anthology for authority.

Yet Philippus and even Agathias did not find it necessary to give an appearance of 'solidity' to their collections by slipping in, say, three or four nicely rounded incidents from the *Odyssey* or *Iliad*, a selected Homeric hymn, a seasonal excerpt from Hesiod, a messenger's speech of Æschylus', a neat piece of stichomythia from Sophocles, a couple of Euripidean choruses, three odes of Pindar's, major poems by Sappho and Alcæus; perhaps also the 'funeral speech of Pericles' or a purple patch from one of Demosthenes' *Philippics*, with an editorial comment: 'Though written in prose this may also be accounted great poetry.' The anthology, though it had degenerated into a text-book of occasional lyrics, had not yet turned into the second-hand clothes shop of poetry.

What has been said about the Greek anthologies applies nearly enough to the English ones. There have been portfolio anthologies of verse from the beginning of English literature: such as ninth- and tenth-century anthologies of charms and riddles, fourteenth-century anthologies of carols and lyrics and the famous 'Percy folio' of ballads – all of these, however, private manuscript collections not multiplied at the copyist-schools: the trade anthology only developed with the advance of printing. Tottel's *Miscellany* of 1557 has at first sight much to recommend it. Tottel, a bookseller, collected the fugitive verses of court-poets of the

elder generation, most of them dead, which might otherwise have been
lost: they were poems which, written in the then new Italianate style, had
been intended merely for manuscript circulation in the limited world of
the travelled nobility. But the *Miscellany* went into eight editions in thirty
years, its subscribers being clearly the country relations and wealthy
would-be neighbours of this fashionable poetry-reading society; and then
became a Classic and a model for such later Elizabethan trade-anthologies
as *England's Helicon*, first published in 1600, which claimed to be a stan-
dard collection of contemporary lyrics, only a few of which, however, had
not appeared in the authors' printed works. These 'Galleries', 'Gardens',
'Paradises' and 'Pageants', containing only poems in the courtly conven-
tion, are comparable with Agathias' collection: they consisted of 'occa-
sional' verse of an amatory and exhibitory kind for people with social
ambitions whose taste in verse stood in need of education and refinement.
A variation from these was the *Paradise of Dainty Devices*, published in
1576, an anthology collected by a printer named Disle, which traded not
in the courtier-market but in the morality-market. Love and Honour are
replaced by graver and more didactic themes – 'Think to Die', 'Our
Pleasures are Vanities', 'Promise is Debt'; it also included a set of pieces
appropriate to Holy Days, and a translation from St Bernard of Morlaix.
Belvedere, or the Garden of the Muses, printed at the same time and by the
same publishers as *England's Helicon* is, to quote A.H. Bullen, 'a collection
of scrappy poetical quotations seldom exceeding a couplet in length',
anticipating, though not effectively enough to do much harm, the
'Beauties' of the late eighteenth century. But for the most part the
anthology of this period kept strictly to short complete poems of the same
general character: there were no lopped-off branches of the *Faerie Queene*
smuggled in, no speeches from *Tamerlaine*, *Gorboduc*, or the *Faithful
Shepherdess*. Nor were Chaucer, Gower, Lydgate and Skelton applied to
for subsidies, or a section of popular balladry added, with an apologetic:

> Rude Rhymers though they be,
>   They boast a native wit:
> And in these gorgeous gardens may
>   Like nimble footmen flit.

Such omissions, however, were chiefly due to the up-to-dateness of the
anthologists, who prided themselves on their modernity, above every-
thing; a generation after the first publication of Tottel's *Miscellany*, which
was a collection of real poems, the anthology was fast becoming a mere
fashion parade. The following lines introduced Proctor's *Gorgeous Gallery
of Gallant Inventions*, 1578:

> See, Gallants, see the Gallery of Delights
> With buildings brave, imbost with various hue,

With dainties decked devised of various wights,
Which as time served unto proportion grew.
By studies toiled with phrases fine they fraught
This peerless piece filled full of pretty pith.

The monotony of these collections led in the seventeenth century to
the publication of various anthologies of *Wit and Drollery*; they were
intended for the same reading public, which had, however, acquired
through the theatres a literary interest in low life and clowning.

Tottel's *Miscellany* and Meleager's *Wreath* both had the advantage of
being the first of their line: they thus contained no poem written for an
anthology public, since such a public could only be created by their
anthologies. Meleager's excellence, however, is more than an accident of
date; he had no trade purposes and, moreover, a love of the poem itself.
Tottel, on the other hand, gets his title as the father of the English
anthology (Dr Johnson called him the Mæcenas of the times) from an
accident of date, not at all from the purity of his interest. Indeed, his scan-
dalous rewriting of many of the poems that he included proves that but for
this accident he would have been only another worse Agathias. It was his
eight editions that stimulated anthology competition and created the
eventual confusion between true anthologies, that confine themselves to
literary rescue-work or have some excuse as works of criticism, or as
private albums, and are not numerous, and the all too numerous trade-
anthologies that turn poetry into an industrial packet-commodity.

A.H. Bullen's *Lyrics from the Elizabethan Songbooks* is a ready example
of a modern true-anthology, fully justified because the song-books them-
selves are very hard to come at and the specimens rescued are obviously
representative. *Lyrics from the Elizabethan Dramatists* may also be
included in this category, though the dramatists are more accessible than
the song-books and the lyric is sometimes too closely related to the play to
make its transplanting to an anthology congruous. Another good example
of the unexceptionable collection is Professor Child's *English and Scottish
Ballads*, which is accurate, definite and well-organized: it keeps within
certain carefully explained limits and, within these, arranges poems that
not only are otherwise inaccessible but gain by a collation of their widely
scattered variants.

Among the less ambitious volumes of the same class is a collection of
songs home-made in the trenches during the War and edited under the
title of *Sing-Songs of the War* by a young airman, Flight-Lieutenant
Nettleship. Professor Lomax's *Cowboy Songs and Frontier Ballads* is
another worthy collection. But in general a great risk is undertaken in
anthologizing raw material of this kind, especially where it is in ballad
form, as in recent collections of hobo and negro songs: the folk music
accompanying such ballads is a temptation to formalize and sentimen-

talize them for popular rendering. *Water Boy, Where are you hiding?* for example, one of the most tragic and humble plantation songs, is now delivered from concert platforms with piano accompaniment as a cultivated, ambitious darkey piece.

Indeed, any field where modifications in the original texts are necessary for popular rendering, more specifically where definite translations are necessary, should be avoided by anthologists. It may be stated as a general rule that an anthology of translations, whatever the merits of the translation, is unlikely to be justifiable as an anthology. This would be true of translations from American Indian poetry in anthology form, or, in fact, of translations from any primitive poetry, where poetry is not an independent creative act capable of being separated from its background, but part of a tribal ritual in which it has a meaning foreign to the authorship-principle of modern popular-anthology verse. The proper place for poetry of this kind is in an appendix to an encyclopaedia of ethnology. This does not mean that such anthologies have not been made which are competent from the literary point of view, as in the recent translations by Miss Eda Lou Walton from the Navajo: but whatever their literary merits, they involve a confusion of communal and individualistic poetry. This confusion is marked in a volume like C. Elissa Sharply's *Anthology of Ancient Egyptian Poems*, which is part of a 'Wisdom of the East' series designed to promote good-will and understanding between East and West – 'the old world of Thought and the new of Action'. Such a sweeping historical generalization about the East – and Egypt is not, of course, the East – does not allow for literary differentiation; and we are therefore not surprised to find bardic battle-pieces and personal love-songs interspersed with ancient religious hymns and extracts from the *Book of the Dead*. The same confusion is even present to a certain degree in anthologies meant to invite wider scholastic research in the original language, like Dr Kuno Meyer's *Ancient Irish Poetry*.

Modern anthologies of foreign poetry fall into two classes. They can be either anthologies in which the incorporated material is left untranslated, such as the *Oxford Books* of German, French, Italian and Portuguese Verse: in which case they merely imitate the vices of the *Oxford Book of English Verse*, of which we shall treat later: or they can be material both selected and translated by a single hand, such as the Deutsch-Yarmolinski translations from the German and Russian: in which case the incorporated material is even more deeply dyed than usual in the anthologist's vat and more unrecognizably recut in the anthology fashion of the language into which it is translated. It is significant that when a representative anthology of a foreign poetry is to be compiled a current native anthology is almost never taken over and translated, but an entirely new selection made of poems that do not so much represent the poetry of the language from which they are taken as the taste of the public for whose benefit they are translated. This reveals a principle that governs not only translation-anthologies but anthologies in general.

A distich recently found scrawled on the door of a flat in the London suburbs suggests the casual nature of a true anthology piece:

> Brother Tradesmen, do not weep!
> They are not dead, they do but sleep.

The signature was 'Hawes' Brothers' Boy'. There must be scores of similar pieces waiting for a place in a portfolio: election lampoons, parodies of popular advertizements, anticipatory epitaphs of public figures, anonymous album verse, barrack-room ballads not by Mr Kipling, and so on. For example, the following epigram appeared in a Base Camp magazine in France in May, 1915:

> *On a Second Lieutenant whose Promotion was Slow.*
>
> O deem it pride, not lack of skill,
> That will not let my sleeves increase.
> The morning and the evening still
> Have but one star apiece.

Mr Rostrevor's recent anthology of *Modern Epigrams* should, we feel, have consisted solely of pieces of this character instead of the studied literary compositions of Messrs Belloc, Squire and others which can readily be found among their Collected Poems. It would be proper to include epigrams like:

> Because the Duke of York is Duke of York
> The Duke of York has shot a huge Rhinoceros,
> Let's hope the Prince of Wales will take a walk
> In Africa and make the Empire talk
> By shooting an enormous Hippopotamus,
> And let us hope that Lord Lascelles
> Will shoot all beasts from gryphons to gazelles
> And show the world what sterling stuff we've got in us –

which the author, a distinguished poet, has omitted from his *Satirical Poems* because of its fugitive character; or Tennyson's summary of the Rosebery-Rothschild wedding, composed for a wager and not to be found in his Collected Poems:

> Venus, Sea-froth's child,
> Playing 'old gooseberry',
> Married Earl Rosebery
> To Hannah de Rothschild;

or the playful lines on Swift attributed to Pope:

Jonathan Swift
Had the gift
By fatherage,
Motherage,
Cousinage,
And by brotherage,
To come from Gutheridge.

These have that fugitive character which makes them everyone's concern but the writer's. It is different from the character that real poems get from being over-anthologized and from that of poems written especially for the trade anthology. The modern fugitive epigram is merely a manifestation of that folk-spirit which has been forced to accommodate itself to the urbanization of wit.

One of the reasons for the growing scarcity of the true anthology is that once a field has been covered well, as Child covered the popular non-literary English and Scottish ballad, as W. Carew Hazlitt in his four-volume *Early English Popular Poetry* and his two-volume *Early Popular Scotch Poetry* covered the black-letter verse fabliau, as Chappel covered the fields of early popular song in his *Popular Music of the Olden Time*, and as Dr Milton Percival has done for the political ballads satirizing the administration of Sir Robert Walpole, in his *Walpole Ballads*, there is nothing left to do but to cross the t's and dot the i's of these extremely conscientious antiquarians and look for remoter fields of research. But there are not enough remote fields of research to go round, and the temptation to make a popular and uncritical compôte of these scholary collections is very strong. And once the research spirit is in abeyance, the conscientious observance of the original texts of fugitive pieces – a morality by the way which first hardened only so late as 1822 with David Laing's *Select Remains of the Early Popular Poetry of Scotland* – is relaxed: and in nine cases out of ten the reconstituted poems, instead of recovering a clarity lost by the carelessness of the original scribe or printer, are further mishandled.

Our definition then of the true anthology has fallen into two classes. First, a strictly non-professional, non-purposive collection, such as the poet's or amateur's scrap-book (the Commonplace Book kept by Woodhouse, the friend of Keats, is a good example). The virtue of such an anthology diminishes with the increase in the number of persons for whom it is made; best if for only one, the private anthologist himself, next best if for only two, as if Meleager had not intended his *Crown* to go further than Diocles, and so on, the bigger the circle of readers, the worse, proportionately, the anthology. Second, the rescue-anthology, the value of which is primarily historical, only incidentally (and not necessarily) sympathetic. Such an anthology may be textual in emphasis, as Hazlitt's

Early English Popular Poetry, or historical, as a compendium of all the political verse of any obvious period, for example the French Revolution. Its object whether textual or historical will be to include as much material as possible, that is, it is committed in this sense to be uncritical; as the first class is also uncritical in the sense that it has only a personal standard. There remains a possible third class of the true anthology – the anthology that is criticism. But a book of criticism could be only incidentally an anthology: an anthology implies a work of pure collection and display. In a critical anthology a conflict is bound to occur between the critical element and the anthologistic element. And the pervasiveness of the popular anthology spirit will as a rule defeat what real critical intentions the author may have had. Roughly speaking, then, the true anthology is one that is in no way likely to become a popular trade anthology, since the general reading public asks from anthologies neither unauthorative examples of private taste, nor historical material in the raw, nor criticism.

CHAPTER II

Anthologies and the Book Market

OF all forms of the trade anthology, the anthology, that is, which treats poetry as a commodity destined for instructional, narcotic, patriotic, religious, humorous and other household uses, the modern publisher's anthology is the most offensive. It comes about something in this fashion. A superstition has hung over from last century when there was, indeed, a practical demand for poetry for household uses, that no general publisher's Spring or Autumn list is complete without at least one volume under the heading of '*Poetry*'. What it is does not matter, so long as it does not run the firm into expense. And the publisher knows well enough that poetry cannot pay its printer's bills except in the form of standard text-books, nursery verse and anthologies. But poetry text-books, unlike scientific text-books, take at least twenty-five years to go out of date. Their market is very close, and made still closer by duplication of texts in America and England, Palgrave's *Golden Treasury of English Poetry* serving as the chief text-book in the secondary schools in both countries, and gems from American poetry – from Whittier, Longfellow, Lowell, Eugene Field (with the addition of Mrs Hemans and Tennyson, of course, on both sides) – providing the chief material for the elementary primer in both. The American market is somewhat more open than the English because of fancy, up-to-the-minute literary courses in the American university curriculum and the *From Whitman to Sandburg* text-books compiled to supply them; in England, recent poetry is considered too recent to be made an advanced academic subject.* As for nursery verse, it must appear in the publisher's list under the heading *Juvenile* if it is to pay for itself. So *Poetry* must again be represented by an anthology this season, the publisher decides.

He runs over the possibilities in his mind. '*Flower Poems*? No, that has been done often, illustrated and plain. *Animal Poems*? Two animal anthologies already this year. *Poems of the Sea*? I might get most of it from

---

* The present Professor of Poetry at Oxford, diving gamely into the waters of modernism, brought up only an old boot – Mr Humbert Wolfe!

Mrs Sharpe's *Sea Music* and slip in a few moderns. But the Sea is going out of fashion since the Air came in; and there is no Air-Poetry to take its place yet.* If I could only hit on something like Mr Hartog's *The Kiss in Poetry*. Perhaps *The Life of Christ, an Anthology*? One of the later Oxford books, I'm afraid. *Child Poems? Lullabies? Drinking Songs? Songs of the Homeland? Book of the Tree? Book of the Inn?* … Can it be that all poems have been anthologized? Then we must dig up the suppressed ones … Ah, an *Anthology of Suppressed Poems*! A quaint Christmas present for the book-lover. About 200pp. octavo in limp leather and with a short introduction by

Mr Squire ⎫   Mr Chesterton ⎫
          ⎬ or   ⎬
Mr Morley ⎭   Mr Mencken. ⎭

Office Boy! Rush this through!'

These publisher's anthologies take many grotesque forms. The arrangement may be one of subject; or of period; or of verse-form, such as *An Anthology of Sonnets* and *A Treasury of Modern Triolets*; or of locale, such as *Manchester Poets* and *The Chicago Lyre*; or of competitive anthology quality, *The Hundred Best Lyrics*, *The Best Poems of Our Time*, and, latterly, *The Second Hundred Best Poems*. All these collections are mere wanton re-arrangement of poetry that has its proper place elsewhere, or nowhere at all; as wanton as if the British Museum were suddenly to change its library system and classify its books according to the colour of their bindings.

Such an anthology-making resembles the tricks that the Victorians used to play with the Bible. They collected instances of the occurrence of odd words such as 'razor' and 'satyr' and 'dragon', and collated curses and references to the End of the World, and compiled 'Biblical Flora' collections and 'Examples of God's Mercy', and so passed many a weary Sunday afternoon; until some thorough-going spoilsport published a *Complete and Trustworthy Concordance*, and the game was over; there were no surprises left. Then they gave it up and read improving scientific books instead on their Sunday afternoons; and so the period of Doubt began. Only the Old Couple remained undefeated. He set himself to tabulate the number of '*Ands*' in the Old Testament, and persuaded her to count the '*Ands*' in the New Testament. *And* they got the answer *and* each checked the other's addition; *and* then they did the *Apocrypha*, book by book, but when they came to *Bel and the Dragon* he died *and* she from a sense of Christian duty finished *and* the grand total, whatever it was, ended in the figures 666, which she thought was unlucky; *and* she was so glad when she checked it to discover that she had overlooked two more marginal '*Ands*',

---

* *A Homage to Lindbergh* anthology, contributed to by some two hundred poets, has however recently been published.

which made it quite all right. *And ... But* by this time Science has invented so many new tabulating games that, though the *flowers* and the *kisses* and the *animals* and the *mysticism* and the *patriotism* and the *alcoholism* have all been used up as far as 666 and beyond, a whole new tabulating-system will soon have been evolved, and we shall be having anthologies of *Vitamine E Poems, Poems of Television, Death-Ray Poems*, and so forth.

Among other ways, the publisher's anthology has varied itself by specializing in publics. In some cases the publisher even allows the public to make its own collection; he, of course, always standing as godfather. School anthologies, for instance, are chiefly compiled in the classroom by and for schoolmasters who like poems that can be readily parsed, recited, and 'got up' with historical notes, that are idealistic in sentiment and that tell a story. Other random examples of the anthology specializing in a public are Canon Langbridge's *Ballads of the Brave*, gallant poems for private reading by English boys of the Mafeking tradition; and *The Open Road* of Mr E.V. Lucas (verse with prose-insertions), a small book for the pocket to ease the sentimental rambler on a walking tour when, shortly after the ninth milestone, conversation breaks down between him and his companion. This last, though accepted as a 'modern classic', smells suspiciously of the publisher's seasonal happy thought, his *Bus-top Treasury*, his *Poems for Convalescence* and his *Business Girl's Garland of Verse.**

Even Dr Bridges' *Spirit of Man* must be classed as a trade anthology, if not as a publisher's anthology, for though the gross commercial view was probably absent from his mind, it was at any rate a public utility volume compiled for a national occasion. It came out in the middle of the War and was dedicated to 'His Majesty the King, by His Poet Laureate'. The preface makes rather sad reading now, when it informs us: 'Prussia's scheme for the destruction of her neighbours was, above all question and debate, long laid and scientifically elaborated to the smallest detail'; and when it suggests that Englishmen should

> turn to seek comfort in the contemplation of spiritual things ... happy even in the death of our beloved who fell in the fight. They die nobly as saints and heroes, with hearts and hands unstained by hatred or wrong,

and that they should find

> joy in the thought that our Country is called of God to stand for the truth of man's hope and that it has not shrunk from the call.

To support such sentiments, the ghosts of the Elizabethans and the

---

* The recent *Sacco-Vanzetti* anthology illustrates how very special the anthology public may be.

Romantic Revivalists are summoned to present their usual verse-offer-ings; but because of the seriousness of the occasion, the reader is asked 'to bathe rather than fish in these waters'.

*   *   *   *   *

In 1777 the Martins of Edinburgh began to print a series of *The Poets.* The London booksellers, alarmed at 'the invasion of what we call our Literary Property', and probably also influenced by the prevailing ency-clopedia movement, determined, with Dr Johnson as editor, 'to print an elegant and accurate edition of all the English Poets of reputation from Chaucer to the present time'. Forty of the most select booksellers met together, pooled their copyrights and got on with the printing: but on a less ambitious plan than first intended, for they decided that the English Poets began with Abraham Cowley. However, in 1810, Chalmers' edition added the earlier poets; and English Literature was at last provided with a *Library* or *Corpus* of Poets. True, it printed Warner's *Albion's England,* Drayton's *Polyolbion,* Daniel's *History of the Civil War* at full length, yet left out Shakespeare's and Marlowe's dramas; it included Ambrose and J. Philips, Watts, Dodsley, Tickell, Mickle, Smith, Jones and Sprat, yet omitted Blake, Crashaw, Campion, Traherne, Vaughan, Marvell; it printed almost all of Smart – except his *Song to David.* But it was a Corpus, the best that the booksellers could command. The general public looked with pride not unmixed with dismay on this new acquisition. It was an impressive shelf-full, but was one really expected to read it all through? If so, did one have to start at the beginning, go on till one came to the end and then stop? The print too, they pleaded, was rather small. So some charitable gentlemen, friends of the booksellers, came to their help with further *Beauties of the Poets* on the model of the guides to previous less complete collections.

Shortly after the publication of Chalmers' edition the great poetry boom began. Not only were the Elder Poets securely indexed in Chalmers crying out to have their 'Beauties' exhumed for contemporary curiosity, but there were exciting Moderns, too – the handsome, wicked, heroic Lord Byron, the romantic 'Waverley' Scott, clever Mr Coleridge and shy Mr Wordsworth, and Mr Leigh Hunt and young Mr... er ... Shelley ('that custody case, you know') and dignified Mr Samuel Rogers. 'Let us have "Modern Beauties" too.' So they had them. Then the fashion arose of putting ancient and recent side by side in manuscript albums, the recent for pleasure, the ancient to counteract the pleasure – this was a period with a growing conscience about pleasure.

The keeping of these private albums of poems that had made a partic-ular personal appeal to the reader, each poem copied out in the reader's own hand, began as a disinterested hobby; and indeed there are people who still continue the custom with pure enough motives. But the tendency to let the album lose its private character, by handing it about among friends and allowing it to come into competition with other albums, soon destroyed the integrity of album-making. The actual personal appeal became confused with the fashionable appeal. Because there was a sentimental cult for Chatterton, or because the elder critics agreed in accepting Shenstone as one of the Masters, or because Mr Lamb and Mr Hazlitt maintained that the Elizabethan Age, even without Shakespeare, had been quite as important an age of poetry as the Augustan, the private anthologist was so busy mechanically copying out page after page of verse that he had no energy left for enjoying it.

Now, the private anthology which grows directly out of serious reading can be valuable to its compiler. It resembles, at its best, creation. A poem particularly chosen and copied down in the reader's handwriting becomes in a sense his own; it is the nearest that a person who is not a poet can get to writing poetry. But a private anthology is only permissible if it remains private. Mr Robert Lynd, in introducing Sir Algernon Methuen's *Shakespeare to Hardy* anthology, quotes 'a young poet of our own time' as testifying warmly to the therapeutic value of a good anthology for sick and disordered minds, and asks Sir Algernon Methuen and every other good anthologist to 'glow with pleasure at so startling a tribute to their usefulness'. But the possible medicinal value of an anthology for sick and disordered minds lies solely in the work which the sick and disordered mind does for itself if it compiles this anthology. And though it is possible to imagine an ideal anthology free of all the faults to which we are calling attention, it must remain ideal. Even an honest private anthology loses most of its value when published as a public anthology. The poems included have become part of the anthologist and have lost their original context. This does not harm the anthologist, but it makes him a bar between the readers of the anthology and the poem and thus prevents a direct introduction to the poem *by the poet himself*, who alone has the right to give it. Mr Walter de la Mare's anthology *Come Hither* is an extreme case. The poems included are so honestly Mr de la Mare's favourite poems that they seem a mere extension of the de la Mare atmosphere backwards through English Poetry. A tyranny which no personality has a right to exercise over the reader; Bryant and Whittier, though their personalities were less fantastic, made typical poets'-anthologies which were open to the same objections.

No matter, then, in what good faith a private anthology is made, it becomes, when published, an organized theft of the signatures of the original poets, for it is the whole intention of a private anthology to make the included poems the anthologist's own. Granted that the publishing of private anthologies is permissible, which we dispute, Dr Bridges, in his *Spirit of Man*, was right in suppressing all signatures to the contributory poems (which occur, however, in an appendix). The alleged reason for their omission, and for the omission of titles to the poems, is that the book has to be read in sequence (as Dr Bridges' new composite epic, we understand) and that titles or signatures 'might distract attention and even overrule consideration'.

The greater the integrity of the private anthology, particularly when the author is a well-known poet, the more dangerous is it when put on the market: by its publication it appears to be an act of criticism instead of a mere expression of taste. Taste is the judgement that an individual makes of a thing according to its fitness in his private scheme of life. Criticism is the judgement that an individual makes of a thing according to its fitness to itself, its excellence as compared with things like itself, regardless of its application to his private scheme of life. With taste, a poem is good because it is liked; with criticism, it is good because it is good. Now, it is not objectionable for a person who has not sufficient originality to make his own criticism to accept another's; for criticism, unlike taste, which is arbitrary opinion, can be tested. The criticism of one person thus accepted can become another person's taste. But for one person to accept another's taste deprives the former of self-respect. Our charge against anthologies is, then, that they have robbed the poetry-reading public of self-respect.

The poet as the private anthologist of his own work provides the only instance in which a private anthology makes a legitimate public anthology. Every single-man volume of verse is a selection of all the poems that were written during the whole or some period of the poet's life. Even a full *Collected Edition* does not contain all the poems he ever committed to paper, let alone those fragmentary poems and versions of poems that were rejected before they ever reached paper.

* * * * *

Of *Beauties of the Poets* there were many collections between 1780 and 1880. Three useful examples are Jane's *Beauties of the Poets*, a late eighteenth-century collection; Campbell's *Beauties of the British Poets*, published in 1825; and William Elwell's *The British Lyre*, published in 1854. Of Jane's anthology, which specialized in eighteenth-century metronomic verse, we have found the following oblique indictment, a paragraph from a letter to Southey by John Jones, the Old Servant; who knew it only too well:

> I soon engaged myself again, Sir, (in 1795) with an old gentleman and his three nieces, whose names were Alexander, uncle and sisters of the present Lord Chief Baron, and I had not been in the family many months before, young as I was, I was made an upper Servant, and as I received a little card-money at times I soon was able to

procure me some books, which I did by subscribing two or three quarters to the library, and the ladies were very kind to me, and often lent me others, and about this time, Sir, I bought the first and almost the only book I was ever master of, which was called Jane's *Beauties* and this I read over several times; but my chief reading now was history, and I made some poetical attempts but I kept copies of none of them excepting the epitaph on Molly Mutton, an old woman very well known about the streets of Bath at that time; but on some of my verses falling into the hands of the ladies, they were much amused with them, and, I believe, expressed regret that I had not been better educated. The housekeeper, Sir, was very kind to me, and on my expressing sorrow at her departure once when she was going to see her friends, she desired me to write something extempore in which my regret might be more strongly expressed, when in a few minutes I remember putting the following lines into her hand:

> There something is, my Martha dear,
> > So amiable about thee,
> The house is Heaven when thou art here,
> > But Hell to me without thee.'

Jones' other poetical attempts were graver and more didactic and show how readily the anthology lends itself to the offices of a poetical horn-book. Campbell's preface we must quote in full:

At no period of our history have we possessed such a galaxy of varied talent evinced in the poetry of the age as at present: and never with some few unfortunate exceptions has the vigorous nerve and intellectual grasp of our bards while throwing 'the drapery of a moral imagination over our poor shivering nature' been more subservient to the interests of religion, or tended more effectually to promote the intellectual as well as the moral happiness of the rising generation. We have therefore in the present selection of the *Beauties of the British Poets* given to the productions of our living authors a longer space than is usually allotted to them in works of this nature: yet not to the exclusion of the writers of the olden time. For it has been our aim to bring together all the principal pieces of acknowledged merit and of intrinsic beauty which have undergone the test of the severest criticism and examination and have received the stamp of public approbation, together with many a charming anonymous production snatched with cautious hand as it floated on the stream of time towards the abyss of oblivion.

While seeking for Beauties we have been careful to ascertain that no poison lurks beneath the flowers. Nothing has been admitted which has a tendency to offend delicacy or injure morality, and we have been as studious to select those passages which convey some solid instruction as those that are merely addressed to the fancy. Occasionally we have introduced a Critical Remark which we flatter ourselves will be an acceptable addition.

The promise of exciting modern work is not borne out by the index. There is no Keats included, almost nothing of Shelley, less of Coleridge, a little inferior Wordsworth, no Blake, of course. The modern writers given most space are Byron, Burns, Rogers, Moore, James Montgomery, Cowper. Not quite so much of Scott and Southey (copyright difficulties?), but their portraits form the engraved frontispiece to the two volumes. The longest poems are Pope's *Rape of the Lock*, Shenstone's *Schoolmistress*, Thomson's *Castle of Indolence* and Stillingfleet's *Essay on Conversation*, which between them take up at least a hundred pages. Shakespeare is represented by five little stock extracts from the dramas, not a hundred lines in all; each extract given a moral heading such as 'Appearances are Deceptive', 'The Power of Music', 'The Course of True Love'. The eighteenth century is strongly represented, and there is a great deal of conventional 'Beauties of' verse-writing in the direct eighteenth-century tradition, of which this extract from Erasmus Darwin's *Upas Tree* is a charming example. He is speaking of 'Java's Isle':

> No spicy nutmeg scents the vernal gales,
> No towering plaintain shades the midday vales.
> No refluent fin the unpeopled stream divides,
> No revolant pinion cleaves the airy tides.
> Nor handed moles, nor beakéd worms return
> That mining pass th' irremeable bourn.
> Fierce in dread silence on the blasted heath
> Fell UPAS sits, the Hydra-tree of Death.

The British Lyre has a readable preface. Note the increased missionary moralistic tone, now at its full, but gradually wearing off (unless in definitely religious or educational anthologies) as the century advances, as the advance of democracy makes the reader's enjoyment the determining commercial factor in the making of books: disguised in critical language as art-for-art's-sake. Note also the increased self-congratulation of the popular anthologist, tending more and more to drive the poets themselves into obscurity:

> Three years have now elapsed since this little work first excited the attention of the Public, and if I may judge by the extensive diffusion it has enjoyed during that period, I have every reason to be satisfied with the appreciation of its readers. Filled with feelings of gratitude for the most hearty welcome allotted to my book, I consider it a

delightful duty to express my thanks to its numerous friends and at the same time inform them that in this new edition I have endeavoured to improve the selection by inserting several modern poems which on account of the richness of their language, purity and beauty of their ideas, truly deserve the warm admiration of all lovers of English poetry. I now again launch *The British Lyre* into the vortex of public opinion, hoping its reception will prove as flattering to myself as in former times. With regard to the arrangement of the poems I need only quote a few remarks of a friend, who kindly wrote the preface to the first edition: 'The book is divided into three parts. The first contains pieces relating to the works of God or (*sic*) the phenomena of "Nature" directing thought to all the lovely and awful demonstrations of the power and wisdom of the Creator, as described by the pen of poetic fancy. The second division relates to Man himself, to "Home and Country", to "Social and Domestic Affections" – and here all the elevated feelings of patriotism (NB this was the date of the "Indian Mutiny"), all the happy scenes of the heart are represented, while those deeper and sadder feelings, inherent to the frailty of man, are not forgotten. But after the praise of the beauties of Nature and the enjoyment of the high hopes of life, the third part, "Devotion", leads us to God Himself, shows us His Grace and Promises, our prospects of immortality, the consolation of public worship and of domestic prayers. Thus the author of this compilation will be found to have carried out the good idea of giving a clear description of "Mankind" by placing his selections under three heads, the first "The Place of our Existence", the second "Our Feelings and Actions during Life", and the third "Our Exit from this World and Our Hopes for the Future".'

In the generation that has elapsed since our previous exhibit, a great change has come over the Beauties. The eighteenth century has been almost entirely cut out. Pope only gets a twenty-line part. Shenstone is dropped altogether. The Upas-Tree is forgotten. Byron, Burns, Rogers, Southey, Moore, hold their own; but Montgomery, Cowper and Scott are yielding pride of place to Wordsworth, Mrs Hemans, Howitt, Barry Cornwall and Henry Kirke White. Coleridge, Shelley and Keats are very gradually creeping up. Tennyson, as Poet Laureate, has established himself in about five pages. Shakespeare still moralizes for a few lines each on 'The Grandfather's Death-bed', 'Mercy,' 'Flattery and Friendship'. The existence of the Pre-Raphaelites is not yet recognized. A few seventeenth-century poets are revived: Waller, Marvell, Quarles, Vaughan, but each only in a short contribution. There are no poems included of any size: though long poems are still represented by proxy of their Beauties. *The British Lyre* is thus transitional to the *Golden Treasury* of 1861, probably the first popular anthology in the modern sense which settled the whole troublesome question of 'Beauties' and their extraction by only claiming to be a 'lyrical' anthology: this with satisfaction both to the compiler and his readers. The compiler was saved the labour of going through the longer works of Chaucer, Pope, Shakespeare, Cowper and company, and the readers were saved the duty of 'looking up' the context of each extract, and could content themselves with a good resolution to read these longer works as a whole at some (indefinite) future date. The *Golden Treasury* was thus an improvement on the *Beauties* in that it did not contain clippings from long poems which, becoming 'star-passages', interrupt their rhythm by a false accentuation. On the other hand, the *Beauties* were preferable as being plainly nothing more ambitious than introductions to the complete works of the poets they included; while the *Golden Treasury* was complete in itself and could be used as a pocket Library of Poets and become very popular as such because it was not moralistic, ranged with greater freedom than its predecessors, and was at least ten years in advance of the literary taste of any rival.

The editor of this 'modern classic' was Francis Palgrave, working with two unnamed assistants; but he was guided in his selection either directly or indirectly by the judgement of Tennyson. Indeed, it was as much the influence of Tennyson through the *Golden Treasury* as the direct influence of his poems that gave the next two generations a Tennysonian view of the progress of English poetry. The *Golden Treasury*, with its later additions, has become the Dean of Anthologies, its original liberalism ossified beyond recognition. Its one serious rival in circulation, Professor Sir A. Quiller-Couch's *Oxford Book of English Verse* (1900), admits its obligations; the compiler 'cannot and does not wish to erase the dye his mind took from the *Golden Treasury*' ('dye' is appropriate, suggesting Palgrave's anthological vat). The *Treasury* is a usurping private anthology, very conscientiously compiled, but all the more formidable for that. For Palgrave was in private life not only an unsuccessful poet but a successful educationalist (the first because of the second); therefore well equipped to impose a personal taste (his own, guided by Tennyson's) as a critical canon on his public.

Palgrave, in the poetical style that marks the preface of practically every anthology – for the anthologist, after months of laborious reading of the works of others, likes to give his own pen a good airing, and this is his only chance – boasts:

> Chalmers' vast collection with the whole works of all accessible poets not contained in it and the best anthologies of different periods have been twice (?) systematically read through: and it is hence improbable that any omissions which may be regretted are due to oversight.

Recent anthologists compiling trade collections have so much respect for Palgrave's industry that they generally use the same list of authors, merely varying it with alternative poems of the same character as those that he (or Tennyson) selected.

The copying of anthologist from anthologist always suggests sheep at a gap. Dr Robert Bridges, after the compilation of one trade anthology, *The Spirit of Man*, an act of genuine if misapplied creation, was persuaded to make another, *The Chilswell Book of English Verse*, which, though it altered the proportionate weight given to the elder poets and included a few rather backward moderns, was only a *Golden-Treasury-Oxford-Book-of-English-Verse* in disguise. One particular poem, John Clare's 'I am, but what I am who cares or knows?' is the only Clare poem in the *Oxford Book of English Verse* and the only one that Dr Bridges printed; one might pass this as a case of great critics thinking alike, if it were not that Clare is far from being a one-poem man, and that Doctor Bridges evidently did not consult Edmund Blunden's recent and authoritative collection of Clare's poetry in which the proper text of the poem is restored. The *Oxford Book of English Verse* version was one rewritten by the asylum doctor who had charge of Clare's affairs at the time he wrote it. Dr Bridges, to speak bluntly, borrowed and borrowed stupidly.

Against *The Chilswell Book of English Verse* may be set Miss Naomi Royde-Smith's *A Private Anthology*, published about the same time. Miss Royde-Smith, in her fear of producing something remotely suggesting *The Golden Treasury* or its stepchild, reacts so violently from the obvious that her collection seems to be competing for a prize as *The Most Individual Anthology*. For instance, she includes nothing of Blake's but his *Address to Tirzah*, and nothing of Siegfried Sassoon's but a very slight poem written in 1910, years before he began any serious work. Miss Eleanor Brougham in her *Corne from Olde Fieldes* does not become quite so idiosyncratic as Miss Royde-Smith, though she introduces her anthology (of pre-eighteenth-century verse) with:

> I am purposely excluding from this anthology many of the master-pieces which have received the homage of a long succession of generations. The poems printed here are mainly chosen from those which have descended so plentifully upon us yet threaten through neglect to disappear altogether.

Much of her choice is fugitive verse proper to be included in an anthology, particularly the early English carols in manuscript in the Balliol College Library; but she finds it necessary to preserve from oblivion pieces so well-known as Herbert's 'Sweet day, so cool, so calm, so bright'; Sidney's 'With how sad steps, O Moon', Drayton's 'Since there's no hope, come let us kiss and part', and Shirley's 'Glories of our Blood and State'. Rochester is represented by a poem really by Quarles, and

Skelton is given only the usual commonplaces from *The Garland of Laurell.*

And now Mr T. Earle Welby publishes his *Silver Treasury of English Lyrics* in America where the *Golden Treasury* is as much a law to anthologists as in England: a case of international bi-metallism in which America, trying to keep her place perhaps, provides the humbler coinage. He admits Palgrave's as the classic anthology and does not try to compete but to supplement. His two tests are 'Is this poem, in its own sort, of rare excellence?' and 'Is it in Palgrave?' But in avoiding the Scylla of Palgrave, he sails dangerously near the Charybdis of Quiller-Couch. It would have been impracticable to admit both as classics, for the average reader cannot do with more than two standard anthologies to give a hand to each.*

In outward appearance a change has begun to come over the popular anthology in recent years, but this is only a change in journalistic technique. Instead of weightiness we tend to get lively sophistication; instead of gentlemanliness, a bland vulgarity; instead of confirmation of established taste, new discoveries not much believed in by the discoverer; instead of pompous flowery language – no, that remains in the prefaces as pompous and flowery as ever. The books are handier to the pocket, more dashing though more perishable in format. But as with the bricking up of journalism, so with the anthologies: they have improved themselves with regard to everything but the one thing necessary, Poetry, as the newspapers with regard to everything but Truth.

---

* Mr J.C. Squire has however appraised the market more cleverly in bringing out an anthology of *Lesser Poets* rather than of Lesser Poems.

CHAPTER III

The Anthologist in Our Midst

THE ideal popular anthologist is one who concerns himself only with supplying his public with what it wants. But, granted for the argument's sake that the popular anthology must be, this idiotic single-mindedness is of the idiocy of genius. For who but an ideal popular anthologist would attempt to say what the poetry-reading public wants?

Does it want to know the sort of poems that were written at different periods in the past or that are being written today? Does it want a nodding acquaintance with all the poets, with or without a desire to enlarge that acquaintance? Or a handy reference collection of best poems as well as the nodding acquaintance? Does it want poems that have already become stock-anthology pieces or will it prefer a less conventional collection, an admitted Not-Quite-the-Real-Best? Or has it no critical ideas of Best and Worst? And after this, what does it want the poetry for? Does it go to poetry as it goes to religion; or as it goes to sport; or how?

His decision on all this, because what the public's interest in poetry really is an insoluble mystery, is bound to be a decision to compromise and to adopt the universally acceptable lie: 'As everybody knows what really good poetry is at first sight, there is no need to define it and no problem to be faced about what to include. Good poems, the poems that everyone likes and understands, never get stale, never clash with each other and are always immediately recognized.' The ideal anthologist is a priest of Poetry to the people, ready to give them any acceptable god. He must be free from prejudices of his own but have a steady intuition of the sort of poems that other people will like from year to year. He must, in fact, to be free from prejudice, actually dislike poetry. He must be merely a barometer of fashion: if today he compiles an authoritative anthology of ancient or contemporary or mixed verse, he must be ready to recast it tomorrow. He will have to be an expert in literary booms. He will have to know, for instance, the exact upward popularity-curve of Donne, Marvell, Skelton, Blake, Clare and others and the exact downward curve of Burns, Byron, Tennyson, Browning, Swinburne, as revealed by an exhaustive historical chart of previous booms and depressions in poets. He will speak with the mock-confident voice of Frederick Harrison:

I protest that I am devoted to no school in particular; I condemn no school, I reject none. I am for the school of all the great men. I care for Wordsworth as well as for Byron, for Burns as well as Shelley, for Boccaccio as well as for Milton, for Bunyan as well as Rabelais, for Cervantes as much as for Dante, for Corneille as well as for Shakespeare, for Goldsmith as well as Goethe. I stand by the sentence of the world.

Our anthologist will also have to appreciate the economy of book-producing: he must pay copyright fees for his key-names if necessary, but the bulk of his material must be either out of copyright or to be had for the asking (in a crafty letter of request). And he will not only be shrewd in the matter of fees; he will take every possible step to prevent the living poet from knowing beforehand in what company he is to find his poems; and will take care to send him no proofs. In this respect all popular anthologists are ideal; we have never yet heard of an anthology whose editor has sent round his proposed introduction and a full list of the poems he intends to include. This would be a tenderness on the poet's behalf that no anthologist with any respect for himself or his public would permit. If the proudest poet were to complain that being put into a popular anthology is like being taken blindfold into a crowded room and then having the bandage removed when the doors are locked behind him, the meanest anthologist would laugh in his face.*

If the poet went on to suggest that the dead poets had any rights and should not be put in company of which they might be expected to disapprove, the anthologist would think that the poet was joking. Poetry, he would say, isn't like money or a business or landed property. The poet's testamentary wishes, to be understood from his work itself, have no force as soon as the short copyright period is over. His poetry is public property because, of course, the poet always writes as a public character and speaks to the universal heart of his beloved fellow-man.

---

* The most playful example of this sort of thing that we have recently met with is the introduction to Mr E.V. Lucas's *Joy of Life*. This production, divided into sections: 'England', 'The Changing Year', 'Birds', 'The Garden', 'The Game', 'Sport', 'Travel', 'The Sea', Lovers', 'Domesticity', 'Children', 'Books', 'Philosophy', 'Theology', 'Thanksgiving and Prayer', 'The Land of Heart's Desire', 'Friends', 'The Old Days', 'Wine', 'Rapture', 'Rest and Slumber', 'Evening Shadow', 'Farewell', is explained as follows:

'I do not pretend that the pages contain, as a whole, the best modern poetry that I could find; but they contain the best modern poetry that I could find with bearing upon my theme: the joy of life. English poets since the war have more often been grave than gay, sardonic than serene, yet I have been able to bend not a few even of the more pessimistic to my cheerful purpose. I hope that none will feel affronted when they see what has been done with them.'

Peep-bo! See what a fool I've made of you!

When dealing with the work of living poets our ideal anthologist may well study Mr Louis Untermeyer, the chief modern American anthologist; who, as a retired businessman, is much more astute than his opposite number in England, Mr Squire, a harnessed literary critic. Mr Squire makes no concessions to modernist poetry; Mr Untermeyer manages to find at least one accidentally easy piece in even the most startling innovators if sufficient pressure from the most advanced section of his public is applied to him. Mr Untermeyer's political tactics in his *Modern American Poetry* have been condemned by superior literary critics; but he is really doing his best to be an ideal anthologist, at a great sacrifice, probably, to his taste. With each new edition the emphasis of his choice shifts: in the latest, for instance, he has at last consented to admit the popular importance of T.S. Eliot and e.e. cummings. It is doubtful whether the superior critic, if he set about making an anthology, could do any better than Mr Untermeyer. As he would be bound not to make way before popular success, he would have to compose his anthology high-mindedly of born failures. But even Mr Untermeyer is not ideal, in spite of his readiness to please everyone. For we cannot regard his criticism, which is in the main a register of the opinions of others, as entirely free from personal indulgencies. For instance, he might get few people to agree that Mr Louis Untermeyer, the poet, should be allotted nearly fifteen pages of the book, which puts him into the same rank with notables like Robert Frost, Amy Lowell, Carl Sandburg and Edwin Arlington Robinson. Nor might everyone agree, that Jean Starr Untermeyer should be given the same poem-space as Emily Dickinson, even though this is only half Mr Untermeyer's ration. Perhaps, too, the ideal anthologist would avoid all detailed prose criticism like Mr Untermeyer's where a simple speculative act of taste on the public's behalf would do: it would save a good deal of rewriting in the next edition if e.e. cummings' stock, say, were to go up and Edwin Arlington Robinson's to fall again.

Among other qualities, the anthologist should have the power of recognizing a valuable old poem, obscured by a dingy setting, with all the acumen of a furniture dealer, and know how to present it properly. He should not be afraid to lop, combine, revise, retitle, respell and repunctuate; and, if there are two versions of a poem, to give the most poetical and suppress the most poetic. Random examples of such popularizing methods are already so numerous that he would not be wanting in encouragement. Barnes' *Woak Hill*, for instance, has been so frequently anthologized in seven stanzas that few of the general public are aware that it has three other stanzas at the end which the poet thought necessary to the poem but which are always omitted. The painful first verse of Lamb's *The Old Familiar Faces* is very seldom given; the *Oxford Book of English Verse* protects us from the too poetic latter half of Donne's *Ecstasy*. The case of the O'Shaughnessy *Ode* should encourage him in philanthropy towards the poet as well as towards the public. 'Palgrave recognizing', to quote a modern anthologist, 'the great difference between the first three inspired stanzas of Arthur O'Shaughnessy's *Ode* and the others, calmly and courageously dropped the final four. William Alexander Percy performed many similar services for this singer and, as he says, 'in O'Shaughnessy's case, it is the only way to save him from himself and for posterity'. A fine bold example of unauthorized revision will be found in Mr J.C. Squire's *Selections from Modern Poets*, where no less than five separate lyrics by Frank Prewett have been run together as a single poem without, as we are informed, the author's consent. Retitling is common. We find Sir Arthur Quiller-Couch retitling Wyatt's poem which appears in Tottel as *The Lover Showeth how he is Forsaken of Such as he sometime Enjoyed* as *Vixi Puellis nuper Idoneus*. This reference to Horace successfully keeps down the passion of the poem, too strong for an ideal anthology, to the commonplaces of which Horace is the Poet Laureate. And the poem as it appears under this title also gives an instance of how an anthologist prefers the most poetical to the most poetic version of a poem. The *Oxford Book of English Verse* rejects the following as the last stanza:

> It was no dream; for I lay broad awaking:
>   But all is turned thorough my gentleness,
> Into a strangë fashion of forsaking;
>   And I have leave to go of her goodnéss
>   And she also to use new fangleness.
> But since that I so kindly am servéd
> I would fain know what she hath déservéd –

in favour of

> It was no dream; for I lay broad awaking:
>   But all is *turn'd now, through* my gentleness
> Into a *bitter* fashion of forsaking;
>   And I have leave to go of her goodnéss;
>   And she also to use new-fangleness.
> But since that I *unkindly so* am servéd,
> *'How like you this?' – what hath she now deservèd?*

We conclude that Sir Arthur Quiller-Couch went to Chalmers' *English Poets* first, following the example of Palgrave, his master, and found the version as he now presents it, though with the original title. Without digging further for the moment into the origin of this version, which is not Wyatt's own, let us see what necessitated it. It was evidently rewritten for a popular audience which could not be troubled with the archaic 'thorough' for 'through', nor the 'strangë' for 'strange', nor the inverted accentuation of 'servéd' and of 'déservéd', nor the satiric use of 'kindly'. 'How like you this' is patched in from a previous stanza to fill out the last line

which, to a popular audience unable to appreciate its satiric meditative
slowness, would read feebly enough. 'I would fain know' is probably
regarded as padding, whereas it is the continued indignation of 'so kindly'.
Sir Arthur was wise in giving the public what it could understand; as it
was unlikely that anyone would go back behind Chalmers, no indication
was given in the anthology that the text was not Wyatt's original. As a
matter of fact, Chalmers, Palgrave and Sir Arthur Quiller-Couch have a
common source: Tottel. Apparently between the writing of the poem
about the year 1536 and its printing in 1557 some hand, possibly Tottel's
own, made these changes. So Sir Arthur Quiller-Couch, in this case at
least, is the ideal anthologist again, copying from the ideal anthologist;
instead of getting the vexatious manuscript reading from Doctor Nott's
edition long ago published from the Harrington MSS.

Respelling is a matter of less importance; even the poet himself will
sometimes allow the printer to have his way in matters of correct usage.
But to do with William Barnes, say, what certain anthologists have done
with him, to transform his fantastically printed Dorsetshire dialect into
educated English, is a service which our hero, however, will not hesitate to
undertake. Examples of daring repunctuation are particularly common in
anthologized versions of Shakespeare's sonnets. We have commented fully
on the treatment of *Th'expence of Spirit in a waste of shame*, in another work.[*]

A further quality necessary in a popular anthologist will be an almost
morbid modesty. He must be able to bring a blush to his own cheeks by
the very thought of all the indecencies and blasphemies he has come upon
in his rambles: he must be as tender of the virgin-mind of his putative
public as an old-fashioned mother of her daughter's, or a new-fashioned
daughter of her mother's. And to this modesty we must add a great gift for
stupidity in face of any difficult passage in a poem. At the first glimmer of
any possible obscurity he must shut his eyes tight and pass on in search of
something easier.

Who are the present popular anthologists? They fall into five common
occupational categories:

1. Irresponsible enthusiasts acting often in the name of a cause.
2. 'Minor poets', disguised sometimes as college professors, who wish
to bully the public into accepting them as major poets through the
leverage of their anthologies.
3. Professional critics who have easy access to the contributory
volumes and are on good enough terms with publishers and poets to get
copyright matter cheap.
4. The publishers themselves.
5. Poets with a reputation which the publishers are anxious to help

---

[*]   *A Survey of Modernist Poetry*: Heinemann, 1927.

them capitalize as an offset against the comparatively poor returns their individual volumes of poetry usually bring in.

Do they in the main fall far short of the ideal possibilities of their task?

Let us observe the popular anthologist in action. He must first settle upon a time and space limit. Let us suppose that he has chosen a grand panoramic view from the earliest beginnings, e.g. 'From Beowulf to Binyon', but that his space is limited to the five-shilling or one dollar-twenty-five cents octavo in stiff boards. He is to provide 'the best' – that is, representative poems by the most desirable authors; to whom he will allot page-space according to their contemporary standing. Since Fitzgerald with *Omar Khayyam* and Coleridge with the *Ancient Mariner* are not all that much better than Landor's usual short contribution of *Rose Aylmer*, *Ianthe* and *I strove with none*, or than John Fletcher's of *Oh fair sweet face*, *Hence all you vain delights*, and *Man is his own star*, it will be necessary for him to cut *Omar Khayyam* as it has been cut in the *Oxford Book of English Verse*, and to omit *The Ancient Mariner* in favour of two unimportant Coleridge items, as the *Golden Treasury* has done (under the pretext that it is less 'lyrical' than *Omar Khayyam*, which is given in full on account of Tennyson's extravagant estimate of Fitzgerald as a poet).

The anthologist, then, decides, on his page-limit, chooses his list of authors according to an imaginary popularity vote and allots his page-space in descending order of generosity. Shakespeare fifteen pages, Keats fourteen, Milton thirteen-and-a-half, Wordsworth the same, down to Southey, Poe, Samuel Rogers and Laurence Binyon one-half apiece. Next he will draw up a list of subjects from which to choose his poems, such as:

> Triumphant Love.
> Renunciation in Love.
> Christian Mystic Love.
> A Hunting Song.
> Farm House Life.
> A Sea Piece.
> A Spring Piece.
> A Garden Piece.
> Remembrance of Childhood.
> Grief for Departed Friends.
> A Pastoral.
> A Poem about a Train.
> A Poem about England, and/or
> A Poem about the Stars and Stripes.
> A Battle Piece.
> A Poem about a Dead Child.
> An Irish Piece.
> Miscellaneous.

In choosing these poems he will look for the following proportion as given in the old punch-brewing recipe:

One of sour,
Two of sweet,
Four of strong,
And eight of weak.

He must go a little further afield than his predecessors, but not too far afield. Though he must not use too much of the material of the two established anthologies – the *Golden Treasury* and the *Oxford Book of English Verse* – the same list of authors must be fairly closely observed, and the same type of poem. For instance, the *Intimations of Immortality* may as a subject be allotted to Henry Vaughan's *Retreat*, as Sir Algernon Methuen has done, while not robbing Wordsworth of page-space. Or, a poem other than *The Old Familiar Faces* may be found to put over Lamb's signature, and 'grief for departed friends' as a subject may be allotted to Siegfried Sassoon's *Twelve Months After*. The new page-length importance of Rupert Brooke being realized, the poem about the Glorious Dead may be allotted to him instead of to Campbell or Collins; and his *Grantchester* may take the place of Browning's *Home Thoughts from Abroad*. The farm-house piece may similarly be entrusted to Edmund Blunden or Robert Frost instead of to Crabbe or Samuel Rogers.

Since there are two divisions of the public to gratify, the public that wants pleasure and the public that wants literary small-talk, the arrangement had better be for pleasure, with the literary references tucked away in a small-print appendix. There must be an index of first lines and one of authors' names; and a list of acknowledgements to publishers. The rest of the anthologizing may safely be left to the printers and binders. The title must be the battle already half-won. So Mr Adam Gowans prefaces his *The Hundred Best Poems* (Lyrical) with: 'Let me frankly admit, to begin with, that the attractiveness and probable selling qualities of the title of this little book proved, when it had once been thought of, too powerful arguments in its favour for it to be abandoned.'

This preface, as it happens, provides a ready model for our anthologist to imitate: 'I am fully conscious of the presumption such a title implies in an unknown selector, but at the same time I submit ... I can assert without fear of contradiction that every one of the poems I have included is a "gem of purest ray serene", that none can be too often read or too often repeated to one's self ... In conclusion my very warmest thanks are due to Messrs Macmillan & Co. for permission ... to Messrs Smith Elder & Co. for a like privilege ... *also to the following gentlemen ...* '

The best introductory preface would be one anthologized from all the anthology prefaces. As follows:

Poetry is the light that never was on sea or land, and the homely glow in the cottage window; the star in the sky and the fire on the hearth; the careless laughter of children and the dreams of the man of business; the glare of the footlights and the sacred flame of the altar; the jewels of the privileged few and the common coinage that everybody handles ...   *The Bookman Treasury of Living Poets*

All the Gems in this volume are not of equal brilliancy: the diamonds, rubies, emeralds and pearls of literature are few; – but there are other gems than these, of inferior value but still gem-like; – agate, cornelian, amethyst, turquoise, onyx and scores of others known to the lapidary and jeweller and prized by the public to whose appreciation they are offered.   *One Thousand and One Gems*

Nor have I sought in these Islands only, but wheresoever the Muse has followed the tongue that among living tongues she most delights to honour.   *The Oxford Book of English Verse*

The poet touches life at every point; he paints all phases of human existence and in moments of exaltation he mounts to ideal regions and sees ... the heavens opened and the angels of God ascending and descending. To such a vision the common man is not wholly blind. He knows without seeming to know what is beautiful and true.   *From Shakespeare to Hardy*

Like the fabled fountain of the Azores, but with a more various power, the magic of this Art can confer on each period of life its appropriate blessing: on early years, Experience; on maturity, Calm; on age, Youthfulness ...   *Golden Treasury*

But there is no arbitrary isolation of one theme from another; they mingle and interpenetrate throughout, to the music of Pan's flute, and of Love's viol, and the bugle-call of Endeavour and the passing-bell of Death...   *Poems of Today*

At this point we might stumble on such contradictions as this:

Every poet writes for the general public or he would not complain when it neglects him, and the greater poets sooner or later make the wider appeal.   *Mr St John Adcock*

and

Poetry is the most private of the arts, the art of the man who can live independently of the crowd.   *Mr Robert Lynd*

But our ideal anthologist would undoubtedly be able to harmonize them somehow.

Perhaps most of all the anthologist must remember that his public loves personalities. A poet's self-portrait will always be welcome. Keats must be presented standing tip-toe up on his little hill; Mr Yeats standing smothered o'wit on the Dublin pavement deliberating a journey to Inisfree; Gray as little Tommy Stout pulling poor pussy sadly out of the water; Milton making decent clutches at his late espousèd Saint (not the one he was so angered at not being able to divorce); Burns interrupting the ploughing of his crooked furrow to address maudlin apologies to the daisies and mice he was disturbing; Shakespeare as Romeo.

In fact, we may conclude that most present-day popular anthologies and anthologists are, after all, not so very far from what they should be. *If* they should be.

CHAPTER IV

The Popular Poem
and the Popular Reader

THE aim of the popular anthologist is to make a single book out of clip-
pings from many books; to create a composite author who shall be a mean
struck between all the poets included. But to strike a mean even, for
instance, between Burns, Rogers, Tennyson and Clough, with only a
century separating the first and last, is plainly impossible. The result is the
choice of a negative type of poem not proper to any of the poets, that is,
not the sort of poem that either Burns and Clough must have written, but
one that neither of them need have written. The intelligent but unread
reader who wishes to find out what poets he would like to know better gets
no help from the popular anthology: in an anthology everything reads
democratically much the same. We would not go so far as to say that every
poem in *The Golden Treasury* is uncharacteristic of the author, but we do
say that even positive poems lose character by being anthologized. Poems
by Shakespeare, Donne, Shelley, Keats, become affected by the same
negative poison, to a point where they are almost unrecognizable; so faces
in the underground or overhead railways are made negative, as faces, by
the spell of the cheap ticket which is the only link between them. In place
of their original quality the good poems acquire the same meaningless
competitive vulgarity as the bad: a conversation between various
anthology favourites would read something like this:

LANDOR'S 'ROSE AYLMER': 'I'm far the most popular of this "Best
  Hundred": I'm so easily learned by heart, I'm so short and sweet.'
SMART'S 'SONG TO DAVID': 'But I'm the longest and I'm good all
  through.'
SHIRLEY'S 'THE GLORIES OF OUR BLOOD AND STATE': 'I have the best
  beginning.'
SHAKESPEARE'S 'FIDELE'S DIRGE': And I'm by Shakespeare.'
MAHONY'S 'THE BELLS OF SHANDON': 'I have the most rhymes.'
HOOD'S 'I REMEMBER, I REMEMBER': 'I appeal to the Universal Heart of
  Man.'
GRAY'S 'ODE TO A FAVOURITE CAT': 'I never fail to get a laugh with my
  little joke in the fourth stanza.'

ANON'S 'SUMMER IS ICUMEN IN': 'I'm the oldest poem in the book.'
MR YEATS' 'INISFREE': 'My bloke's still alive and he's got the Nobel
   Prize for being the best poet IN THE WORLD.'

It is doubtful whether even the 'masterpieces' can weather the effects
of being anthologized. The reprinted poem is not like the copied art-trea-
sure. Every accurate reprinting of a poem is the original. If this were
clearer, perhaps, some appeal might be made to the anthologist against
debasing the poem in what is seldom more than commercial exploitation –
or at best the distribution of masterpieces as an aristocratic largesse to the
reading populace.

Apart from the general damage suffered by 'best poems' in being
herded together in anthologies, there are particular ill-effects arising from
the forced association of the poets themselves. The Countess of
Pembroke's *For the Healing of the Nations* was published during the War
in aid of the Red Cross; a Wiltshire anthology which, suffering from a
traumatic neurosis, overflowed into 'all climes and ages' and may be taken
as type of the honestly irresponsible collection. Here is the list of contrib-
utors in full, and the editor's note:

Beaconsfield, Earl of (Benjamin
   Disraeli)
Binyon, Laurence
Bridges, Robert
Brooke, Rupert
Bunston, Anna (Mrs de Bary)
Coleridge, Miss Mary E.
Confucius
Corneille
Crewe, Marquis of
De la Mare, Walter
Diane, Comtesse
Dostoievsky
Ecclesiastes
Elizabeth, Queen
Engleheart, George
Epictetus
Euripides
Fonblanque, Ethel M. de (Mrs
   Arthur Harter)
Gales, R.L.
Glenconner, Lady
Hamilton, Lord Frederic
Harte, Bret

Henniker-Major, Hon. Ethel
Herbert, George
Johnston, H.F.
Jonson, Ben
Jones, I.W.
Keble, John
à Kempis, Thomas
Kipling, Rudyard
Lyttleton, Hon. Mrs A.
Malone, W.
Meynell, Mrs Wilfred
More, Thomas
Morley, Viscount
Newbolt, Sir Henry
Pawlowska, Yoi
Pembroke, Sidney, Earl of
Pound, Ezra
Remizov, Alexey
Richardson, Mrs H.
Robinson, W.F.
Rogers, Samuel
Sackville, Lady Margaret
Seaman, Sir Owen
Shakespeare, William

Slow, Edward
Taylor, Jeremy
Tennant, Hon. E. Wyndham
Theresa, St
Thoreau

Traherne, Thomas
Trench, Herbert
Underhill, Miss Evelyn
Voltaire
Williams, Alfred

'If I have inadvertently committed any breach of copyright I must beg forgiveness, stating at the same time that in every case I have tried my best to trace the owner and to print nothing without permission.'

Euripides, Samuel Rogers, Confucius, Voltaire and St Theresa, etc., must certainly have generously waived this little question of copyright-fees, for it was all for the Good Cause. But they must have had great difficulty keeping up the conversation. When Ecclesiastes and Disraeli exchanged

> Remember also thy Creator in the days of thy youth;

and

> It is a holy thing to see a nation saved by its youth;

even their common nationality and the common rhythm of their sentiments can hardly have reconciled them. Shakespeare probably felt a similar embarrassment with Sir Owen Seaman. After hearing the latter's

> England, in this great fight to which you go
> Because, where Honour calls you, go you must ...

he must have felt like a cad in making this contribution:

> Let me not to the marriage of true minds
> Admit impediments. Love is not love
> Which alters when it alteration finds
> Or bends with the remover to remove.

Shelley, Sidney, Suckling, Scott and the other S's, even Siegfried Sassoon, he had met before and could comfortably exchange handshakes with, but the Editor of *Punch*! He would rather admit himself Bacon and 'bear it out even to the edge of doom' in the company of Laurence Binyon and T.E. Brown. This particular anthology is obviously too diffident to have lasting ill-effects on the better poems. But the regular anthology on which it is modelled is not redeemed by any such weakness.

The technique of the anthology is particularly apparent in the arrangement of poems. If the alphabetic arrangement has been chosen we always, for instance, get the same poem of Lamb's run up against the same three of Landor's; or if the arrangement is according to date of birth and date of death we always get the same three poems of Landor's run up against the same one of Lamb's. Lamb and Landor become twinned in the mind as inevitably as Scylla and Charybdis, Sacco and Vanzetti, David and Jonathan, Mutt and Jeff. Yet what real connection is there between Landor's poetry and Lamb's? One would say none at all. Landor was austere, select, ambitious, restrained; Lamb was open-hearted, unassuming, a punster, not ashamed of having common sentiments and setting them down simply. How then does the more ingenious anthologist fit them into his scheme of composite-authorship? As follows. Lamb's *Old Familiar Faces* (which occurred in every anthology but nine of the sixty-eight that we examined for this purpose) can be supplemented by his uncharacteristic *Hester*, which makes a perfect bridge between Landor's uncharacteristic *Rose Aylmer* and *The Old Familiar Faces*.

That is the trick at a glance. But let us take further examples. Collins and Pope are near enough contemporaries to be worth tuning together. A careful choice of their poems will therefore be necessary. Collins'

> How sleep the brave who sink to rest
> By all their country's wishes bless'd!

is near enough in style to Pope's *Ode on Solitude*:

> Happy the man whose wish and care
> A few paternal acres share –

to give the necessary illusion of composite authorship. Pope may, as in a short anthology like Mr Gowans' *Hundred Best Poems (Lyrical)*, be alphabetically cast on the same page as Samuel Rogers. What then? Well, that same poem of Pope's is one of the few things he wrote short enough to anthologize, so Rogers must be searched for a companion piece. Mr Gowans has managed splendidly. He has found a poem which can actually be interdigitated with Pope's without interrupting the sense of either. It is called *A Wish*. So the title of the doubled poem which we shall print for fun will be

Ode to Wished-for Solitude

> Happy the man, whose wish and care
>   A few paternal acres bound,
> Content to breathe his native air
>   In his own ground.
> (*Mine* be that cot beside the hill.
> The bee-hives hum shall soothe *my* ear.
> A willowy brook, that turns a mill,
> With many a fall shall linger near).
>
> Whose herds with milk, whose fields with bread,
>   Whose flocks supply him with attire,
> Whose tree in summer yield him shade,

In winter fire.
(The swallow oft beneath *my* thatch
Shall twitter from her clay-built nest.
Oft shall the pilgrim lift the latch
And share *my* meal, a welcome guest).

Blest who can unconcern'dly find
    Hours, days and years slide soft away
In health of body, peace of mind,
       Quiet by day.
(Around *my* ivied porch shall spring
Each fragrant flower that drinks the dew,
And *Lucy* at her wheel shall sing
In russet gown and apron blue).

Sound sleep by night; study and ease
    Together mixed; sweet recreation;
And innocence which most does please
       With meditation.
The village church among the trees
Where first our marriage-vows were given
With merry peals shall swell the breeze
And point with taper spire to heaven.

       Envoi
Thus let us live, unseen, unknown,
    Thus unlamented let us die,
Steal from the world, and not a stone
       Tell where we lie.

A happy combination. Pope's Ideal Man does the milking, ploughing and wood-chopping. Rogers' Lucy minds the spinning-wheel and does not interfere with the study, ease and recreation which her goodman finds time for in intervals of husbandry. Rogers' Ideal Man does not add any tasks to Pope's except bee-keeping, and supplies abundance of local amenities. But do you find a discrepancy between Pope's solitude and Rogers' pilgrim and his Lucy? It is all right really. Do not think that Pope's Ideal Man was intended to live literally unseen and unknown, any more than Rogers intended his Ideal Man to entertain pilgrims. Pope's man knows well enough that as a farmer he will need a wife to make butter and the beds, and that he will have to show himself at markets occasionally, and that as a reader he will have to go out and buy books. Rogers' man knows well enough that the age of pilgrimages is long over in England and that vagabonds will not presume to take him literally. The only textual change that we have made is in the *Envoi*, where we have included 'Lucy'.

All this is not primarily a criticism of Pope or of Rogers but of the anthologist who discovered the poems and threw them together close enough to let them grow into a single piece; and again of the anthologist who described both these poems in his preface as 'gems of purest ray serene' instead of disregarding them in the first case as ineffective and false, as he would admit if confronted with the history of their authors in relation to such idealistic pictures of simple life.

Need we take the chain of composite authorship farther forward or backward? We could show how, in alphabetical anthologies, Collins' *How Sleep the Brave* will pair with Campbell's *Toll for the Brave*; and how Rogers and Wordsworth are close enough in date to get thrown together in unalphabetical anthologies, so that Wordsworth's 'Lucy' will get somehow identified with Rogers' 'Lucy' poem given above; and how in a subject-anthology, under the heading of 'Lost Maidens', the 'Lucy of the Springs of Dove' will get confused with Kingsley's 'Mary of the Sands of Dee'.

Once these confusions start, there is no checking them. Byron's praise of his mistress:

> She walks in beauty like the night
>   Of cloudless climes and starry skies,
> And all that's best of dark and bright
>   Meet in her aspect and her eyes ...[1]

is infected by and infecting Sir Henry Wotton's praise of his:

> You meaner beauties of the night
>   That poorly satisfy our eyes
> More by your number than your light,
>   You common people of the skies ...[2]

Shirley and Shakespeare, alphabetically allied, get entangled:

> ... There is no armour against fate,
>   Death lays his icy hand on kings –
>   Sceptre and Crown
>   Must tumble down
> And in the dust be equal made
> With the poor crooked scythe and spade.
>
> Only the actions of the just
> Smell sweet and blossom in their dust;[3]

and

> Fear no more the frown of the great,
> Thou art past the tyrant's stroke!
> Care no more to clothe and eat;
> To thee the reed is as the oak:

> The sceptre, learning, physic, must
> All follow this and come to dust.[4]

When the anthology is used for recitations in schools and Goldsmith's *Deserted Village* and Gray's contiguous *Elegy* and Arnold's *Scholar Gipsy* are as usual learned by heart, further unfortunate associations occur:

> This said, he left them and returned no more:
>   But rumours hung about the country-side
> That the lost scholar long was seen to stray,
>   Seen by rare glimpses, pensive and tongue-tied …
>
> Shepherds had met him on the Hurst in spring …
>
> Haply some hoary headed swain may say,
>   'Oft have we seen him at the peep of dawn
> Brushing with hasty steps the dew away
>   To meet the sun upon the upland lawn' …
>
> One morn I missed him on the customed hill …
>
> How often have I loitered o'er thy green
> Where humble happiness endeared each scene …
>
> But times are altered …
> Usurp the land and dispossess the swain;
> Along the lawn where scattered hamlets rose …

until there is nothing left of these poems but confused recollections of Dr Thomas Arnold's *Elegy in a Deserted Schoolyard*.

Through likeness of title and nearness of date poems so fundamentally unlike as Keats' *Nightingale* and Shelley's *Skylark* affect each other strangely; the rhythm of the one 'vibrates in the memory' and unsettles the other, and it requires a serious mental effort to assign the right bird to the right case.

The fact that both poems are sonnets and written about the same period will link up Keats' On *first looking into Chapman's Homer* with Wordsworth's *The World is too much with us*:

> Then felt I like some watcher of the skies
>   When some new planet swims into his ken,
> Or like stout Cortez when with eagle eyes
>   He stared at the Pacific, and all his men …

with

> So might I, standing on this pleasant lea,
>   Have glimpses that would make me less forlorn,
> Have sight of Proteus rising from the sea;
>   Or hear old Triton blow his wreathed horn …

although by themselves Keats' sonnets read like Keats, and Wordsworth's like Wordsworth without the possibility of confusion.

Between Ben Jonson and Burns there seems little danger of mistaken identity; yet after a course of anthology-reading 'Drink to me only with thine eyes' is indistinguishable in manner from 'O my luve is like a red, red rose' and 'Go fetch to me a pint of wine'; Milton's *Nativity Hymn* becomes an intimation of Wordsworthian Immortality, and Herrick writes lyrics for the Elizabethan dramatists.

If *Annie Laurie* is included it is long odds against the original version (*not* by Lady John Scott but by Douglas of Finland in 1680) being included even in an appendix, as Colonel John Buchan has done in his *Northern Muse*. Instead of

> She's backit like the peacock,
> She's breastit like the swan,
> She's jimp aboot the middle,
> Her waist ye weel micht span:
> Her waist ye weel micht span
> And she hath a rolling ee ...

we have a censored version in which Annie Laurie appears demure rather than wild:

> Her brow is like the snaw-drift,
> Her neck is like the swan,
> Her face it is the fairest
> That e'er the sun shone on:
> That e'er the sun shone on.
> And dark-blue is her ee ...

an opportune bridge between Burns and Moore.

The reader whose first approach to poetry is through anthologies usually acquires the anthology habit for life; he cannot distinguish poets from each other by what may be called the *handwriting quality* in their poems. It hardly occurs to him that there is such a quality, or that it is worth discovering by reading poetry in its original setting. If you ask him who wrote 'God's in His Heaven, all's well with the world', he will likely enough reply: ' I don't know the name, but it's on page 856 of the *Oxford Book of English Verse* – didn't he also write " *Where the Mayne glideth*" and that nice poem about *"The pleasant waters of the river Lee'*? I'm bad at names.' He has never read a long poem or anything much longer than the *Scholar Gipsy* and the abridged *Love in the Valley* by George Meredith. He cannot read any poem which presents the slightest difficulty of thought, which demands, that is, more than one reading. He regards poetry as a patent food, 'Just add hot water and serve'. He calls himself a lover of poetry if he has stored up a few rhetorical plums such as Lovelace's

> I could not love thee, dear, so much
> Loved I not Honour more;

or Jonson's

> Death, ere thou hast slain another
> Learn'd and fair and good as she
> Time shall throw a dart at thee;

or Keats'

> Beauty is truth, truth beauty – that is all
> Ye know on earth, and all ye need to know –[5]

for social occasions. But take the first quotation. The sentiment is neatly rendered but fundamentally dishonest. Merely preferring martial honour to his mistress' arms did not help Lovelace in any way to love her so much. He loved her less, in fact, because she had, as a woman, lower social rating than the sword, the horse, the shield. There is no causal relation here between love and honour – artful cavalier flattery disguises a set of brutal sentiments that might otherwise disgust even an anthologist and his public. Then the second quotation. The Countess of Pembroke had been a generous patroness to poets and Jonson's prophecy that she would have no rival to the end of time might pass if he had contented himself with a simple and dignified recital of her personal qualities. Instead, however, he closes his tribute with a poetical flourish that robs it of seriousness. For, though visitors to the church-memorial or readers of a popular anthology may be impressed by these fine words, Death won't. As for Keats, the equation between Truth and Beauty, together with the conclusion, is just a clumsy attempt at a serious proposition in logic. Compare it with these two inspired formulas by Mr W.E. Johnson:

> The factual universal may be expressed in the form 'Every substantive in the universe of reality is Q if P'; while the assertion of law assumes the form 'Any substantive in the universe of reality would be Q if it were P.'[*]

Our remarks on the effect on the poem of being repeatedly anthologized, its slow spiritual breakdown, may be considered fanciful. But of the bad effect on the reader of repeatedly reading the same poem there need be no dispute; we have only to try the following experiment: If you say the same word, any word – say, if you say the word 'word'; say it – 'word', 'word', 'word', like that a few times over: then you have 'word' for awhile stripped clean and new. You realize its character, its sound, the letters that compose it, as you haven't done for years. But then go on, a hundred times more, saying the word 'word' – 'word', 'word', 'word', and it gets

---

* W.E. Johnson, *Logic, Part III*, p.6, quoted by R.B. Braithwaite, *The Idea of Necessary Connexion* (II), Mind, vol. xxxii, no. 145.

completely ga-ga as a word. In fact the word 'word' has already in this paragraph begun to fail in its habitual organization, to change colour and suggest other similar words like 'wood' and 'ward' and 'wort' and 'wart', until you will soon not be able to recognize it as your old friend 'word'. This curious obliteration is, of course, the common fate of prayers. When the bedesman has said ten thousand *ave*'s for the repose of a rich man's soul there is no telling what the ten-thousand-and-first *ave* will mean to him.

There are three stages in repetition: the first when the sense still persists; the second when it wavers and breaks and free association begins; the third when free association itself breaks down and the thing repeated becomes a pure incantation. When you get a pure incantation, it is no longer a case of the word or prayer having any soul of its own, even its friends (that is, the associated ideas) have deserted it: it becomes an empty lodging in which any strange creature may choose to nest. That is why clergymen often have such haunted faces. In the technical religious phrase the arrival at this stage in prayer is called 'accidie': it is the time when the Belgian-looking devils slip in. The first act of black magic is to empty a prayer of religious meaning and so smuggle something anti-religious in. You can always tell by listening to a clergyman when he has reached this stage of 'accidie'. He may be able to repeat all the prayers word-perfectly; but there is a note (like the note of the churn when butter has at last begun to form) which is unmistakable. Usually, however, as in a musical-box a note gets broken, so a word will break in a prayer. We know a parish church where the parson Sunday after Sunday intones: 'Who *desireth the death* of a sinner, but rather that he should turn from his wickedness and live'; and the congregation, as spell-bound as he, never notices the disappearance of an important negative.

A rather worse case was that of a lecturer during the War who was employed by the War Office to address troops on the subject of 'Our War Aims'. It was at first, in 1914, quite a good lecture. The lecturer did not let it harden into a formula until late in the Spring of 1915, when he nevertheless gave it accurately and with conviction and without personal strain. In 1916 it was still word-perfect, but the lecturer had lost reality: he looked dim on the platform. Late in 1917 it had begun to fray: there was no actual break of sense, but the words were strangely clipped and slurred and the lecturer was in a complete state of self-hypnosis. Shortly before the Armistice there was a nervous breakdown. There had been some violent disturbance during the lecture (an Australian audience had begun to barrack) and the hypnosis had been interrupted. The lecturer had tried to get into familiar touch again with his own lecture, but the result was a bad short-circuit. The catenation broke and the lecture degenerated into a recurring sequence of three sentences, including the joke (always sure of a laugh) about the Entente Cordiale and King Edward VII's 'love of French Institutions'.

Consider, then, in the light of these effects of repetition, the case of the anthology poem, as *L'Allegro* or Shakespeare's 'When in disgrace with fortune and men's eyes', which probably had a bad beginning with the anthology reader when he first learned them by heart in the class-room. In the class-room meaning could obviously not have mattered, but memory and 'expression' did. And what the adult reader recognizes when he reads these poems in an anthology again are not meaning-echoes but memory- or expression-echoes of what, in recitation, received most emphasis. He will greet again such phrases as 'Come and trip it as you go, On the light fantastic toe', or 'Trouble deaf Heaven with my bootless cries', and get nothing from them but repetition-pleasure. By the time he has repeated them to himself a few dozen times (a particular line often getting associated with a habitual act such as shaving, or posting a letter, or eating the breakfast egg) and has seen the 'light fantastic toe' quoted a few dozen times in theatrical journals and 'Trouble deaf Heaven with my bootless cries' quoted a few dozen times on the comic pages of fiction monthlies, he will be unable to realize that 'fantastic toe' and 'bootless cries' have real meanings. He will have the same blank feeling towards them as towards words like *peppermint* or *hedgehog* which he never by any chance breaks up into their original parts, 'mint' and 'pepper', 'hog' and 'hedge', but remembers by a vague sensuous image. The popular anthologist makes a practice of including as many poems of this exhausted character as he conveniently can; they give neither himself nor the reader any trouble.

'Beachcomber', of the *London Express*, knows all about anthologies:

ANOTHER ANTHOLOGY

Mr Dribble's 'Hundred Best Telephone Numbers' is all that an anthology should be. It is comprehensive and free from prejudice. Moreover, it includes many new numbers, the compiler having gone to the little-known outlying exchanges for fresh talent. 28443 Pobham, for instance, is a genuine discovery. Nearly all the favourite West-End exchanges are well represented, but one misses the superb 00010001 Mayfair. Also, one could have done with more Park numbers. It must be admitted, however, that the compiler has done his work so well that he has included numbers to suit all tastes. And if I were condemned to a life in prison or on a desert island, and were allowed to take six numbers with me, I should find them all in this anthology. One may conclude with the hope that each one of these hundred numbers may find an answering echo in at least one exchange.

*   *   *   *   *

I understand that the success of this anthology has emboldened Mr Dribble to prepare a similar work, which will be called the 'Hundred Best Trains'.

CHAPTER V

The Perfect Modern Lyric

THE effect of anthologies on the general reader extends into criticism: the professional critic is in most cases merely a more than usually infatuated reader of anthologies. The critic's business has come to be to condone the general reader's wilful inertness; to reprove or neglect poets who do not take these into account; and to bear out his assumption that the poet's first thought in writing a poem is its eventual inclusion in an anthology. How general this assumption is can be seen by a glance at Mr Norman Ault's* *Elizabethan Lyrics*. (On the whole this is quite a scholarly and honest piece of editing; if it had been content to include only the ten hitherto unpublished pieces and the two or three hundred pieces otherwise difficult of access it would have been worthy of even greater praise. But the editor's scholar's-conscience has not been proof against the popular-anthology temptation of using *Elizabethan* in an 'aesthetic' sense. The Elizabethan age closed abruptly with the death of the Queen and the accession of the unlovable, unfearable and un-English James I. And about a third of the poems are Jacobean in date, or probably more, including one or two of Shakespeare's sonnets. A number were written in the 1530s and are only made Elizabethan by the doubtful expedient of printing Tottel's versions rewritten twenty-five years later to suit contemporary taste. The only connection between poems written in the middle of the reign of Henry VIII and those written at the end of the reign of James I is, indeed, that they are both un-Elizabethan.)

Mr Ault writes in his preface (the italics are ours):

The poems are arranged neither in the order of the birthdays of the authors, nor according to subject matter: but year by year according to the dates at which each poem *first became known to the public for which the author wrote*. This plan renders it possible to see each poem *in relation to its proper historical background of contemporary song and thus to estimate its comparative as well as its actual quality*;

---

* Author of *Dreamland Shores*, *The Poet's Life of Christ*, and *The Podgy Book of Tales*.

and in the case of the *better known* poets (who are *of course* repre-
sented by more numerous selections) to study the development of
the work of the individual author.

We have here then the editor in a dual anthology role: as a modern
anthologist catering retrospectively to Elizabethan public taste and as an
Elizabethan anthologist catering prospectively to modern public taste.
The result is a two-fold distortion: not only the distortion of textual mate-
rial into aesthetic material but the distortion of the aesthetic material as
well. An Elizabethan anthologist turning the same textual material into
aesthetic material would have studied a taste very different from Mr
Ault's twentieth-century high-brow taste. Instead of Shakespeare forty-
eight poems, Breton nine, he would have made it Shakespeare nine,
Breton forty-eight.

The little dedication of *Printer to Reader* which Mr Ault puts at the
beginning of his collection, borrowing it from the Elizabethan anthologist
of *A Handful of Pleasant Delights*, 1584, may be touching; but it is most
inappropriate when made to introduce a number of poems by Vaux,
Wyatt, Shakespeare, Donne and others which do not correspond with the
anthology taste of the book to which it was originally attached:

> You that in music do delight
>   Your minds for to solàce,
> This little book of sonnets may
>   Well like you in that case.
> Here may you have such pretty things
>   As women much desire:
> Here may you have of sundry sorts
>   Such songs as you require.
> Wherefore, my friend, if you regard
>   Such songs to read or hear,
> Doubt not to buy this pretty Book,
>   The price is not so dear.*

Mr Ault, in spite of what he writes about his arrangement, does give a list
of authors with dates of birth, and does give a careful subject-concordance
with such headings as *Time* (see also 'Beauty' and 'Gather the Rose-bud'),
Tobacco, *Town Life*, *Trade*, *Travel*, *Tristia*, *Toilet*. He will be much preyed
on by future anthologists. 'And by God's Body', in Wyatt's words, 'I
would he might be so served, and then were he well served.' He makes this
subject-arrangement because he knows that the reader, finding it impos-
sible to connect poems with the names of their authors, is inclined to

---

* Longmans, Green & Co., 10s. 6d.

group poetry in his mind according to subject (as 'Thus the Mayne glideth' is grouped with 'The pleasant waters of the river Lee' and various Skylarks with various Nightingales).

The effect of this practice on criticism will, we hope, be made clear by instancing several modern poems that have gained undeserved reputation by it. The first is a poem of which we have a right to speak more severely than others because one of us first met it in a popular anthology and the other wrote it. It was written in a crowded room when the author was just nineteen, with official stationery and gramophone intermissions. The subject was suggested by a reproduction, in a Christmas supplement, of Holman Hunt's 'Scapegoat'. This public setting for the birth of the poem may have had something to do with its subsequent popularity: public sentiment somehow infiltrated. We would not say that the poem was originally dishonest in its conception, but it certainly is made to appear so by its being anthologized; and now even its author can only with difficulty remember the genuine feelings that provided it with a nucleus.

The story was simple; a supposed tender encounter between Christ and the yearly scapegoat in the Wilderness. Little thought was necessary after the first three lines; it only required a quaint assemblage of desert animals recalled from Isaiah, and a grafting of the love-of-animals theme on the Christ theme to help it out. There is a loose equation of Christ with the scapegoat, and the scapegoat weeps like Blake's Lion when he found himself in an equally tender relationship with Lyca in the *Songs of Innocence*. And that is all. The only flaw in it as an anthology piece has been that in one line the definite article was found wanting. But the anthologists soon put that right (without the author's consent) and the perversity has never been allowed to return. The poem has been in at least seventeen English anthologies and several more in America. Its increment by this means has been six or seven times as much as the total proceeds of the three editions of the volume in which it first appeared.

It is very accommodating as an anthology-piece. It is a poem about animals, it is a poem about Christ, it is a poem about comradeship, it is a 'Shorter Lyric of the Twentieth Century', it is in rhyme, it is easily learned in schools, and it takes you nowhere quite safely after giving you the feeling that you have been a long distance. Because of the author's alphabetical position it always forms such a pleasant little curtain-raiser to Gray's *Elegy* that the children love it. With a single not serious lapse, a poem fancifully combining natural history with unhappy love, this author has written no other successful anthology-piece, and so remains for the public, in spite of all that has happened since, the author of 'that poem about the Goat'. Emile Cammaerts, the Belgian critic of English poetry, has written of him as 'one of the rising modern religious poets of England' solely on the strength of these lines. A press-cutting recently received informs us:

The King Alfred School of Hampstead has its own printing press, from which a fascinating anthology has emerged with a squirrel on the cover. It is an anthology of beasts and birds, and it faintly adumbrates what might be collected and embalmed for the delight of naturalists and animal lovers ... it is an unconventional and what is called an 'experimental' School. Anyway, there are two quotations from Tennyson and all of Gray's lines 'On a Favourite Cat, Drowned in a Tub of Gold Fishes' ... and Mr W.H. Davies' 'Kingfisher' and 'Jenny Wren' ...

And, of course, the 'Scapegoat' is there (though without permission).[1] Now if that little poem had been left alone it would not have been a bad little poem, though rather muddled and young and silly. But it has gone to the devil now and fancies itself as a perfect lyric, and nothing will bring it to its senses short of putting it back again among the other rather muddled and young and silly pieces of the book which first included it.

The other author of this book has had the similar experience of being represented in popular anthologies only by juvenilia. The editor of a 'Best Poems' anthology has recently written to apologize that the poems he asks for are not her best or most characteristic, but that he fears for the saleability of his collection. This apology does not, however, occur in his preface.

The popular anthology-piece, like the best-seller novel, is usually achieved in the dark; but certain critical regulations can be made for it. It must be fairly regular in form and easily memorized, it must be a new combination of absolutely worn-out material, it must have a certain unhealthy vigour or langour, and it must start off with a simple and engaging statement of a sentimental character. Somewhere there must be a daring poetical image such as:

> If ye break faith with us who die,
> We shall not sleep, though poppies grow
> In Flanders fields;

or,

> The Master said:
> 'I have planted the Seed of a Tree,
> It shall be strangely fed
> With white dew and with red,
> And the Gardeners shall be Three,
> Regret, Hope, Memory!'

It must have as many 'subjects' in it as possible, so that it can be easily shifted about by the anthologist from one section of his book to the other wherever fattening is required.

Mr Yeats' 'Lake Isle of Inisfree' is a striking example of a poem that started in innocence, but the progress of which from anthology to anthology suggests that of the 'simple village maiden' of the ballad, 'Victim of a *Squire's Whim*'.

> So away she went to London
>   For to hide her sin and shame,
> But she met *another* Squire,
>   And *again* she lost her name.

Note the applicability of the ironic end of the ballad:

> In a cottage in the country
>   Her old honest parents live,
> Drinking champagne which she sends them –
>   But they NEVER can forgive.

The ordinary reader is inclined to take 'Inisfree' for granted as a 'perfect lyric' on the assurance of the critics, and will be surprised, when he examines it out of its anthology setting, to see what a misery it really is. True to anthology-type, it begins with the necessary simple sentimental statement: the Biblical 'I will arise and go unto my father' is padded with the poetical repetition of 'and go':

> I will arise and go now, and go to Inisfree.[2]

The name 'Inisfree' is a romantic invention, with the syllable 'free' slipped in to help the reader to the conclusion that Inisfree isn't the name of an up-to-date private nursing-home or the prodigal's father's house; but an island refuge, somewhere remote and solitary, in Ireland of the legends.

> And a small cabin build there, of clay and wattles made.

The smallness of the cabin suggests the complete enervation of the poet who could not even trouble to build himself a roomy retreat, and his complete improvidence against the damp of an Irish winter: this fatalism is likely to meet with a ready response from the reader who has been already enervated by an extensive course of anthology-browsing. The most miserable touch is the proposal to *build* a cabin which he magically finds already *made* before he reaches the end of the line: suggesting the wish-fulfilment mechanism of the ordinary fatigue-dream. Anthology lyrics are as a matter of fact the only form of poetry that can be rightly compared with the dream, which in general may be regarded as the unchecked running-down of a theme (first suggested in waking life) to a finish either of exhaustion and indecision or of false, because disorderly decision. Dreams are born of the will to disintegrate physically, such poems of the will to disintegrate mentally. In both you find the same surrender to sensuality, a sleepy luxuriousness which is what is commonly meant by 'poetic ecstasy'. And as in dreams one constantly finds oneself making witty jokes which, when one wakes up, do not hold together as jokes at all, so in this type of poetry one gets, as we shall see, the poetic conceit which does not hold together either.

> Nine bean-rows will I have there, a hive for the honey-bee.

Nine, because that is a mystic number. How long in extent the bean-rows were, does not appear. The reader is expected to react to the mystic 'nine' and say, 'Probably some deep Hermetic mystery is intended, or some strange Celtic allegory.' But Mr Yeats is only dreaming, not exercising thought; this 'nine' is a plain confession of muzziness, justifying our continued line by line prose-analysis. The 'honey-bee', too, is just a mysterious synonym for the ordinary bee; and when the phrase 'a hive for the honey-bee' is put in apposition to 'bean-rows', it can only mean that the poet, being too lazy to build his own skips, lets the bees swarm among his beans. But even so, the bees will never make their hive in the beans but will choose a hollow tree at some distance from the cabin. Note the ugly clash between *bean* and *bees*.

> And live alone in the bee-loud glade.

Bee-loud is another would-be poetical phrase, suggesting rather the police-court report: 'Your worship, defendant used improper language while I was at my piano-practice. "Dee you," she said, "you're making too bee-loud a noise for *my* peace and quiet."' As for the sentiment, it is only a weak repetition of Pope's *Ode to Solitude* and Rogers' *A Wish*, cutting down the simple necessities desired by those earlier sentimentalists to a point far below subsistence level.

> And I shall have some peace there, for peace comes dropping slow,
> Dropping from the veils of morning to where the cricket sings.

Again the poetical repetition concealing the impoverishment of thought. In this second line we have the showy conceit necessary to suggest profundity. Presumably the veils of morning are the dawn-clouds, and the place where the cricket sings is the cabin hearth: 'peace comes down the chimney every morning' is what Yeats really meant. The second half of the first line, because of 'for', must grammatically explain the first half: because of the slowness of peace as it drops, the poet will be able to catch some of it at least as it comes slowly down the chimney every morning.

> There midnight's all a glimmer, and noon a purple glow,
> And evening full of the linnet's wings.

This is further extravagance to set off the 'veils of morning'. A-glimmering midnights are rare in Ireland; you wouldn't get linnets in a flock except in the late summer migration which is incompatible with the bee and bean-flower context, nor are linnets particularly active in the evening. But 'midnight', 'glimmer', 'evening' and 'linnet' are poetical words and must go in, despite the sense: so is 'purple', the easiest colour-disguise for feeble workmanship both in painting and poetry (and for that matter in music) – purple began as the colour of kingliness and ended as the colour of anaemia and half-mourning. 'Linnet' is chosen from all the other birds because it begins with 'L', and part of the lullaby quality of the poem is got by an over-proportion of l's to natural requirements. No modern poet, it is safe to say, with the exception of Edmund Blunden and Robert Frost, can distinguish a linnet from any other small bird with a squeaky little voice: but the linnet is as fashionable in contemporary nature-verse as the lark and nightingale used to be.

> I will arise and go now, for always night and day
> I hear lake water lapping with low sounds by the shore.

This is an attempt to pull the poem together, before it dissolves into mush, by reintroducing the action idea: but not real action, only a repetition of the resolution in the opening line, which has not yet been and indeed never could be translated into practice. The over-alliterative description of noises in the head reads as pathological, especially in view of the poet's previous auditory absorption in the buzzing of bees and the whirring of linnets' wings.

> While I stand on the roadway, or on the pavements grey,

Is there here an antithesis between the roadway and the pavement? If so, it is not clearly made. And how does 'while I stand' square with 'I will arise'? Perhaps he stood on the roadway but sat on the pavement. Why the 'pavement grey'? Is that an inversion for the sake of the rhyme, or does 'grey' refer predicatively to the poet? Why all the 'ey' sounds? Are they intended to create a melancholy urban sound in contrast with the Tennysonian vowel-variation of the preceding line; or is it just carelessness, and is the internal rhyme of 'way' and 'grey' unintentional? It was foolish, anyhow, to mention the 'pavement grey' because this definitely introduces the time-note and accentuates the hopelessness of the fancy.

> I hear it in the deep heart's core.

What he means is either 'in the core of my heart', or 'deep in my heart'. But, unable to make the verse fit with only one of these phrases, he combines the two metaphors of *depth* and *centrality* of emotion in a way that defeats his meaning; for he has had to leave out the important word 'my' (it would have made the line end in too many heavy syllables running): so that the possessor of the heart may be anyone or anything. Certainly with whatever qualities the hero of such a simple-life romance might properly adorn himself, depth or centrality of emotion is not one of them (nor ordinary common-sense).

Still, as anthology material 'Inisfree' is invaluable. It can be classified under 'Rustic', 'Mystic', 'Thoughts from Town', 'Irish Sentiment', 'Solitude', 'Exile', 'Love of Animals', 'Natural Religion' and other anthology headings, and must have proved a little gold-mine to its author. We conclude our criticism by a fugitive epigram:

Inisfree on its Author

In the Senate house in Dublin
   My old honest author sits
Drinking champagne on the proceeds
   Of his early loss of wits.

Mr de la Mare's 'Arabia' hangs together better than most anthology pieces because it is *all* muzzy:

Far are the shades of Arabia
   Where the Princes ride at noon
'Mid the verdurous vales and thickets
   Under the ghost of the moon.
And so dark is that vaulted purple
   Flowers in the forest rise
And toss into blossom 'gainst the phantom stars
   Pale in the noonday skies.

If we are to trust travellers, there are no shades in Arabia, particularly at noon, except in sand-storms. There are no forests. The moon and stars are not visible at noon: except in the rainy season, which lasts for a week or two, the sky is as bright as brass at noon. The Arabians, princes and all, do most of their riding at night. Flowers do appear in certain districts each spring, but grow low on the ground and are soon burned up.

Sweet is the music of Arabia
   In my heart, when out of dreams
I still in the thin clear mirk of dawn
   Descry her gliding streams;
Hear her strange lutes on the green banks
   Ring loud with the grief and delight
Of the dim-silked dark-haired Musicians
   In the brooding silence of night.

Streams are not characteristic of Arabia except in the short rainy season, when they rush rather than glide. Lutes are not native to the East in spite of the Authorized Version of the *Book of Daniel* (where they occur with harps, sackbuts and psalteries); and Arabian music is not in any sense

sweet like the music of people who live in wooded countries and have
singing birds such as the thrush to model it upon, but harsh and bare and
monotonous like the desert.

> They haunt me – her lutes and her forests;
>   No beauty on earth I see
> But shadowed with that dream recalls
>   Her loveliness to me:
> Still eyes look coldly upon me,
>   Cold voices whisper and say –
> 'He is crazed with the spell of far Arabia,
>   They have stolen his wits away.'

This poem is a clear proof of the justice of the comparison that we made
between the anthology lyric and the dream, particularly the fatigue-
dream. If this poem had been written as poetry and not as poetic ecstacy,
the word Arabia would never have been allowed to enter; either an actual
place would have been chosen like Cambodia, where much of what he says
in the poem applies, or a new name would have been coined. But Mr de la
Mare has had a confused, luxurious dream in which the hackneyed lines
'I'll sing thee songs of Araby and tales of far Cashmere' have developed
without any wakeful restraint into this foolish fantasy which combines the
silken Prince of Araby with the forests, flowers and silks of Cashmere and
identifies the 'songs of Araby' with the Victorian song which celebrates
them. The last stanza which admits the craziness of the dream and its
distortion of waking life, is the best argument against the poem as a poem
and its best ticket of admission into the anthology, where it will continue
for many years to *cheat* people of a sigh and *charm* them to a tear. The
desire of certain poems to leave the company of their fellows in the indi-
vidual volume, seek their fortune and finally end their lives as perfect
lyrics in a standard popular anthology comes not from enterprise but
depravity. 'Why poems leave home' is a story of disgrace rather than of
glory. For it can be laid down as a fairly fast rule that any modern piece
that has achieved the popularity of 'Inisfree' or 'Arabia' must be function-
ally half-witted or contain at least one crucial perversion of thought.

Mr Ralph Hodgson's much anthologized *Bells of Heaven*, with its
humanitarian appeal for 'wretched, blind pit-ponies and little hunted
hares', is easily recognizable as a black sheep of the Hodgson menagerie. It
offends us certainly to think of pit-ponies being kept down in the dark
until they lose the use of their eyes, and so it should; but not dispropor-
tionately to other crimes of civilization. Pit-ponies are more lovingly-
treated than most of their kind above ground; so that, indeed, the pit-pony
often shows fewer signs of wretchedness than the average miner or
miner's wife and family. Thus the adjective 'wretched' can only apply
fairly to certain particular pit-ponies who happen to be wretched: and the

cause of their wretchedness is not specified. We would not insist on the weakness of 'wretched' if it were not matched by the 'little' hunted hares. The hares hunted are not singled out for sport *because* they are usually small in size. Nor should mere size in any case induce pity: mice are much smaller than hares and just as charming: but we destroy them without protest from Mr Hodgson. Bugs are smaller still. The ugliness of hunting the hare is in the way that its wantonness is sportingly disguised, not in the relative *size* of man and hare: bigness in man does not mean relatively greater speed. The first part of the poem is:

> 'Twould ring the Bells of Heaven
> The wildest peal for years
> If Parson lost his senses
> And people came to theirs
> And he and they together
> Knelt down with angry prayers
> For tamed and shabby tigers
> And dancing dogs and bears ...

The conceit about losing one's senses and coming to one's senses bears the whole burden of poeticality for this little piece and must be supposed to be wittily intended: but when one examines the antithesis it falls to pieces like the witticism of the dream examined in daylight. If Parson is at present in his senses, and 'people' are out of theirs, one would think that all that was necessary was for Parson to kneel down and say the necessary prayers, and for the people thereupon to come to their senses. No, Parson has first to *lose* his senses. But if Parson lost his senses there would be no sensible prayers. Mr Hodgson probably intends that there is a callousness about Parson in his sensible moods that would allow such things to continue without protest. But if in Parson, why not in the Congregation? Why shouldn't they too lose their senses? If the first part of the antithesis is meant ironically, why not the second? Why should Parson come in for all the irony? And why should the bells of Heaven be so enthusiastically rung at the receipt of these prayers which are not contrite but definitely indignant, and addressed to the Deity. Must we suppose that the angelic bell-ringers dare to sympathize with 'people' in their new-found indignation, the Deity corresponding in callousness with His representative on earth, Parson? Must the Deity be persuaded to lose His senses in order to preserve the logic of Mr Hodgson's humanitarianism?

This piece cannot be judged as poetry any more than 'Inisfree', it has to be judged as propaganda verse. The first test of propaganda verse is whether it gives the message clearly: and we have found that 'The Bells of Heaven' are, in Mr Hodgson's hands, cracked. The next test is whether its remedial suggestions are plausible. Now, there is figurative sense in Shelley's

Men of England, wherefore plough
For the lords who lay you low?

There is superficial sense in the temperance hymn beginning:

Cold water is the best of drinks ...

There is even a homely if fanciful wisdom in the eighteenth-century catch:

Slaves to the World should be tossed in a blanket
If I might have my will ...

But all that Mr Hodgson can suggest to remedy the sufferings of (*a*) caged tigers, (*b*) performing bears and dogs, (*c*) pit-ponies, (*d*) hunted hares, is prayers to God by callous congregations miraculously converted to Sunday humanitarianism. The very inefficacy of the solution makes the poem delightful for anthology readers, for they realize that they are not expected to do anything for the poor animals but read it.

Dr Bridges' most anthologized poem is another piece of careless carpentry:

I love all beauteous things,
    I seek and adore them;
God hath no better praise,
And man in his hasty days
    Is honoured for them.[3]

Of course he loves all beauteous things. He loves them because he considers them beauteous, or he considers them beauteous because he loves them – it doesn't matter which. Naturally he seeks them and adores them. He seeks them because he adores them or he adores them because he seeks them – it doesn't matter which. Naturally also, this being the next thing on the list, he gives God praise, and he then gives man honour – it doesn't matter which. The question, however, arises: do the beauteous things belong originally to man or to God? Or must God and man litigate?

I too will something make
    And joy in the making;
Altho' tomorrow it seem
Like the empty words of a dream
    Remembered on waking.

'I too' can only mean that Dr Bridges wishes to be classified as neither God nor man. 'And joy in the making' – by adding a new quality to his proposed creation, not known to God or hasty man, Dr Bridges suggests an antithesis, i.e. 'God and man make beauteous things and are praised and honoured for them, but get no joy; I, on the other hand, am determined to get joy, although the impermanence of my creations gets me no praise or honour.' The 'dream remembered on waking' is a reminiscence of the seventy-third Psalm.

Of Rupert Brooke's famous *England* sonnet, 'If I should die think only this of me', and the remainder of that sequence, the final comment was already made in April, 1915, by Charles Sorley, himself a soldier, killed in action five months later.

> I find it overpraised. He is far too obsessed with his own sacrifice, regarding the going to war of himself (and others) as a highly remarkable sacrificial exploit, whereas it is merely the conduct demanded of him (and others) by the turn of circumstances where noncompliance with this demand would have made life intolerable. He has clothed his attitude in fine words; but he has taken the sentimental attitude … His early poems are his best.

And what of Mr Masefield's 'Cargoes'? It is his most anthologized poem, one that has even been included by Dr Bridges in his *Chilswell Book of English Verse* (a collection, by the way, that omits Donne, Marvell, Vaughan, Marlowe, Skelton and the three Fletchers, for the benefit of Newbolt, Moore, Lang, Longfellow, Arnold, Kipling, Campbell, R.W. Dixon who has four, Scott who has six, Byron who has eight and Tennyson who has ten pieces included).

> Quinquereme of Nineveh from distant Ophir
> Rowing home to haven in sunny Palestine –

Nineveh has possibly been linked up with the sea on Jonah's account, Mr Masefield remembering that the prophet, afraid to pronounce doom on Nineveh, took ship from Tarshish. But Nineveh is hundreds of miles from Palestine, so why a quinquereme of Nineveh should row *home* to Palestine is mysterious. Let us charitably assume that by Nineveh Mr Masefield means Assyria; but though the Assyrians conquered Palestine and held it for a while, Nineveh was not then the political centre of their empire; moreover the Phoenicians, not the Assyrians, had command of the Palestine coast; and anyhow the route from the land of Ophir to Palestine before the days of the Suez Canal was one no quinquereme could take unless it first casually circumnavigated Africa – Hiram's Phoenician fleet was sensibly built on the Red Sea with Solomon's right-of-way permission. And anyhow Nineveh had fallen before quinqueremes were invented.

> With a cargo of ivory,
> And apes and peacocks,
> Sandalwood, cedarwood and sweet white wine.

The circumnavigation of Africa is here lengthened by a voyage to the East

Indies or perhaps Polynesia in search of sandalwood; but why these Assyrio-Phoenicians were such fools as to go to Ophir (where the gold came from) and to bring back not gold but cedarwood and wine, which are among the chief riches of Palestine, we cannot well make out. The ivory, apes and peacocks are clipped of course from the *Book of Kings* but from a different chapter than the one dealing with Hiram: and they then came sensibly cross-country with the Queen of Sheba. It is strange how many of these perfect lyrics crib their effects from the Bible. There is no finite verb in this stanza.

> Stately Spanish galleon coming from the Isthmus,
> Dipping through the Tropics by the palm-green shores,
> With a cargo of diamonds,
> Emeralds, amethysts,
> Topazes.

Cargo is rather a heavy term for this: consignment would be more plausible. The cargo would have been something bulkier; for instance, cotton, cacao, nuts, silver ingots, hard woods, Jesuits' bark, and so on. Oh, no, we see –

> … cinnamon and gold moidores.

Well, then the bulk of the cargo was cinnamon: the galleon was coming home from the Isthmus of Panama (?) after unsuccessfully trying to plant a cargo principally consisting of cinnamon (from Ceylon) on the Mexicans. But why in the world were moidores among the cargo? Again some unsuccessful commercial transaction is indicated. The Spaniards took their chests of coined gold to the New World and were told, 'No, thank you, we have plenty of that yellow metal here.' Which so chilled their stately hearts that they did not think of asking for some ordinary unworked bars of gold in exchange for steel knives, guns and other European manufactures. But they got the jewels all right, perhaps in barter for a small amount of cinnamon; unless these also came from the East Indies with the cinnamon. There is no finite verb in this stanza either.

> Dirty British coaster with a salt-caked smoke stack
> Butting through the Channel in the mad March days,
> With a cargo of Tyne coal,
> Road-rails, pig-lead,
> Firewood, iron-ware and cheap tin trays.

And still no finite verb; so we are evidently intended to hang up these three nautical sketches on the wall and compare them. The main differences in the three exhibits are as follows: Fig. 1, Oars; Fig. 2, Sails; Fig. 3, Steam. Fig. 1 and Fig. 2, Romantic, scented cargo, long calm voyages;

Fig. 3, Prosaic cargo, short voyages, dull travelling. The natural deductions to be drawn from these tabulated contrasts can only be that improvements in methods of marine transport do not necessarily make for long, pleasurable voyages. Which is not a sublime thought; and we therefore look farther for a meaning of greater subtlety. The Tyne coal and road-rails give the clue. Where was the coaster taking them to in the mad March days? Think a moment! Fig. 1, Cedar and wine to Palestine; Fig. 2, Moidores to Spain. Fig. 3? Why, of course, iron and coal back to Newcastle again after a rattling voyage round the British Isles; in the course of which the cheap tin trays were re-imported into South Wales at a somewhat dearer price. And the moral? Is it the 'Changeless Mystery of the Sea'? Perhaps we may take a couplet of Mr Masefield's scandalously out of its context and refer it to the Sea:

> All I have learned, and can learn, show me this:
> How scant, how slight, my knowledge of her is.[4]

A frequently anthologized poem of Mr Humbert Wolfe's begins:

> *Morning*
>
> If all of us were doomed to die
> When we had lived a minute,
> I think I know what Anne and I
> Would wish to happen in it.

An archly expressed fancy which may be rationalized as follows: 'If a mysterious disease or functional failure were to destroy all human beings one minute after birth, then I and Anne' – the poet's daughter as we read elsewhere – but of course there would not be a daughter Anne, there would not be time, or Mr Wolfe would have to waste several seconds of his minute begetting her – anyhow 'I and my daughter Anne, mysteriously co-eval in babyhood, with our first comforters in our mouths and our first swaddling clothes about us, would like to have what happen?'
      The poem continues:

> We'd let our sixty seconds run
> Where chestnut-blossoms harden
> Some early morning, at Kensington,
> When Spring is in the Gardens.

And that is all. After all the agony of this tragical proposition we are left with only an arithmetical formula, which we may be expected to have already known – that one minute is the equivalent of sixty seconds – and a little bit of mystical natural history which we could not be expected to have already known. For chestnut-blossoms do not really harden. The buds soften as they turn to blossom and the blossoms soften further as they wither and fall off, and then the fruit hardens. Whether or not this mysterious phenomenon, the hardening of the blossom, is more notice-able in the Gardens in the early morning before the gates open when Peter Pan is still piddling about on his lawful errands, the context does not make clear.

Grammatically, the only conclusion is that these baby-folk, if put in the unfortunate position of having to meet their God only sixty seconds after having taken leave of Him, would choose to be born under a spreading chestnut-tree and would spend their time each with one eye on the second-hand of a watch, the other on the chestnut-blossom, to note exactly how much hardening took place in their life-time of research. They would then report their observations to St Peter. But perhaps what Mr Wolfe really means is that if you let sixty seconds run, among the perambulators, where the brain softens, some early morning at Kensington, when Spring is in the Gardens, you are likely to achieve a perfect modern lyric.

Modern American anthology-pieces are not quite so successful as their British counterparts, because the Free Verse movement has made it diffi-cult to use worn-out material in quite so hypnotic a manner, and the true bad-vigour quality only comes with rhyme. Still, Mr Sandburg manages successfully enough in his 'Cool Tombs'.

When Abraham Lincoln was shovelled into the tombs, he forgot the copperheads and the assassin ... in the dust, in the cool tombs.

'Shovelled' is intended as a confidential colloquialism, 'tombs' as a poet-ical enlargement of singular into plural. But the colloquial and the poetical obstruct each other: the verse reads as though poor President Lincoln had been assassinated with dynamite and had to be distributed with a shovel among the different state-cemeteries. There, such as it is, the poem really ends, but it is protracted as an anthology-piece by the old ballad device of three parallel statements and a conclusion – 'I said it once, I say it again, what I say three times' (in slightly different ways) 'is true'.

And Ulysses Grant lost all thought of con men and Wall Street, cash and collateral turned ashes ... in the dust, in the cool tombs.

Sandburg here cites a second typical American citizen who has undergone multiple burial. To complete the mystic trinity we must search out an inevitable third to this great-hearted and hard-headed pair. John Brown? Virginia Dare? Barbara Frietchie? Uncle Remus? Who else is a dead American?

Pocahontas' body, lovely as a poplar, sweet as a red haw in November or a pawpaw in May, did she wonder? does she remember? ... in the dust, in the cool tombs?

Evidently Pocahontas' body (since Mr Sandburg puts it as a question) has a possible sense of memory which Lincoln and Grant (or their bodies) lack. Is it because she was a woman and, though respectably married, of middle age, and a mother, beautiful still? Or because she was buried not in America but in a London church? It is interesting to note as an example of the practical effect of the bad poem that there has been a patriotic movement started for exhuming Pocahontas and transferring her to America. Will she wonder? Will she hell! By this time Carl Sandburg himself no longer remembers. Though he has not yet been shovelled into the cool tombs.

> Take any streetful of people buying clothes and groceries, cheering a hero or throwing confetti and blowing tin horns ... tell me if the lovers are losers ... tell me if any get more than the lovers ... in the dust ... in the cool tombs.

The question 'Are the lovers losers?' means just what? Losers in comparison with the hero-cheerers and the grocery-buyers? Or losers in comparison with Lincoln, Grant and Pocahontas? Or losers in regard to love? The supplementary question is equally indistinct. Does it mean 'Do any others get more than the lovers get when the lovers are in the cool tombs?' Or does it mean 'Do any others get more than the lovers get – when they themselves are in the cool tombs?' But the anthology reader doesn't mind; he is fagged out by his own cash and collaterals, he is too weary to remember his Country's heroes or even that women are beautiful. In fact, he too might just as well be ... in the dust ... in the cool tombs ... like Pocahontas, Carl Sandburg, and everybody else.

One of Miss Edna St Vincent Millay's most notorious anthology-pieces begins:

> I shall go back again to the bleak shore
> And build a little shanty on the sand
> In such a way that the extremest band
> Of brittle seaweed will escape my door
> But by a yard or two, and nevermore
> Shall I return to take you by the hand.
> I shall be gone to what I understand
> And happier than I ever was before.[5]

This ends the octave of the sonnet. It is really extraordinary how many poets, when feeling thoroughly low-spirited, revert to childhood and think of going out into the wilder parts of the world and building a *tiny tiny* house JUST TO SHOW HOW I HATE YOU ALL, and how constantly they choose to be near large sheets of water, not to drink or to wash in, but just to give them that nice melancholy feeling that eighteenth- and early nineteenth-century anthology lyricists used to get more directly by crawling about in country graveyards. Miss Millay however is more careful than Mr Yeats in particularizing her little shanty. She says nothing about it that sounds ridiculous except to those frivolous readers who find her 'brittle seaweed' amusing just because it is a piece of exact and cheerful natural history ('the farther from the sea, the more brittle is the seaweed found') incongruous to the atmosphere of bleak despair the poem is supposed to convey. Is the brittle seaweed to serve as thatch for the shanty; as bedding; as food? They trust not. Similarly they find Miss Millay's careful calculation of the neap-tide limit even more diverting than Mr Yeats' romances about linnets and bean-rows. For 'Inisfree' might one day slowly settle to the bottom of the lake – cabin, poet and all, or be engulfed by a Piastre (not the Turkish coin, but the fabulous Irish lake-monster), or spirited away by the Sidhe (pronounced 'Shee' in a footnote) to Hy Brazil (where the nuts do not come from); and they wouldn't laugh, or not very much. But if one late September evening a big big BIG wave did come and go splash against Miss Millay's tiny tiny house and she got her shoes and stockings wet, and the fire was put out, and the roof began to sag, now that would be something to laugh at.

> The love that stood a moment in your eyes,
> The words that lay a moment on your tongue
> Are one with all that in a moment dies,
> A little under-said and over-sung;
> But I shall find the sullen rocks and skies
> Unchanged from what they were when I was young.

The poem, then, is apparently a rhetorical spite piece, a goodbye from a woman to a man who has only loved her momentarily. Notwithstanding her assurance that she is going to be happier than she ever was before, we are not convinced that she really loves the sea or living in a shanty on the seashore. (All she can see in this life is the sullen rocks and skies and seaweed.) What she seems to want is to be thoroughly miserable, so miserable that she'll make him sorry, and repentant; and perhaps he will come back. Our little lady, we begin to feel, is just playing a game. She is teasing: she will build her shanty so near the sea that she will always be on the verge of being washed away, but always there the next morning to go on teasing. And the nasty sandfleas that breed in the seaweed will come right in at her front door and make her more miserable and him sorrier. But evidently she is used to that, having lived in a little shanty when she was a child; or perhaps in a converted hulk like Peggotty's in *David Copperfield*. So it is easier than it seems. She left her home early in life and went to the city, perhaps, where she took him by the hand. And he liked it for a little while, but then got tired: for she was only a simple fishermaid and they had nothing in common after all. What seems to have happened is that she went on holding his hand; and he *said* very little and she *sang* a great deal, too much, perhaps – he didn't like poetry and was really simpler than she. So she gave it up, or seemed to give it up; and ran away, or seemed to run away. Or doesn't the poem mean this at all? Or what does it mean? Or isn't it supposed to mean anything? Or is it supposed to mean just anything, so that the reader can make what he wants of it? And is this why it is a perfect lyric? And what is a perfect lyric anyway?

There will be indignant protests against our treatment of these perfect lyrics 'as if they were prose': for there is a popular superstition that a poem, like the legendary female mind, is charming because it is illogical; that it need not tally with itself (come out right), or, as the Germans say in a single word which the English language badly needs, that it need not 'stimm'. Whereas it is prose which does not need to stimm, or needs to stimm only in a few directions: it can use dead metaphors, toy with false analogies, and can record a succession of events bound together only by space or time propinquity. It describes something; it does not make something. So that any means by which it may strengthen the description will pass. It is the idea not the thing itself that matters. Poetry must stimm in all directions: every metaphor must be alive and reconciled to its neighbours; analogies must work out precisely; its events must have so complete interdependence that a single idle word would spoil the cohesion of a poem. Poets unable to make everything 'stimm' conceal their shortcomings in a facile artistry. Indeed, a cleverly metrified poem is scarcely asked to stimm even in an elementary prose sense, let alone in a poetic sense.

CHAPTER VI

'Best Poems'

THE expressed critical aim of the anthology has come to be the sifting out of the 'best poems'. And the material used by the anthologist has come to be poems written especially to supply the demand for them. His 'best poem' is the best of a best-poem type. We have then two general classes into which poems fall, the best-poem class, including good and bad 'best poems', and the large indefinable class of poems not of the best-poem type. This latter class is left largely to its own fate. But certain kindly provisions are made for the most deserving of the rejected 'best poems'. Many find their way into Fireside Anthologies, consoled by the company of a few decrepit veterans, such as Lamb's *Old Familiar Faces* and Hood's *Song of the Shirt*. An ingenious way of disposing of them has been employed by Mr C. Lewis Hind in his volume *One Hundred Second Best Poems*. He begins well by discussing the Fireside poem, the poem that makes an irresistible appeal to the heart of the great uneducated public and is always asking for its author and for missing lines in the literary pages of the Sunday papers. A good example he gives is Cecil Frances Alexander's:

> By Nebo's lonely mountain
>   On this side Jordan's wave,
> In a vale in the land of Moab
>   There lies a lonely grave ...

and Charlotte Bickersteth Ward's:

> Child of My Love, lean hard
> And let me feel the pressure of thy care.
> I know thy burden, child; I shapèd it ... etc.;

and Thomas Bayly's:

> She wore a wreath of roses that night when first we met:
> Her lovely face was smiling beneath her curls of jet.[1]

But these typical instances of parlour verse are curiously confused with vigorous old rhymes which are not in the competitive best-poem tradition at all:

'Tis well to be merry and wise,
'Tis well to be honest and true,
'Tis well to be off with the old love
Before you are on with the new;

and

'Tis a very good world to live in,
To lend or to spend or to give in,
But to beg or to borrow or get a man's own
'Tis the very worst world that ever was known;

and

Love me little, love me long
Is the burden of my song.
Love that is too hot and strong
   Burneth soon to waste.
Still, I would not have thee cold,
Not too backward or too bold:
Love that lasteth till 'tis old
   Fadeth not in haste ...

Why these are here classified as second-best rather than best poems is that they were not written for the sophisticated 'best' reader: Mr Hind therefore includes them, disregarding their quality, in the hope that they will vulgarly please the second-best reader. But even in his well-meaning snobbery he is not consistently generous in giving his public what it wants. For he has funked putting in Sir Henry Newbolt's 'Play up! play up! and play the game' and Mr Kipling's 'If' and Wordsworth's 'We are Seven', the first, as he admits, because he hadn't the courage, the second because 'Kipling – is Kipling', and Wordsworth's 'We are Seven' because Wordsworth is 'among the Immortals'. No such courtesy prevented him from including Sidney Dobell's 'Tommy's Dead', a poem rather marred in the making but not a second-best poem or yet a 'best', and one by Gerard Manley Hopkins, a poet who sometimes makes Wordsworth look like a real second-best poet; nor from setting the unpretentious Negro spiritual 'Swing low, sweet Chariot' side by side with the farcical wedding-hymn of Mrs Gurney's 'O perfect Love, all human thought transcending'. Mr Hind closes his preface by saying that, after all, since a Second Best Poem is one that the reader likes not because he has been told to but because he really does, a few of the one hundred examples of *Second Best Poems* should be really included in an anthology of Best Poems. In other words, Mr Hind suggests, though the anthologist's first object is to flatter his readers that they are 'best' readers, they should perhaps be made a little comfortable with a few real favourites, such as:

God and I in space alone
And Nobody else in view.[2]

He has given away the secret that the 'best' reader is a homely second-best reader at heart.

The point about Best and Second Best is really this (and we are grateful to Mr Hind for illustrating it so conclusively), that though poetry which submits to a public standard may be appropriately judged by this standard and given blue and red tickets as first-class and second-class, for poetry that is not thus dapperly professional there must be a separate standard for each poem, a standard supplied by the poem itself. Now, the anthology standard would be convenient and just if applied only to poems which properly fall under it. It serves for the sub-logical 'best poem' (the perfect modern lyric), which is held together by pseudo-magical sleight-of-pen; and for the 'best poem' which is held together by common prose logic. Take, for example, Kipling's 'If'. As M. André Maurois has shown, it translates easily into French and makes a better poem there than in English. Therefore, since French poetry is inflated prose,* 'If' must have originally been in English a mere prose fancy without any poetic construction; therefore again, a poem to which the 'best poem' standard may properly apply itself – a professional effort. But by applyi ng itself to *all* poems this standard is capable of classifying as first-class a poem which is not professionally classifiable: as with Wordsworth's poem on the death of Lucy, which, though rated as first-class, should in all justice rather be put out of the running. Because of its subject, because of its picturesque last two lines, and because it was written by Wordsworth, however, it is generally included in most *Best Poems* anthologies:

A slumber did my spirit seal;
    I had no human fears:
She seemed a thing that could not feel
    The touch of earthly years.

No motion has she now, no force;
    She neither hears nor sees;
Rolled round in earth's diurnal course,
    With rocks, and stones, and trees.

As a prose fancy this poem is confused and illogical; and if it were translated into French it would be no poem at all. The contrast between Lucy's once active evasion of the touch of earthly years and her present

---

* Mr Humbert Wolfe, who defines all poetry as 'prose in flight' (the *New Criterion*), should have all his own poetry immediately flown into France.

passive acquiescence in earth's diurnal course is the main argument. But
from the prose view it may be facetiously pointed out that Lucy never
in her most active days could have gone to counteract the daily rolling
of the earth. The details are even more illogical than the main
argument. Apparently what Wordsworth has in his mind is that 'I
thought once that she was non-human in a spiritual sense, but now she is
dead I find her nonhuman in the very opposite sense.' But all the words
have got misplaced. 'Spirit' has got attached to Wordsworth when it
should go with 'Lucy', 'no human' likewise. There is a false comparison
made between 'A slumber did my spirit seal' and 'She neither hears nor
sees'. 'Trees' is an irrelevant climax to 'rocks and stones'. 'Thing' should
not qualify the first Lucy but should be with the second Lucy among the
rocks and stones. As a French poem it would run, more logically, some-
thing like this:

> A slumber sealed my *human fears*
>   For her mortality:
> Methought *her spirit* could withstand
>   The touch of earthly years.
>
> Yet now her spirit fails, she is
>   Less sentient than a *tree*,
> Rolled round in earth's diurnal course
>   With rocks and stones and *things*.

Indeed, if we could get the rhymes to match the revised sense, this
could properly be rated, according to the 'best poem' standard, as a first-
class poem. The fact is, this poem, judged by its own idiosyncratic stan-
dard, has great uncanonical beauty: it is not logical, but neither is it
sub-logical. The poet has not induced a professionally confused, clap-trap
frame of mind in which to write a fitting (but false) poem like Jonson's
'Epitaph on the Dowager Countess of Pembroke'. He is obviously writing
a private, not a public poem, which is under no obligation to be tapholog-
ically [*sic*] fitting. It has rather a supra-logical harmony, by identity of the
theme, which shows the inability of the mind to face the actual reality of
death, with the expression, which shows an inability to get the right words
to pair off in a logical prose manner. Had the mind been able to face lyri-
cally the fact of Lucy's death and had the words been illogically placed; or
had the mind not been able to face the fact and had the words been logi-
cally placed – it would not have been as true a poem as it now is in its
distortion. That is, though at first we may judge the poem as bad because
it is not 'the best words *in the best order*', according to Coleridge's defini-
tion, the *best order* in the logical prose sense would have been as false here
as a more professional disorder. A poem like this, then, slight as it is, and
false as the bulk of Wordsworth's work is, should not be submitted to the

indignity of being put in company with Kipling's 'If', on the one hand, or Jonson's 'Epitaph' on the other.*

The anthology-habit betrays anthologists into cataloguing even poets who never entered their poems for literary competition. So Mr Louis Untermeyer, in his *Modern American Poetry*, prints large quantities of Emily Dickinson, who avoided publishing anything in her life-time, and calls her 'possibly the greatest woman-poet', 'of the colossal substance of Immortality'. He says that she wrote chiefly on four topics, 'Love, Nature, Life, Death', and agrees with another critic, Mr Aiken, that she was incorrigibly perverse in her refusal of the accepted technique of verse, that *'one even suspects that these lapses were deliberate'* (!!). Mr Untermeyer deals in much the same way in his *Modern British Poetry* with Gerard Manley Hopkins, who was as reserved and even secretive about his poems as Emily Dickinson; no poem of his appearing until thirty years after his death. He finds in Hopkins 'verbal excesses, irritating oddities' and agrees with Dr Bridges, Hopkins' editor, that 'the beauty in his least peculiar poems makes it lamentable that he died when to judge by his latest work he was beginning to castigate his art into a more reserved style ... For even in the cloudiest of his poems there is a splendour, a rush of rhyme, a cataract of colour attained by *scarcely any of his clearer-speaking contemporaries.'* Mr Hind showed a clumsy appreciation of Hopkins' proud shyness in hiding him among the Second Best poems. Mr Untermeyer, who is a businessman rather than a sentimentalist, pulls him out on the Best Poem stage and makes him yield Best Poem returns. But though the anthologist can exploit almost any material to his ends, he prefers regular best-poem talent. He wants intelligence, not genius. In comparison with talented writing most works of genius are unintelligent from the anthology view-

---

* The question of the relation of logic to poetry, and especially of the difference between French and English poetry in this respect, is discussed by Albert Thibaudet in the *Nouvelle Revue Française*, January, 1928. English lyrical poetry, he says, is far removed from everything logical, French lyrical poetry has an oratorical sympathy with logic – *'le flot oratoire roule sur la pente de la logique'.* But he makes no distinction between sub-logical and supra-logical oppositions to prose logic; between the pseudo-magical 'best poems' of Poe and Swinburne, for example, and the 'stimming' though illogical poems of Shelley and Shakespeare at their best. Mallarmé, reacting under English and American influence against what M. Thibaudet calls *'l'intermédiaire oratoire, didactique, logique, qui s'interpose toujours plus ou moins entre le poète français et la réalité poétique'*, improvised in the illogical Poe manner rather than in the illogical Shakespeare manner. But as it is not in the French nature to be supra-logical, so also they fail as sub-logicians: their perfect modern lyrics are only scientific, synthetic imbecilities, their sleight-of-prose is logical, not pseudo-magical. For better or for worse no French poet could have achieved the sub-realistic immateriality of 'Inisfree' or 'Eldorado'.

point. And as so many people nowadays have intelligence and, having it, use it to their profit, the anthologist is not obliged to make many raids on genius.

Perhaps the first test of talent in the anthology lyricist is whether he can do his turn in no less than eight and no more than thirty lines – the daily newspaper and the weekly literary journal are the trying-out places. For the more solid 'best poem' a longer unit is stipulated, from about fifty to two hundred lines; and the trying-out places for these are the academic monthlies and quarterlies. This latter type is the declamatory as opposed to the lyrical poem; it takes a central argument through a number of rhetorical digressions and clinches it with a felicitous lyrical summary. It is sober, deliberate oratory rather than light-headed variety – the dull, weighty parts of the anthology programme. Whether ode, elegy, descriptive or narrative verse or philosophic disquisition, the method is the same: *'le flot oratoire roule sur la pente de la logique.'** An exercise in this type might be helpful.

The title proposed is a fine eye-taker – 'He Died Today'. The subject is a scrap of a clay pot recently found by archaeologists in the sands of Egypt, and dating about A.D. 300. It was apparently sent by a runner as a sort of telegram between two unknown persons. It says simply 'He died today', and may be found in the Bodleian Library at Oxford exposed in a glass case.

This makes an ideal subject for a long anthology poem. There is in it the suppressed story element referable to the reader and waiting to be enlarged in the manner of Edwin Arlington Robinson in his 'Man Against the Sky'. (Who was he? Where was he going? Was he really a man? Could it have been this? Or that? Or the other? And then the end.)[3] The central argument is: 'Here is Death; a brief, poignant message that does not actually hurt you because it is remote in time and place, yet a symbol of the Universal Sorrows of Man, so that it may stand for a tragedy of yours that is not poignant to other people. How little do we know of other people's affairs, and yet how much: even after a lapse of centuries!'

The scheme is the same, whatever the period-mannerisms. The introductory stanza would run 'I loitered in a dim Museum when suddenly my wandering eye, etc., etc. I felt chill, etc., etc. And walking home through the quiet streets I asked myself: "Who was he?" ... when today ...

> ... today is always today ...
> ... Clay is always clay ...

And you go on to say (in the second stanza): 'Who sent the message to whom?'

... 'Perhaps' (in the third stanza) 'it was a dissolute Alexandrian

---

* See preceding footnote.

waiting for the death of his rich uncle, now sending this joyful message to his creditors or to his mistress.'

'Perhaps' (the fourth stanza) 'it was a new-born child; his nurse sent this message to his absent father.'

'Perhaps' (the fifth stanza) 'a wife sent this message to the mistress of her husband, who was about to desert her. Perhaps she poisoned him in jealousy.'

'Perhaps' (the sixth stanza) 'it was sent by the Master of the Prison to a man's wife, when she sent him the Pardon that she had got from the Governor at the price of her chastity.'

'Perhaps' (the seventh stanza) 'it was sent by the Merchant to the mother of his apprentice, an only son. She had heard a rumour that the lad was killed falling from a ladder three weeks before. He died *today*. (!!!)

This last 'perhaps', being dramatically the most effective, may end the sequence. In the eighth stanza comes the lyrical summary.

Now cast this subject in its simplest possible form: for instance use the nearest Western equivalent to the *hokku*, the most usual short form in Japanese anthologies. The *hokku* has only seventeen syllables and is arranged in lines of five, seven, and five syllables apiece. Something like this:

THE ARCHAEOLOGIST

A shard of Nile clay
I found, in haste antiquely
Scrawled 'He died today'.

And we have the bare but adequate poetical sketch to which our hypo-thetical 'best poem' may be reduced – the least exceptionable inflation of the original prose idea.

Now to consider an actual longish 'best poem'. A subject that immedi-ately occurs is Wordsworth's 'Intimations of Immortality from Recollections of Early Childhood', which Hallam thought 'perhaps the most perfect ode in the English language':

The rainbow comes and goes
And lovely is the rose;
The moon doth with delight
Look round her when the heavens are bare;
Waters on a starry night
Are beautiful and fair:
The sunshine is a glorious birth;
But yet I know, where'er I go,
That there hath pass'd away a glory from the earth.

The prose-idea is fully contained in the title; what is the legitimate length of the poetical sketch? In this stanza, whose verbose mock-simplicity is typical of all the other stanzas, we have a topic last line (an inflated quotation from the Old Testament) qualified by five parallel poetical commonplaces. One such would have made the stanza merely a 'lyrical' passage; five puff it into philosophy. Or if Wordsworth had set himself the task of rendering an honest poetical sketch of his prose idea, he could have justified one of these commonplaces in the clear antithesis it established between itself and the topic line. But the relevancy of 'The sunshine is a glorious birth', for example, is compromised in advance by the sentimental dishonesty of the six preceding lines and further by the makeweight line following it. If we had the sunshine line by itself 'birth' would have to go, no longer supported by the general confusion of the coming and going rainbow and the constant rose and the bare heavens on a moony night and the fair waters and the beautiful waters on a starry night – in which it passes unchallenged; or if it remained it would have to square itself with 'passed away' by an acknowledgement of the fact that sunshine passes away, and also that it is renewed; it could not at any rate stand as an idle word. In the same way 'glorious' would have to go, as merely the end flourish of a promiscuous adjectival sequence; unless it squared itself accurately with 'glory'. This may seem a somewhat wanton and futile indictment of a well-entrenched 'best poem'. If it were patiently sustained throughout the whole poem, if all rhetorical falsities were struck out, all gratuitous cataloguing, all irrelevant conceits and all plagiarisms, very little, it is true, would get by. The point of disagreement is, whether or not it is better to pass over the solecisms of our 'best' poetry in order to have any poetry at all. Granted even that we were anxious to save what we could, just for the sake of having poetry, and that it were possible here to rescue the poem from the solid masonry of imitation Milton and Dryden in which it is immured, the result would probably be another Vaughan's 'The Retreate' – or rather 'The Retreate' in sixteen lines instead of thirty-two.

Or take Milton's *Hymn on the Morning of Christ's Nativity*. Here are two typical stanzas:

> And sullen Moloch, fled,
> Hath left in shadows dread
> His burning idol all of blackest hue;
> In vain with cymbals' ring
> They call the grisly king,
> In dismal dance about the furnace blue;
> The brutish gods of Nile as fast,
> Isis, and Orus, and the dog Anubis, haste.
>
> Nor is Osiris seen
> In Memphian grove or green,

Trampling the unshowered grass with lowings loud,
  Nor can he be at rest
  Within his sacred chest;
Nought but profoundest Hell can be his shroud;
In vain, with timbrelled anthems dark
The sable-stolèd sorcerers bear his worshipped ark.

Milton is a more finished orator than Wordsworth; but underneath the swaddlings of mythological quaintness there is to be found only a rather tuneless Christmas carol. The first stanza makes it quite plain what Milton was at:

... Nature in awe to Him
  Had doffed her gaudy trim,
With her great Master so to sympathize.
It was no season then for her
To wanton with the Sun, her lusty paramour.

Occasionally an oratorical 'best' poem appears in lyric length, as T.E. Brown's ten-line *My Garden:*

A Garden is a lovesome thing, God wot.
Rose plot,
Fringed pool,
Ferned grot –
The veriest school
Of peace; and yet the fool
Contends that God is not –
Not God! in gardens! when the eve is cool?
Nay, but I have a sign.
'Tis very sure God walks in mine.

This might be hokku'd into:

'There is no God.' 'Fool!'
He walks my lovesome garden
In the evening cool.'

From which, if we were not interested in saving the pieces, just for the sake of having poetry, it could be coué'd away altogether, God wot.

CHAPTER VII

Poetry and Anthology Labels

THE salad-mixing of a popular anthology is intended to give the reader a composite picture of the poetic world. There must be flowers, birds, land-scapes, and in contrast a few grim glimpses of urban life, and a balanced representation of emotions new and old. A lark-poem, for instance, would be included not because it was a good poem but because it was a good poem about a lark. It would be chosen not so much as a particularly distin-guished contribution by a given author as a particularly distinguished example from a hypothetical lark-anthology.

Imagine such a lark-anthology, compiled, say, by Mr Hartog as a companion volume to his *Kiss in Poetry*. Let us give him a start with the ancient Irish 'Song of Summer':

> ... A timorous, tiny, persistent little fellow
> Sings at the top of his voice,
> The lark sings clear tidings.
> Surpassing summer time of delicate hues!

Skelton's

> The lark with his long toe,
> The spink, the martinet also.

Lyly's

> what is't now we hear?
> None but the lark so shrill and clear,
> How at heaven's gate she claps her wings!

Shakespeare's

> Hark, hark, the lark at heaven's gate sings!

Henry Lawes'

> Swift through the yielding air I glide.
> ... Teach the young lark his lesson out,
> Who early as the day is born
> Sings his shrill anthem to the rising corn.

Pope's lines from 'Windsor Forest':

> He lifts a tube and levels with his eye.
> Straight a short thunder breaks the frozen sky.
> Oft as the mounting larks their notes prepare
> They fall and leave their little lives in air.

Wordsworth's

> Mount, daring warbler ...

and

> They pay the price who soar but never roam,
> True to the kindred points of Heaven and Home;

and his earlier 'Up With Me!' in which the lark is called the 'drunken lark' and made a symbol of irresponsible gladness;

Shelley's

> Hail to thee, blithe spirit,
> Bird thou never wert ...

Clare's 'Above the russet clods ...' ending

> ... Oh, were they but a bird!
> So think they, while they listen to its song
> And smile and fancy and so pass along
> While its low nest, moist with the dews of morn,
> Lies safely, with the leveret, in the corn.[1]

The lark-anthology is well on its way already. But when it is done what has it accomplished? Nothing except to collect a stock of larks for future popular anthologists to turn over in search of a suitable specimen for their Composite Poetic World. There is no common factor in these poems except the word 'lark': it would be as reasonable to garner all the poems beginning 'There is a ...' e.g. 'There is a flower, the lesser Celandine'; 'There is a garden in her face'; 'There is a lady sweet and kind'; 'There is a glory on the apple-boughs'; 'There is a pigeon in the apple-tree'; 'There is a sweet music here that softer falls.'[2] Indeed the 'There is a ...' poems are probably more closely allied than the lark poems. All that one can get from the lark-anthology is a number of critical notes such as that in ancient Ireland the lark was not yet a literary bird, nor in England in the reign of Henry VIII, but grew so in Elizabethan times; that Shakespeare in need of a song for one of his comedies was not above stealing from Lyly; that the seventeenth century made the lark purely literary; that the eighteenth century had less feeling for birds as birds than even the seventeenth, regarding them alternately as food and incidental music; that the early nineteenth century sentimentalized the lark as a moral or philosophical symbol, and paid no attention to the reminder of a man like Clare, who knew larks personally and not through literature, that after all larks were larks (as they had been in ancient Ireland). It is a socio–literary–critical work, not a book of poems.

Poetry has no intrinsic categories, though for its arrangement in volume form the author-category is obviously necessary; or, in the case of fugitive poetry, the period-category. The author-category, however, is made to support the anthology-system if the author can possibly be represented as a specialist in some poetic department. The period-category is generally perverted in the same sort of way to exploit some specialized historical appeal. Thus Mr Norman Ault's *Elizabethan Lyrics* might have passed as a legitimate anthology if it had merely included loose anonymous and virtually anonymous pieces strictly of the Elizabethan Period. Likewise Mr Massingham's *Seventeenth Century English Verse*, which contains a number of fugitive pieces for which we can be very grateful, such as:

> Hic jacet John Shorthose,
> Sine hose, sine shoes, sine breeches:
> Qui fuit, dum vixit,
> Sine goods, sine lands, sine riches;

and the catch:

> The Wise Men were but seven, ne'er more shall be for me.
> The Muses were but nine, the Worthies three times three,
> And three merry boys, and three merry boys are we.

Between Mr Ault's period (1558–1603) and Mr Massingham's period (1600–1700) there is only a Debatable-land of three years: that is, if each had made a true anthology of his set period they would have together tidied up the poetic scraps of a century and a half. But Mr Ault reaches anthologistically forward to William Basse's panegyric on Shakespeare, written in 1616, which also appears in Mr Massingham's book; and Mr Massingham reaches anthologistically back to Donne for love poems like 'Go and catch a falling star!' that he wrote in the 1590s and which are also used by Mr Ault. 'Period' to the anthologist is an appealing trade label rather than a genuine means of classification.

The political category is a refinement of the period-category. Morley's *The King and the Commons* is an anthology of Cavalier and Puritan pieces, divided up like a game of French-and-English, with Milton, Marvell, Wither, Bunyan on one side, and Suckling, Crashaw, Davenant, Waller on the other. Marvell – to point to only one discrepancy – could only be properly represented in a political anthology by both Roundhead and Royalist pieces. He kept on good terms with Cromwell, but remained independent. His 'Horatian Ode upon Cromwell's Return from Ireland' is more Royalist, indeed, than Puritan. But the joke turns against the anthologist not the poet when we find Marvell's 'To make a final conquest of all me' and Wither's 'Shall I, wasting in despair' registered as Puritan poems.

Next, the ethnological category. We have Mrs Sharp's *Lyra Celtica** built up on a popular theory of the consanguinity of Bretons, Manx, Cornish, Irish, Scots, Welsh: which are now distinguishable as racially either P Celt (Brythonic) or Q Celt (Goidelic) – two very antipathetic races – or casual mixtures of these and other races. Even as a muddled survey of muddled P and Q there might be scientific justification for *Lyra Celtica*, leaving poetry out of the question: but an unfortunate desire for symmetry led the editor to fatten the Manx section with what she calls 'Anglo-Celts' like T.E. Brown and Sir Hall Caine, and the Cornish with Sir Arthur Quiller-Couch and Riccardo Stephens. These in the same book with Deirdre's 'Lament for the Sons of Usnach' and Taliesin's 'Song of the Wind'! Ethnology is clearly too complicated to provide a criticism for poetry and poetry too complicated to provide a criticism for ethnology. But pseudo-ethnology of the Pan-Celtic type agrees well enough with the anthology-system, which is as crude a caricature of poetry as such movements are of ethnology.

The regional category of poetry returns as twisted an image as the pseudo-ethnological category. A poet is not a poet because of his origin, nor even a special kind of poet because he has had a special kind of origin. So long as the language used is more or less the same there may be a greater affinity between a poet born and living in, say, Dayton, Ohio, who is not wilfully Daytonian, and a poet born and living in, say, Oxford, but not wilfully Oxonian, than between the former and any Dayton-proud poet, or between the latter and any Oxford-proud poet. The only excuse for a regional anthology is where the language and psychology of the region selected varies very considerably from those of other regions, and where an accumulation of uncollected poetry exists which may be regarded as the product of the region rather than of individual poets. For instance, 'Manchester Poetry' is a false category because it implies that there is an inherent cultural force in Manchester that absorbs individual authorship and that enables one to distinguish a Manchester poem from one composed in Liverpool. Whereas the reason of such an anthology would only be that the commercial enterprise of Manchester is expected to make the anthology saleable in two or three editions. Northern English as opposed to Southern English poetry is a different matter: poetry composed in Northern English (usually called 'Scots') by people to whom Southern English is not the ordinary spoken language, is very different in character from Southern English poetry; and this difference is most

---

* And more recently another Celtic Anthology by Mrs Rhys on the same lines.

clearly marked in the fugitive and anonymous pieces for which the
anthology is the natural home. The following rhyme, even though trans-
posed into Southern English, betrays its origin at once:

> There was a piper had a cow
>   And had no hay to give her:
> He played a tune upon his pipes
>   'Consider, old cow, consider!'
>
> That old cow considered well
>   And promised the piper money,
> Would he but play his other tune
>   'Corn Rigs are bonny'.

Whereas the following verses by Miss Elinor Wylie, an American writer,
are only Northern English in decoration – Southern English in feeling:

> Now haud your tongue, ye haverin' coward,
> For whilst I'm young I'll go flounced and flowered,
> In lutestring striped like the strings o' a fiddle,
> Wi' gowden girdles aboot my middle.
>
> My silks are stiff wi' patterns o' siller,
> I've an ermine hood like the hat o' a miller,
> I've chains o' coral like rowan berries,
> An' a cramoisie mantle that cam' frae Paris.[3]

Before compiling an anthology of dialect poetry a careful distinction
must be made between dialect by inheritance and dialect by sentimental
adoption. Mr John Buchan's *The Northern Muse* succeeds well enough in
including poems only Northern English by inheritance. But it also
includes poems by Scott, Stevenson and others to whom, though Scots by
birth, Southern English was the normal literary language; and poems by
other well-known authors, such as Burns, whose works stand by them-
selves and should not be (as in the disfiguring subject-category employed
by Mr Buchan) set side by side with poems by authors whose works could
not stand by themselves, or with the anonymous anthology-pieces in
which Northern English is very rich. Of these *The Northern Muse* contains
so many that the faults which it shares with all popular anthologies are
more easily forgiven. Here are two pieces from *The Northern Muse*:

> Kiss'd yestreen and kiss'd yestreen
> Up the Gallowgate, down the Green:
> I've woo'd wi' lords, and woo'd wi' lairds,
> I've mool'd wi' carles and mell'd wi' cairds,
> I've kiss'd wi' priests – 'twas done i' the dark
> Twice in my gown and thrice in my sark;

But priest nor lord nor loon can gie
Sic kindly kisses as he gae me;

and

Happy the craw
That biggs in the Trotten shaw
And drinks o' the Water o' Dye –
For nae mair may I.

Much the same may be said about Mr Padraic Colum's *Anthology of Irish Verse*, which is well-edited, with notes, and is intended to call attention to the qualities characteristic of Anglo-Irish verse. Mr Colum likewise makes use of subject-categories, mixes the individual with the not strongly individual poets, and sets the work of men like Moore and Swift, to whom Southern English was the normal literary language, next to popular ballads like 'The Night before Larry was Stretched', 'The Peeler and the Goat', 'The Shan Van Vocht', and 'I know my love by his way of walking'.

The regional label is to be as much distrusted in American poetry as in English. One of the first propagandist acts of statehood is to take stock of state-poets and marshal them in an anthology. The only qualification for inclusion is a six-months' residence in the state: no doubt if poetry were financially more profitable there would be the same heavy transfer fees and bribes as are paid in American professional baseball (and English professional football). The usual anthology of Californian poets, for instance, begins with Edwin Markham who, though Oregon-born, did spend the first part of his life in California in the pioneering days, continues with George Sterling, who only came to California in 1895 at the age of twenty-six, and finishes with a batch of younger writers, many non-Californian, who attended Mr Witter Bynner's class in verse-writing at the University of California – Mr Bynner being a product of Harvard. Even Edwin Markham, however, never wrote verse that was in any sense Californian; except for a few casual references his early poems might have been written almost anywhere – even in Staten Island, his home for twenty-five years. His commonplace humanitarianism comes strangely from the most boisterously plutocratic, commercially freakish and cruelly reactionary state in the Union. George Sterling's Victorianism belonged neither to old-world San Francisco nor to new-world Hollywood. Younger 'California' poets might be just as fittingly classified as New York City nature poets, Chicago bums, Iowan or Virginian lyricists or Tennessee metaphysicians: on the assumption that it is not possible to get to one state without travelling through most of the others, and that all Americans are always travelling. And California, for poets as for prospective film stars, must be the shortest stop-over in the world. Californian poetry magazines are generally filled with the work of Easterners,

Southerners and Middle Westerners who have failed with the Eastern, Southern or Middle Western magazines, or who wish to branch out, or by Westerners who can't get a hold in the Eastern, Southern, Middle Western magazines. But what is a Westerner?* Merely someone who happens to be living in the West. In California a pedigreed 'native' son or daughter is an esteemed curiosity; and in the other Western States native sons and daughters are taught to sing at State universities predominantly staffed or inspired by the cosmopolitan East.

As Californian poetry is only inferior American poetry, so modern negro poetry so labelled is only inferior white poetry. Mr Countée Cullen, the youngest and most sentimentally advertised of contemporary negro poets, writes just a little worse than the usual versifying white undergraduate. The negro was perhaps the one American population-unit with a just claim to a spiritual regionalism. But he whitened himself in order to be able to express his blackness; and so was left with nothing to express. Or else he cynically blackened his blackness in order to bring a few material comforts into his spiritual region; and so became a white man's negro, a burnt-cork minstrel.

Separate regional portfolios, then, should be only allowed where the regional idiom is unmistakable, and used for fugitive pieces only. As soon as the regional flavour undergoes literary diffusion – as, for example, when the industrialization of the South destroyed its eccentric provincial culture – the regional category must be abandoned by the conscientious anthologist. Local sentiment nowadays (except in the case of local units too insignificant and too mute to be gathered in by time) is either a dingy hangover from the past or commercial opportunism or journalistic opportunism or the dissatisfaction of a group of literary theorists with vulgar literary diffusion. A stock-label, in fact, is only too often the mark of an inferior poet, or of an inferior critic. It may mean, as with the label 'peasant-poet' or 'poetess', that there is no more to be said about the work than that it was written by a peasant, or by a woman. But it may also mean, on the other hand, that the critic is either weakly or maliciously shirking his responsibilities; if John Clare, say, is dismissed as a peasant or Edith Sitwell as a woman; or if a woman critic dismissed *all* men poets as men.

Certain terms might seem justifiable as a necessary part of the anthologist's critical apparatus, where they contributed to the accuracy of his definition of a poet's work. Yet even the respectable term 'metaphysical' falls among the cant labels. Though it might be used, without prejudice, to suggest by simple analogy that the poet's method resembled the metaphysician's in its analytical thoroughness and in its almost business-like seriousness, as a matter of fact it generally expresses a critic's irritation

---

* Or what is a Southerner? One of the authors of this book spent a little over a year in Kentucky and has since been generally labelled a Southern poet.

with a poet too difficult for his poor powers, such as Johnson's irritation with Donne, or his self-congratulatory satisfaction with a poet difficult enough for his large powers, such as Eliot's satisfaction with Donne. In neither case is 'metaphysical' a disinterested critical term: a disinterested critical term is concentrated on the work rather than on the critic, whose job it is (if he wants the job) to describe, not to enjoy himself. So an anthology of metaphysical verse would be a flattering assemblage of light conceits, heavy philosophizings, airy speculations, dreary finalities – in which Mr Eliot for one would set Donne and Poe side by side to be conversationally incomprehensible to each other. To make such an anthology possible it would have to be disregarded (and an anthologist could disregard it quickly enough) that 'metaphysical' is critically mean-ingless except as a term of simple analogy – that poetry and metaphysics are professionally incompatible. The object of a professional metaphysi-cian is to talk without saying anything. A poet's object is to talk and say something. An anthology of metaphysical verse would therefore consist of those poems or fragments of poems which, its editor would be proud to say, meant nothing to him.

'Mystical' would seem to be more easily sustainable as an anthology label, the analogy between poetic mystical experience and religious mystical experience being fairly close and a strong sympathy rather than a strong incompatibility existing between the two processes: here indeed is an accurate term all ready-made for the anthologist with critical preten-sions. But as a critic he must maintain his prestige by begging criticism: if critics were really to practise criticism they would reveal it to be a matter of library routine rather than of belles-lettres. So with 'mystical' verse: the anthologist shirks the responsibility of applying his term accurately as at once too laborious and too humble. The preface to the *Oxford Book of Mystical Verse* reads:

> In sending out this anthology we have no desire to venture on a definition of what actually constitutes mysticism and what does not, since such an attempt would be clearly outside our province. But ... we have been governed in making our selection by a desire to include only such poems and extracts from poems as contain intimations of a consciousness wider and deeper than the normal.
>
> That is the connecting link between them – the thread, as it were, on which the individual pieces are strung ...
>
> Our attempt has been to steer between ... uninspired piety on the one hand and mere intellectual speculation on the other.

And we get a few truly mystical poets, such as Richard Rolle, Vaughan, Traherne and Phineas Fletcher, introducing Victorian dead-heads and living sap-heads who have played with mystic-making at the same time as they have played with poetry-making. As Alice Meynell wrote in a preface to another not much better 'mystical' anthology, *The Mount of Vision* (which, however, she did not compile):

> It is ominous to hear the name of mysticism so easily used, given and taken without a thought of its cost. Visions are thought easy to come by, and revelations and such extreme things as 'the unitive life' – things for which the Saints thought fifty years of self-conquest and self-abandonment a paltry price – are discussed as incidents of well-read aspiration: with no mention of the first step, much chatter of the last.

Now in a larger sense than merely Christian mysticism, with its implied asceticism and retreat, there is in a poetic sense the mysticism which the editors of the *Oxford Book of Mystical Verse* have defined as 'intimations of a consciousness wider and deeper than the normal'; yet though concessions are here made to other non-saintly and gross-feeding poets, such as Tennyson, Emerson, Browning, Swinburne and Matthew Arnold, there is not a line of Shakespeare's given – not even his *Phoenix and Turtle*, which is obscure enough and passionate enough for the editors to have passed off as even Christian mysticism. From the end of the seventeenth century onward, with the exception of Blake, Hopkins and Francis Thompson, who were religious persons and also poets, the collection consists almost wholly of the library-Victorians just listed as discovered writing sentimentally about religion, and dozens of dim little people, chiefly Anglo-Catholics, hiding their dimness and littleness behind the bright capital-letters of Mystery, Eternity, King of Kings, Perfect Soul, Immortal Truth, Body, Word, Dwelling, Watcher, Night, God. There are many styles; these are typical openings:

> The Lion, he prowleth far and near
>   Nor swerves for pain or rue ...
> And a little Lamb with aching Feet,
>   He prowleth too ...
>   *Ruth Lindsay*

> Before me grew the human soul,
>   And, after I am dead and gone,
> Through grades of effort and control
>   The marvellous work shall still go on
>   *Archibald Lampmann*

> Snowflakes downfloating from the void
>   Upon my face,
> Spilth of the silent alchemy employed
>   In deeps of space ...
>   *Walter Wilmshurt*

The Voice of a Man
   What of the Night, O Watcher?
The Voice of a Woman
   Yea, what of it? ...
                   Madison J. Cawein

A list which bands together as (even occasional) mystics such writers as Clifford Bax, Robert Buchanan, G.K. Chesterton, Aubrey de Vere, Eva Gore-Booth, Sir Edmund Gosse, W.E. Henley, Jean Ingelow, Laurence Housman, George Macdonald, John Masefield, Sir Henry Newbolt, Alfred Noyes, John Oxenham, Alexander Pope, Sir James Rennell Rodd, Arthur Symons, Evelyn Underhill and Oscar Wilde, can only move us to wonder why anybody has been left out at all by the ambitious anthologist.

'Mystical', then, as stock-label, besides putting the critic who uses it under suspicion, may merely indicate a mental muddiness in the poet, the celebration of vagueness by minds incapable of clarity. However, though there are inferior mystics posing as poets and inferior poets posing as mystics, the mystic function need not be called in question. Mystical experience is an arrival at a proved state of sublimity; and men have been sublime. There is a close resemblance, moreover, between mystical contemplation and poetic concentration: the difference is principally in the object, which in the first is predictable, in the second unpredictable. A critic might profitably occupy himself in showing where these experiences coincided and where they diverged and thus give himself a critical excuse for anthologizing. But he would hesitate to admit the need for an excuse; believing it safer for his prestige to go on occupying himself unprofitably – and so it is.

All poetical categories reduce to the subject category. For poetry is most easily digested as a parallelism in song of all the headings of the encyclopaedia of rational prose life – a compressed pocket-universe. A poem is something quite new. The critic, a self-appointed busy-body and guardian of ancient peace, suppresses the heresy by showing it to be something quite old; the anthology makes poetry conform as far as possible to the conventions of stereotyped appearance. Hence the anthology-label, under whose reassuring stamp poetry reads like a twice-told tale.

CHAPTER VIII

Anthologies and the Living Poet

THE anthology meets with two different kinds of reactions in living poets. They will write either toward the anthology or away from it. Anti-anthology poets often overreach themselves, inflicting self-protective distortions on their work – as parents in old Central Europe often deliberately maimed their sons to save them from compulsory military service. But the problem of remaining outside the anthology system should be to the poet no other than the problem of writing as it is best for him to write. Once it becomes a separate problem, his work is distracted with snobbish considerations. The charmlessness of some of the best poetry of our time is in part due to a militant disdain of anthology standards and criticism.

But in the long run it is almost impossible to hold out against the anthology. One of the 'romances of modern publishing' is the success of Messrs Benn's set of sixpenny modern English poets, *The Augustan Books of Modern Poetry*, also published in America by Messrs Stokes – with a corresponding set of American poets by Messrs Simon & Schuster. The less popular poets of these series are naturally glad of a chance of freeing themselves from the anthology and of finding a few new intelligent readers among the greater public which they could otherwise never reach. A number of these small volumes, which average two thousand lines apiece, can be bound together to make a very good *introductory* anthology to the works of the various poets concerned; for in each case the poet has approved of the selection and arrangement. But only introductory; seldom representative of the whole body of a poet's work. The general editors have a very clear idea of what the sixpence-in-purse public will stand, and are particularly bound to respect the limitations of the school-teacher. Hence the poet is only permitted to include his 'sweetest' and, because of the word-limit, his shortest poems, so as to give an appearance of variety. In fact, the majority of these poems approximate closely to the demands of the anthology reader, though they were not originally written toward the anthology.

A poet like Edith Sitwell, however, should come off better than most in this series because she has written very few anthology pieces. Also, because she is included in the series as a notoriously modernist poet (about whom the public, which pretends to but does not buy her individual volumes, is glad, for sixpence, to satisfy its curiosity), she can put in more or less what she likes, except naughty poems in which Bishops, Beelzebub and Queen Victoria occur. She is even at liberty to omit the only poem, an uncharacteristic one, by which she is known in the anthologies, 'The King of China's Daughter', a fancy restatement of a simple nursery rhyme, done in the days before she had found herself as a poet. Yet from polite condescension she feels constrained to print 'Colonel Fantock' and 'The little Ghost who died for Love', instances of charming and completely traditional writing. And now the pleasure of being popularly received in spite of herself has led her, in *Rustic Elegies*, to write, one would say, definitely toward the anthology.

Similarly James Joyce, in *Pomes Penyeach*, published after *Ulysses*, capitulates to the success of the early *Chamber Music*, which was represented in Mr Colum's *Anthology of Irish Verse* by stanzas like the following:

> This heart that flutters near my heart
>> My hope and all my riches is,
> Unhappy when we draw apart
>> And happy between kiss and kiss;
> My hope and all my riches – yes! –
>> And all my happiness.

The unanthological Joyce is to be found hidden away in his unanthological prose work.[1] 'The Ballad of Joking Jesus', for example, in *Ulysses*:

> I'm the queerest young fellow
>> That ever you heard,
> My mother's a jew,
>> My father's a bird …

One of the most recently dated of the 'pomes' is:

> *Bahnhofstrasse*

> The eyes that mock me sign the way
> Whereto I pass at eve of day,
> Grey way whose violet signals are
> The trysting and the twining star.
> Ah star of evil! star of pain!
> High-hearted youth comes not again
> Nor old heart's wisdom yet to know
> The signs that mock me as I go.

The high-brow success of *The Waste Land* brought T.S. Eliot into the anthologies with the 'Conversation Galante' and other ingratiating early pieces:

> I observe: 'Our sentimental friend, the moon!
> Or possibly (fantastic, I confess)
> It may be Prester John's balloon
> Or an old battered lantern hung aloft
> To light poor travellers in their distress.'
>   She then: 'How you digress!'

And now, captured by general fame, he is busy wiping out his waste years with poems like the 'Journey of the Magi', pursuing his anthology career in earnest.

Anthology pressure is indeed difficult to resist. Poets who have happened to have a popular success with a poem are tempted to repeat themselves with another on the same model; and the second is often equally popular in anthologies. So Burns' 'Wee modest crimson-tipped flower' and his 'Wee sleekit cow'ring tim'rous beastie', candidates for the contemporary Beauties of the Poets; and so de la Mare's 'Far are those tranquil hills' and his 'Far are the shades of Arabia'. So at first sight Shakespeare's early song, 'When daisies pied and violets blue' and his later 'When daffodils begin to peer'. Shakespeare not only repeated a popular success of his own, but he was not above repeating a popular success of someone else's. He did it, for example, with Lyly's poem 'What bird so sings yet so does wail?' popularized by the play *Alexander and Campaspe*, which is full of 'reminiscences' of Shakespeare's later borrowings from it. But Shakespeare's songs were intended for his not very serious comedies. Furthermore, they were never offered by him as anthological poems. 'When daisies pied' and the other 'when' poems are definitely satiric of the properly anthological poems of Breton, Barnfield and others. No such excuse can be found for Tennyson's 'When cats run home and light is come',[2] a plagiarization of Shakespeare's 'When icicles hang by the wall' with an ambitious anthological cast.

So John Clare, when taken up by literary London and put into the peasant-poet category of which Burns was then the leading example, was cajoled into writing:

> The bloom's on the brere, bonny lassie oh!
> Oak apple's on the tree, and wilt thou gang to see
>   The shed I've made for thee,
>   Bonnie lassie oh?

> ... with the woodbine peeping in ...

and even into trying his hand at drawing-room stuff in the manner of Moore and Byron:

> Maid of Jerusalem, by the Dead Sea,
> I wandered all sorrowing, thinking of thee:

Thy city in ruins, thy kindred deplored,
All fallen and lost by the Ottoman sword —³

when he could write and had already written better poetry than Burns, Byron and Moore at their best. But poor Clare, in financial straits, had his eye on the heavy fees then paid by the yearly Keep-Sake anthology.

The present-day Living-Poet anthology sorts itself into four general types. The first is the schoolroom anthology supplementing the usual Dead-Poet anthology, including only the works of poets who write best poems in the tradition of thirty years ago. This entombment of the Living-Dead has its merits: these poets, jealous of each other with a rancour not to be found among their juniors, are glad to be safely in port 'among the *English Poets'* – as poor Keats hoped some day to be. And their removal from life to literature clears the decks somewhat for a new generation which may do no better, but could hardly do much worse. *Poetry of Today*, published in England by the English Association principally for use in English Schools, is more up to date than the usual anthology of this sort. Its object is to brighten the Poetry Lesson in the Freubelized school where they hang up orange curtains in every room and do Eurhythmics at the proper interval after a carefully caloried breakfast. This sort of anthology exhibits all the worst traits of the ordinary popular anthology. It does not present the poetry of a real 'today' but of a rejuvenated yesterday. Its message is. 'Now this morning, dear children (and any of you older people who like to listen to my little chat), I have a wonderful secret for you. *The poets are not all dead* as you have been accustomed to think. Shakespeare is dead, alas, and so are Byron, Tennyson and the heroic Robert Brooke [*sic*] of whom I spoke yesterday in my talk about the Meaning of Patriotism. But great poets are still alive today, walking among us with their marvellous heads full of the same marvellous magic for us. There's a hill near Oxford where no fewer than three of them live quite close to each other: Dr Bridges, the Poet Laureate (like Tennyson was); and Mr Gilbert Murray, whose wonderful translation of *Alcestis* we are going to act as a play next term; and Mr John Masefield, perhaps the greatest poet of our day, who writes so beautifully of the Sea and Hunting and Racing and other exciting subjects – sometimes so sadly, but always so beautifully.⁴ And then there is Mr Laurence Binyon, the great master of the modern Ode, and the musical Mr De la Mare, and Mr W.H. Davies who was once a tramp – which shows that the Spirit of Poetry blows unaccountably about like the wind and may light on any man: who knows, it may one day, please God, fall on one of you here ...' etc. The corresponding American poetry lesson exists, with post-Stedman American Anthologies and Poetic Worlds ranging in gentle gradation from Edwin Markham's *Man with the Hoe* to Vachel Lindsay's *Chinese Nightingale* – modern, in the American secondary-school sense, means nearly dead

American. There was this to be said for the old-fashioned straight-classical education, that what corresponded in the curriculum to the modern Poetry Lesson, the making of Latin Verses on the model of Ovid and Virgil, was never felt by the child to have any connection with poetry and was rather an amusing game, like the crossword puzzle. Lucretius was too early to be a model and Catullus too un-Latin (having broken many of Virgil's and Ovid's rules): so poetry was spared from the school-boy as he from it; and if in the play-hour he read or even wrote English poetry, the shadow of the blackboard did not darken the page.

A second type of the Living-Poet anthology is the subscription anthology and is closely connected with the Poetry-Magazine movement. It is a simple money-making matter, cleverly exploiting the inexperience and ambition of young and old fools of both sexes who have read too many anthologies and are thrilled at any prospect of seeing their own work in print. The usual method is to collect a clientele through a poetry magazine with a publishing house attached; to solicit manuscripts, which is always encouraging; to propose the publication of a slim single-man booklet for which must be guaranteed a sum equivalent to five times the actual cost of printing the book – the publisher, from his high opinion of the work, promising to take half the risk in an edition of five hundred copies. The little poet is delighted at the idea and raises the money. After a long delay about a hundred copies are really printed, at trifling cost; they are not advertised. The author's friends buy up about fifty or sixty, but no others are sold. The publisher shakes his head in pretended disappointment at the sales, the author feels sorry to have cheated him out of his half-share in the risk, admires his unselfish declaration: 'But it was an honour to have published the book!' and is then ready to 'advertise' the book in the subscription-anthology in which, with his hundred fellow-gulls, he is enrolled at the cost, say, of two guineas or ten dollars a poem. Here the expense of publishing is somewhat greater, but the gulls and their friends buy up enough copies to make the venture a very profitable one to the publisher, who uses the anthology as a net for further fish.

Sometimes the subscription-anthology is published by the committee of a literary society on behalf of its members. *The Bookfellow Anthology*, Chicago, 1926, may be an example of this, though it is not clear whether the not-inconsiderable profits of the previous issue went to the copyright holder, Flora Warren Seymour, or to George Steele Seymour who wrote the introduction, or to the general funds of the Bookfellow Association, of which the Seymours are officials, possibly paid officials, or to the funds of the Bookfellow poetry-magazine, *The Step Ladder*, of the editorial staff of which (it is possible to deduce from the anthology) they are members. At all events:

The terms for entry into this volume were the same as for the 1925

Anthology. Contributors were required to be Bookfellows [that is, to pay a membership fee, which included a subscription to the *Step-Ladder*] and to purchase three copies of the book for each page contributed, the price of the book being fixed at two dollars per copy. Not more than ten pages might be contributed by any one person.

It appears that the 'co-operating publishers' of 1925 sent their spare copies free to the libraries and newspaper offices. 'As our plan had not contemplated the giving away of free copies at the expense of increased cost of production, this generous act of our associates at once surprised and pleased us.' And this edition, and another too, was sold out.

A few of the contributing authors were themselves newspaper-writers, and they lent their efforts with a will to the task of putting it over ... We shall say little of the imitations that at once sprang up, for they were palpably imitations in every respect save one – that the power of co-operative publishing which we Bookfellows command was not behind them. And as they languish unsold and uncirculated – the inevitable fate of the book that is not wanted – we come forward again with our 1926 Anthology –

whose pages of verse number 235. Multiply that by six and the answer in dollars is the *certain* takings of the volume, that is, 1,410 dollars. Further takings from actual sales should bring in at least another two or three hundred dollars. As the cost of producing the book itself (it was printed at a private press), with no distribution expenses beyond the postage of the copies to the authors (perhaps even these were carriage forward), could not have exceeded, at the most, five hundred dollars for the edition of eight hundred copies, someone seems to have made a nice little sum out of the 'co-operative venture'. As it is not so recorded, we may not take it for granted that the contributors or 'associated publishers' were each sent back two-thirds of their subscription. But such contributors are not captious about returns: this is a consolation-anthology. They believe that a printed book has more lastingness than the files of a poetry-magazine and that when the printed book gets round to newspaper critics this may be the beginning of a poetic career for each of them – a still higher rung of the step-ladder. Such a dream may be worthwhile even at six dollars a page, and even if, as in the case of Jessie E. Williams, who contributed six pages, the average printed on each page is only ten lines. But it should be commercially possible to dream it more cheaply.

A third type of Living-Poet anthology deals in the marketable sentiment aroused by some event of public importance – the murder of President McKinley, the death of Edward the Peace-Maker, the Sinking of the *Titanic*, the Outbreak of War, the Victory. That President

McKinley, the puppet-nominee of the Trusts at their most cynically corrupt stage, was murdered by a maniac; that Edward the Peace-Maker, personally responsible for the English Entente with France and therefore for the destruction of the Anglo-German alliance which was keeping the peace of Europe, died after a life not particularly distinguished for the qualities which his idealistic German mother and father had tried to inculcate in him; that the *Titanic* was sunk as a result of culpable negligence on the part of the staff and that its sinking was attended by scenes that, to say the least of it, compared unfavourably with those at the sinking of the *Birkenhead*; that the English Liberal Government was able to justify by the German invasion of Belgium its own secret commitments to and preparations for a war that had as its object the crippling of a commercial rival; and finally that this War was technically won by weight of numbers and munitions after a gross display of atrocities on both sides – all this is history. But the anthologist and his poet have no more respect for history than for poetry, for public than for personal truth.

Mr Braithwaite's *Victory! Celebrated by Thirty-eight American Poets* begins with a series of panegyrics on the heroes of the time, of the quality of which this sestet of a sonnet to Marshal Foch is a fair example:

> Focus of freedom – Foch! Your mind has made
> Reason – religion's theme, intelligence –
> An anthem rising from the blood-dark sod.
> Your brow – a temple where the world has prayed,
> Your brain – of myriad souls the single lens:
> A burning glass, held in the hand of God.

Since King Albert, Sir Douglas Haig, General Diaz, General Pershing and Cardinal Mercier have each to be celebrated as the unique heroes of Victory there is some discrepancy – but never mind, they were all jolly good fellows, even – guess whom! – General Leonard Wood!

> Had not your spirit led, our ardent youth
> Had faltered leaderless, their eager feet
> Attuned to effort for the valiant truth,
> Through your command alone, rushed to complete
> To hold on high the torch of Liberty
> Great visioned soul, yours is the victory.

This marketable sentiment is chiefly Franco–American (the literary references to Lafayette and Joan of Arc are not tactful, but may be set off against the English victory hymns recollecting Waterloo and the Flanders campaigns of Marlborough). The victory mood in America yielded precedence in valour and sacrifice only to the French, exalted Château Thierry into a major military operation and concealed the fact that the total casualties of the British Forces were between eighty and ninety times greater than the American. Sometimes not even to France, as when Edgar Lee Masters writes of

> the glory of England, glory of Italy, glory of France
> And the imperishable glory of America.

The introduction, again, begins tactlessly:

> Lowell's great lines ring as true today as at the close of the Civil War:
>
> > 'Come, Peace! not like a mourner bowed,
> >   For honour lost and dear ones wasted,
> > But proud, to meet a people proud
> >   With eyes that tell of triumph tasted.'

This is rather hard on the Southern regiments who also marched to glory at Château Thierry.

The moral of the collection is also confused: undying hate against Germany on the one hand, eternal peace on the other; 'Sew the flags together' (Vachel Lindsay) and American nationalism triumphant; and liberal rhetoric like Mr Untermeyer's

> Soon these battered heroes will come back
>   The same, yet not the same.
>
> They who have bandied words in No Man's Land
> Will never be the old and abject crowd.
> They will not grovel and they will not stand
>   What used to keep them cowed.

Mr Untermeyer's battered heroes unfortunately fulfilled his promise only too literally: e.e. cummings, for instance, in his charming portrait (not included in *Victory*):

> A tear within his stern blue eye
> upon his firm white lips a smile,
> one thought alone: to do and die
> for God for country and for Yale
>
> above his blond determined head
> the sacred flag of truth unfurled,
> in the bright heyday of his youth
> the upper class American
>
> unsullied stands, before the world:
> with manly heart and conscience free,
> upon the front steps of her home
> by the high minded pure young girl

much kissed, by loving relatives
well fed, and fully photographed
the son of man goes forth to war
with trumpets clap and syphilis.[5]

A fourth type is the yearly Best Poem anthology which is generally conducted for the publisher by a minor anthology poet, such as L.A.G. Strong, author of *Dublin Days*, *The Lowery Road*, *Difficult Love*, and Thomas Moult, author of *Down Here the Hawthorn*. It purports to give an annual summary of the 'best' poetry that can be winnowed from magazine verse. It never assigns more than two poems to any individual author, and by giving the public which 'wishes to be informed of contemporary verse-tendencies' ready-made taste in names kills any critical interest in poetry itself. All these volumes are of a uniform size: which gives away the game at once. If there was any real critical interest in their compilation the 1925 volume would have been perhaps a thin pamphlet, the 1926 volume a still thinner one, while in 1927 an official announcement might have been issued to subscribers: 'We regret that this year the vintage has failed and no anthology will be printed.'

The financial history of these 'Best Poems of ...' anthologies – which as a matter of fact are only commercially successful in the sense that they pay the publisher better than volumes by individual authors – is interesting: though no contributors are invited to pay their fee for inclusion, to become 'co-publishers' at six dollars a page, not many are given any fee other than their presentation-copy. There are, however, a few 'names' which must be secured in order to give the collection an air of respectability. Each 'name' is paid for according to the owner's awareness of its exact market-value. An unwholesome situation is thus at once created: the anthologist, on behalf of his publishers, either offers to print a poem free as a favour, or, as a greater favour still, offers a small fee for it. In cases where a fee is demanded and the name is uncertain, the anthologist punishes the shylock by omitting him. For the most part he takes advantage of the 'uncommercial spirit' of grateful verse-writers.

Many of the features of the more general popular anthology are to be found in this type. The same salad-mixing of subject, for example, the same Composite Picture of the (Modern) Poetic World. Indeed, if we are to have more of these anthologies of *Living and Willing Poets*, and if the reading public continues to support them, we may as well have 'Bespoke Yearlies', in which the poems are written (by poets who have 'made good') to the order of the anthologist.

Once this system was inaugurated an English committee might get in touch with an American committee, and a combined Poetical Budget might be made out on the first of April every year. To Mr Conrad Aiken would be allotted the Garden poem; to Miss Edna St Vincent Millay, the

Old Woman poem; to Mr T.S. Eliot, the Old Man Poem; to Mr Wolfe, the Lamb poem; to Mr Chesterton, the Love Song; and so on, each with one or if necessary two competent understudies. This would mean a high standard of writing and no overlapping or jealousy. The Official Anthology would appear punctually on 5 November each year and would be on sale at all railway bookstalls, leading stationers, army canteens, Woolworth Stores, etc.; and it would be possible to pay each poet as much for his quota as he makes in a year from private volumes and from book-reviews. It would be pointed out in the first issue that poetry is now an important public service and that private enterprise is to be considered anti-social and uneconomic; and that the aim of this Official Anthology is to protect the public from freebooting poets and freebooting poets from themselves.

CHAPTER IX

Conclusion

THE growth of the modern popular anthology in England can be traced through the stage of medium-sized 'Beauties of the Poets', which were guides to Chalmers' twenty-one volume *English Poets* published in 1810 (or to the less complete Libraries of Poets that went before), to a final condensation in the miniature *Golden Treasury*, 1861, which also contained the cream of the poetry of the new century. This abridgment of the *English Poets* was so well received that Chalmers went out of print and has had no successor: the publishing unit for poetry in the bulk is now the abridgement itself.

America, which never had a Chalmers, was content throughout the nineteenth century with a series of compendiums of mixed verse, very much larger in size than the English anthologies. These were really popular in feeling; they were compiled for the American average reader at a time when the gap between his taste and that of the advanced reader was not great, when it was therefore not necessary to anthologize either up or down to suit a particular public. One of the earliest of these volumes, first published in 1842 at Philadelphia, consists entirely of American writers – *The Poets and Poetry of America*, edited by Rufus Wilmot Griswold. It was described as a survey of the beginnings of a true American literature in the first half-century of freedom: 'until the spirit of freedom began to influence the national character very little verse worthy of preservation was produced in America. The poetry of the Colonies was without originality, energy, feeling or correctness of diction.' Griswold's method is to give the work of over a hundred poets – practically all there were – allotting generous page-space and a biographical note to each; and since the contributors are not strongly differentiated in style and subject he covers the field well enough. Griswold in 1849 later divided up the book into two parts, separately published, *The Poets* and *The Female Poets* of America. The male poets given most space were Charles Hoffman, Bryant, Percival, Whittier, Holmes, Brainard, Pierpont, Pinkney, Emerson, Longfellow, Sprague, Poe; in that order. Hoffman has thirty-six poems, Poe fourteen: which is very fair when you read them both without prejudice. The female poets of this half-century are forgotten names: Sarah Josepha Hale, Emma

Willard, Lavinia Stoddard, Lydia Sigourney, Maria Brooks, Sarah Helen Whitman and Frances Osgood (the two last-named of Poe-ish fame), Elizabeth Kinney, Mary Stebbins, etc.

Griswold's collection unfortunately prepared the way for others less harmless: trying to cover too much ground, they had to arrange their material according to subject-categories in order to handle it, and to mutilate poems to save space. Charles Dana's *Household Book of Poetry*, first published in 1856, was a quarto of over eight hundred double-columned pages of the combined gems of American and English verse. Dana arranged the poems for household uses, like kitchen stores: Poems of Nature, Poems of Childhood, Poems of Friendship, Poems of Love, Poems of Ambition, Poems of Comedy, Poems of Tragedy and Sorrow, Poems of the Imagination, Poems of Sentiment and Reflection. A solid book, successful enough to produce many solid imitations, including Whittier's *Songs of Three Centuries*, Emerson's *Parnassus*, and Fields' and Whipple's *Family Library of British Poets*. The household as a reading-unit was a discovery of American Victorianism and did not survive it (it was also discovered in Victorian England, but Archbishop Trench's *Household Book of Poetry*, published in the Fifties, had few, if any, English imitators). The biggest and most ambitious of all these family compendiums was Bryant's *Family Library of Poetry and Song, Being Choice Selections from the Best Poets, English, Irish, Scottish and American, including Translations from the German, Spanish, French, Portuguese, Persian, Latin, Greek, etc.*, a quarto of over a thousand pages. He keeps Dana's arrangement but adds new categories: Poems of Temperance and Labour, Poems of Patriotism and Freedom, Poems of the Sea, and so on. Nearly all these compendiums are grangerized with poetical engravings, depicting Scottish Maidens, Drowned Maidens, Storms, Bouquets, the Stricken Stag, the Convent Cloister and the birthplaces and libraries of well-known American poets. But it is difficult to feel severe about these books: though they show not the slightest suspicion of what poetry is all about, they have other simple virtues of which honesty and undifferentiating kindliness are the chief; and they were genuinely read and enjoyed; and they are no longer published; and, if they survive at all in remote parlours, give comfort where comfort is needed.

Griswold's *Poets and Poetry of America* was superseded by Edmund Clarence Stedman's *An American Anthology, 1787–1900*, a more ambitious version of his earlier *Poets of America*, as his *Victorian Anthology* was of his *Victorian Poets*. But as Stedman's page-length was less than Griswold's in spite of the addition of sixty years of poetry the result is unsatisfactory. Griswold printed just as much as was historically pertinent; his was, in fact, a true period-anthology. Stedman fell into the anthology trap because he wanted to be critical, as he rightly believed Griswold had not been. 'But if this anthology were modelled upon his

"Poets and Poetry of America" it would occupy a shelf of volumes'; which it should have done.

In the new century, in place of the large family compendium, America adopted the shorter sample-anthology of the English variety, which professes to be merely a guide to, not a substitute for, the works of the poets represented. But the difficulty in both countries is that of ready access to the poets, the absence, in fact, of an up-to-date Chalmers. There have been several partial Libraries of the Poets published, with a single volume for each poet: the *Globe* series, the *Muses' Library*, the *Everyman* series and the *Mermaid* series. But no publishing house has undertaken to print a definite corpus on the Chalmers' model. Yet copyright troubles are not so serious as they were a hundred years ago because, except for a few odd pieces lately discovered or texts 'established' of ancient poets, one may reprint almost anything. And much more compendious works have been frequently attempted, brought to conclusion and kept up to date. The *Encyclopaedia Britannica* and *New English Dictionary* are immediate instances – not to mention the many historical and scientific encyclopaedias or series; and the *Loeb Classical Library*, a collection which in spite of its great value is of far less importance to the English-speaking world than a library of English Poetry, makes steady progress.

Our first suggestion for the defeat of the popular anthology is that the publishers should meet in the friendly way that their predecessors the booksellers met in Dr Johnson's day, sinking their separate financial interests for the occasion, and agree to share the labour, expense and profits of a new standard *English Poets* to be published co-ordinately in England and America. Any publisher who has commercial interests in any particular poet should, of course, have these assessed by an impartial committee. Since the collection when complete would consist of perhaps thirty large quartos, each containing a number of poets, the harm done to handy individual volumes in series like the *Globe* and *Everyman* would be inconsiderable. The poets chosen would be mostly out-of-copyright poets; the latest at any rate need be no later than the day before yesterday. There would, we believe, be an immediate and satisfactory demand from all libraries, colleges, clubs of any size and from a number of private persons. Given this representative Corpus of dead poets, including those omitted by Chalmers, the whole situation begins to clear. We become independent of the tyranny of anthologies; if we want to read and judge how much of a poet Matthew Green or Thomas Flatman or Robert Henryson was, we are no longer forced into probably fruitless search in the Municipal Library, or into eating the few dry crumbs that we find or do not find in the *Golden Treasury* or *The Oxford Book of English Verse*. As things are, if we wish to buy the volume there is no means of finding the publishers of the most authoritative edition; if we apply to a large bookshop we cannot be certain whether its critical judgement is to be trusted. If we write to the *Reader's*

Guide of a literary review we shall, after about six months, get an evasive answer. Or even if in some cases such editions not only exist but are easily obtainable, the expense will be great – very great if our interest in the lesser-known poets is broad. Suppose Skelton is wanted, Dyce's edition, a very good one indeed published in 1843, may cost as much as five pounds; Richard Hughes' edition of 1924, though it contains a poem not known to Dyce, is only a selection. Other poets are also published at prices which mount up prohibitively – Hopkins, Blake, Traherne, Smart, the Scottish Chaucerians. In the Corpus we would have each poet, complete and in his place, from Cynewulf onward: and for people with small libraries this would be a great economy in money, time and shelf-space.

One of the greatest benefits of the Corpus would be the disappearance of the 'comers' of knowledge by which the critic contrives to dupe and impress the general reader. An obscure and almost worthless poet is cried up as a neglected genius on the strength of a few better lines: the reader cannot check the judgement, and perhaps allows himself to be convinced, adding another name to his list of snobbish literary mentions. Not only these, but better-known poets, such as Dryden or Ben Jonson, never read but taken for granted on the critic's word, would have to be at least looked at because they were there. The usual anthology blur would be avoided, because all the work of each poet would appear. The oppressiveness of the great names, moreover, which generally upsets the balance of the anthology, would be counteracted by the size of the Corpus itself.

Educationalists should encourage such a collection. Much of the artificiality of English literature courses at the universities is due to the inadequacy of the local library, in which the English poetry representation consists of random and non-uniform volumes, with many gaps. Students are thus obliged to get their critical views from second-hand sources like W.J. Courthope's *History of English Poetry* and *The Cambridge History of English Literature*. And frequently the professors themselves have had no other sources but these. With the Corpus, students would be able to discard such text-book lies as 'The Age of Shakespeare', 'The Age of Dryden', 'The Age of Wordsworth'. Poetry would show itself to be not a sequence of fashions, but of individual poets who are poets only to the extent to which they are outside the sequence of fashions.

This full Corpus would include all poets who had a certain recognizable minimum of credibility: there is poetry which is not even historically significant and about which everyone, whatever his literary politics, agrees. Thus Spratt, Lyttelton, Cawthorn, John Cunningham, Boyse and a dozen more eighteenth-century writers included by Chalmers would be probably unanimously omitted from the Corpus by a representative committee, as others omitted by Chalmers would be included. If there were any disagreement at all as to whether or not a poet should be included, he would naturally be included. Where it was agreed to include a poet, disagreement as to his relative merit would not matter, as each poet would be printed entire and in a uniform manner. If a poet in his old age has, like Wordsworth, rewritten the poems of his youth, both versions should be given. The texts should be correlated with great accuracy and the universities called upon to help in this matter. Candidates for a degree in English Literature, who are always at a loss for a suitable thesis-task, might well be set to work on this.

Given such a collection, with its particular volumes devoted to the anonymous waifs and strays of a given period (the true anthologies), the popular anthology loses much of its power to vulgarize poetry. Even Palgrave and his rivals could be restrained from doing serious damage if the Corpus included a skeleton appendix of these anthologies, reducing them to mere Recommendations for Reading in the Corpus: a list—of page and volume references with such notes as 'stanzas 4 and 5 omitted' and 'text reformed as follows for use in school'. If private manuscript-anthologies were kept again they would remain private; at the most, they might be condensed into page-references and included at the end of the Corpus as 'Miss So-and-so's' or 'Mr So-and-so's' Reading Recommendation.

Every ten years it would be found necessary to print a supplement bringing the Corpus up to date, as with the *Encyclopaedia Britannica*, and at longer intervals complete new printings. This would mean not only the improvement of texts –the Corpus could provide a much-needed international clearinghouse for variorum readings, newly discovered poems, re-attributions of poems, re-datings and so forth – but the inclusion of further poets, both older ones revived and more recent ones who had just passed through the thirty years' purgatory qualifying them for admission. University bodies might further be employed in providing a grand Poetical Concordance, on the lines of the Biblical Concordance. All the *Larks* and *Solitudes* and *Kisses* and so on could be thus assembled far more effectively than by a single editor at present. Even with a poetical concordance there would be plenty of minor tricks left for the amusement of private scholars. But besides a concordance, there is the enormous task of making a cross-reference index of unconscious or deliberate plagiarisms and adaptations. Let the editors print Lady John Scott's version of 'Annie Laurie', but refer back to Douglas of Fingland's original; let them print Chaucer in the original, and then show by Dryden's adaptations what the late seventeenth-century preferred. Let them print Shirley's 'Glories of our Blood and State', and refer back to Shakespeare's 'Fidele's Dirge'. Let them mark Herrick with the back-references to Skelton's 'Philip Sparrow', mark Burns with back-references to the popular ballads; mark Clare with back-references to Burns and Moore, and refer his 'Skylark' back to Shelley's. Let them print Shakespeare's songs in the dramas as they occur, and then refer to the borrowings. Let them, in a full bibliographical index, show in the case of poets whose works were not collected in volume-form in their own day at what point they became part of literary history; or, in the case of poets like Donne and Campion, at what point they were restored to literary history after a lapse of popularity.

The collection need not be as trying as Chalmers, although printed at four times his length: Chalmers did not have India paper at his disposal and so was obliged to use very small print. Nor would it be beyond the interest of the general reader. For the general reader of poetry is a *general* reader. The skimmer in poetry is not a reader, as with the popular novel: the reader either reads poetry and reads it generally, or he is no reader at all. The popular anthology, indeed, is composed not for readers, but, like the popular novel, for skimmers: the purchaser's interest is not in *reading*, merely in *seeing* who is in it, what the titles are like, what look the poems have. Yet the general reader need not be an expert reader. For the inexpert reader the skeleton anthologies printed in the appendix at the end of the Corpus could act as guides. And when he turned, say, to 'Woak Hill' by Barnes or 'I am but what I am who cares or knows' by Clare, he would find these usual anthology poems in their right setting, in their right version, in their right spelling, and entire.

The new Corpus, then, would present past poetry in the bulk, poetry, that is, removed by at least a generation from the politics of contemporary literature; it would introduce order into quantity by giving the quantity complete. But it is a question whether it could be profitably extended to contemporary poetry: it might introduce into it an order which was qualitative rather than quantitative, a liberal order of taste. If not, how might contemporary authors come up for eventual election to the Corpus? Rather by waiting two hundred years in manuscript like Traherne than registering themselves in popular anthologies of the present Living-Poet variety; anthologies which are mostly compiled from magazine-material, so that the work included is the least characteristic work of the better poets and the most characteristic of the worse – the most anthologizable of both. The anthologist has used the magazines merely as the cheapest and laziest means of getting his material together; he rarely consults the individual volumes of the poets themselves – if he does, he still keeps magazine standards. Moreover, because of these standards, it is very difficult indeed for an uncommercializable poet to get his work published in any form. Undistinguished but old-fashioned and undistinguished but new-fashioned poetry can get printed easily enough as dressing to a publisher's list. There are publishers who specialize in new-fashioned poetry as there are others who specialize in old. But poetry of an unorthodox and yet not aggressively sensational type often remains unpublished for years, because it is without obvious commercial value.

Suppose, for the moment, that poetry of even an unpopular character were freely printed: why could not the Corpus do for contemporary poetry what it could do for past poetry: print every so many years a supplement of contemporary poetry? Such a supplement might contain, with the authors' permission, all the poetry printed in volume-form in the period covered, omitting work in each case which the author wished to discredit. If obviously inconsequential volumes were excluded according to the same principle that was suggested for the Corpus itself (but none because they seemed difficult to label or otherwise difficult, the object of such a supplement being not critical but to include as much as could be decently included), the size and expense would not be prohibitive. Especially when one considers the expenditure made on various bulky directories published yearly and even twice yearly – telephone directories, street directories, Who's Whos, Peerages, Landed Gentries, Fraternity Year Books, College Year Books, Blue Books, Business Directories, Garden, Clothing and Furniture Catalogues, Literary Year Books, Publishers' Catalogues, Guidebooks to Hotels and Pensions of France, Patent Medicine Almanacs, etc. The expense of such a supplement could be considerably reduced, moreover, by making it a subscription edition. Incidental financial problems would remain – the value of contemporary poems varies with critical wire-pulling and first-edition speculation and unaccountable fashion and would be difficult to assess. But even if the financial question could be adjusted, a committee would not be likely to agree as to what contemporary poetry was inconsequential as a similar one could about past poetry. Indeed, it would be impossible at the start to form a committee representative of all legitimate tastes in contemporary poetry: the same economic forces that govern the publishing of poetry at the present time would also govern the definition of legitimacy.

Why could not poets themselves combine to form libraries? Principally because most poets belong to cliques and would be prevented by personal feeling or critical bias from combining in a large way. And the few independents would be indifferent. Small co-operative anthologies are usually just advertising organs for a new brand of poetry; like the *Imagist* series; or tea-parties of co-opted popular-anthology successes raised above clique-jealousy, like the *American Miscellany*. The recent *Fugitive* anthology is perhaps as inoffensive as a small co-operative anthology may be; it is in the nature of a memorial volume to the friendliness of a few poets once temporarily associated – by geography rather than by programme. It is difficult to decide whether the co-operative clique-anthology is better or worse than the publicity anthology conducted on behalf of poets by the poetry enthusiast or the professional anthologist, who create cliques. It is exceptional to find an editor of the integrity of E.M., the founder of *Georgian Poetry*, which began as an attempt to call attention to certain poets who had not come so far under public notice and continued biennially for ten years. E.M. kept in the background with a most unusual restraint, wrote no purple prefaces, paid his contributors generously, exercised no patronage and, when he found that the task that he had set himself in the 1911–1912 volume had been accomplished and that the newer generation of writers had aims unintelligible or unacceptable to him, decided to discontinue the series though it was still in popular demand. He never associated himself with any poetry-magazines or societies and published no verse of his own until the series was over. However, even *Georgian Poetry*, like the *Imagist Anthology* did little in the long run but institute a fashion in verse-writing and make it difficult for the poets included to shake off the fashion or the label.

The rejection of a supplement to a Corpus of poetry, the rejection in fact of the Living-Poet anthology in any disguise, seems to bring the fate of contemporary poetry with contemporaries to a dead halt. Yet nothing could be more desirable. For the worst fate that contemporary poetry can have is to have any fate, however unarbitrary, with its contemporaries. If the popular anthology were removed, if contemporary poetry in general were removed as a subject of journalistic reference, and the magazines devoted to such reference removed as well, there might be nothing left but a few plainly printed volumes, to be found out by those who were meant to find them out, exercising no persuasion but that of being between their two covers, from line to line and page to page, for whoever should happen to open them.

Notes

Chapter IV

1. Lines from one of Byron's *Hebrew Melodies*, 'She Walks in Beauty'.
2. Lines from Sir Henry Wotton (1568–1639), 'On his Mistriss, the Queen of Bohemia'.
3. These lines are from James Shirley (1596–1666), 'Death the Leveller'.
4. Lines from Guiderius' and Arviragus' song, Act IV of Shakespeare's *Cymbeline*.
5. Lines from: Richard Lovelace (1618–1658), 'Song. To Lucasta, Going to the Warres'; Jonson, 'On the Countess Dowager of Pembroke' (sometimes ascribed to William Browne); Keats, 'Ode on a Grecian Urn'.

Chapter V

1. The reference is to Graves' much-anthologized poem 'Scapegoat'.
2. Lines from John McCrae, 'In Flanders Fields', and from Robert Williams Buchanan, 'The Tree of Life'. Riding and Graves misspell Yeats' 'Innisfree' throughout, and seem unaware that it is a real place.
3. The first stanza of Robert Bridges' poem 'I Love all Beauteous Things', from *Shorter Poems in Five Books*.
4. The closing lines of John Masefield's poem 'Ignorance'.
5. The opening lines of Edna St Vincent Millay's Sonnet XXXIII. The remaining lines are quoted later.

Chapter VI

1. Cecil Frances Alexander (1818–1895), lines from 'The Burial of Moses'.
   Thomas Haynes Bayly (1797–1839). Lines from his poem 'She wore a Wreath of Roses'. The lines are properly trimeter, as follows:
   > She wore a wreath of roses,
   > The night that first we met,
   > Her lovely face was smiling,
   > Beneath her curls of jet.
2. The opening of 'Illusion' by Ella Wheeler Wilcox (1850–1919). The poem is collected in *Poems of Power* (1901). The lines should properly read:
   > 'God and I space alone
   > And nobody else in view.'

3. Edward Arlington Robinson (1869–1935). His poem 'The Man Against the Sky' was published in 1921.

Chapter VII

1. John Skelton (1460–1529), from 'The Book of Philip Sparrow'.
   John Lyly (1554?–1606), from 'Spring's Welcome'.
   Shakespeare, 'Song' from Act 2 Scene III of *Cymbeline*.
   Henry Lawes (1600–1662), 'The Lark'. The final quoted line should properly read 'Sings his shrill anthem to the rising morn'.
   Alexander Pope, 'Windsor Forest'. Riding and Graves have not indicated the ellipsis between 'sky' and 'Oft', where two lines of Pope's poem are elided.
   Riding and Graves quote twice from William Wordsworth, 'To the Skylark'.
   Percy Bysshe Shelley, 'To a Skylark'.
   John Clare, 'The Sky Lark'. Riding and Graves are probably quoting from Blunden's edition.
2. The 'There is a'… poems are as follows: Wordsworth, 'The Small Celandine'; Thomas Campion, 'There is a Garden in her Face'; 'There is a Lady Sweet and Kind' from Thomas Ford's *Music of Sundry Kinds* (1607); Madison Julius Cawein (1865–1914), 'There is a glory in the apple boughs' (this particular poem is anthologized in *The Oxford Book of English Mystical Verse*, eds. Nicholson and Lee, 1917); Tennyson, 'There is sweet music here that softer falls' – 'Choric Song I' from *The Lotus Eaters*.
3. Elinor Wylie (1885–1928). American poet. Two stanzas from 'The Prinkin' Leddie', from her collection *Nets to Catch the Wind* (1921).

Chapter VIII

1. James Joyce, *Pomes Penyeach* were first published in 1927, the year before the publication of *A Pamphlet*. The quoted text is the first stanza of poem XXIII from Joyce's *Chamber Music* (first published in 1907).
2. 'When cats run home and light is come' is the opening line of Tennyson's 'The Owl'; 'When icicles hang by the wall', from Shakespeare's *Love's Labour's Lost*.
3. The two John Clare poems are 'Bonny Lassie O!' and 'Maid of Jerusalem'.
4. 'There's a hill near Oxford…'. Graves and his family lived themselves on Boar's Hill, when he first went up to Oxford in 1919. In *Goodbye to All That* he writes: 'Not an unfurnished house could be rented anywhere within the three mile radius. I solved the difficulty by pleading ill health and getting permission from St John's College to live five miles out, on Boar's Hill – where John Masefield, who thought well of my poetry, had offered to rent us a cottage at the bottom of his garden.'
5. From cummings' poem 'come, gaze with me upon this dome', collected in *is 5*. Riding and Graves here regularize the typography in the line 'a tear within his stern bluE.E.ye'.

List of Principal Anthologies

Ault, Norman	*Elizabethan Lyrics*, 1925
Bridges, Robert	*The Spirit of Man*, 1916
Bridges, Robert	*The Chilswell Book of English Poetry*, 1924
Brougham, Eleanor	*Corn from Olde Fieldes*, 1918
Buchan, John	*Northern Muse*, 1924
Bullen, A.H.	*Lyrics from the Elizabethan Song Books*, 1887
Campbell, F.	*Beauties of the British Poets*, 1824
Child, Francis	*English and Scottish Ballads*, 1861
de la Mare, Walter	*Come Hither*, 1923
Deutsch, Babette and Yarmolinsky, Avraham	*Modern Russian Poetry. An Anthology, chosen and translated by B. Deutsch and A. Yarmolinsky*, 1921
	Contemporary German Poetry; an anthology, 1923
Gowans, Adam	*The Hundred Best Poems*, 1903
Griswold, Rufus Wilmot	*The Poets and Female Poets of America*, 1849
Griswold, Rufus Wilmot	*The Poets and Poetry of America*, 1842
Hartog, W.G.	*The Kiss in English Poetry*, 1923
Harrison, Henry	*The Sacco-Vanzetti Anthology of Verse*, 1927
Hind, C. Lewis	*One Hundred Second Best Poems*, 1925
Janes, Thomas	*The Beauties of the Poets*, 1790
Langbridge, Canon	*Ballads of the Brave*, 1890
Lomax, John Avery	*Cowboy Songs and other Frontier Ballads*, 1911
Lucas, E.V.	*The Open Road*, 1899
Methuen, Algernon	*From Shakespeare to Hardy*, 1922
Meyer, Kuno	*Ancient Irish Poetry*, 1911
Moult, Thomas	*Down Here the Hawthorn*, 1921
Palgrave, F.W.	*Golden Treasury*
Quiller-Couch, Arthur	*The Oxford Book of English Verse*
Rhys, Grace Little	*A Celtic Anthology*, 1927
Royde-Smith, Naomi	*A Private Anthology*, 1925
Sharp, William	*Lyra Celtica*, 1896
Sharply, C. Elissa	*Anthology of Ancient Egyptian Poems*, 1925
Squire, J.C.	*Selections from Modern Poets*, 1918
Stedman, Edmund C.	*An American Anthology, 1787-1900*, 1900

Stedman, Edmund C.	*Poets of America*, 1885
Strong, L.A.G.	*Difficult Love*, 1927
Strong, L.A.G.	*Dublin Days*, 1921
Strong, L.A.G.	*The Lowery Road*, 1923
Trench, Charles	*Household Book of Poetry*, 1921
Untermeyer, Louis	*Modern American Poetry*, 1925
Walton, Eda Lou	*Dawn Boy. Blackfoot and Navajo Songs*, 1925 Introduction by Witter Bynner
Whittier, John Greanleaf	*Songs of Three Centuries*, 1876

Index